SHELLS
Guide to the Jewels of the Sea

By GIORGIO GABBI

ABBEVILLE PRESS PUBLISHERS
New York London Paris

First published in the United States of America in 2000 by Abbeville Publishing Group, 22 Cortlandt Street, New York, NY 10007

First published in 1999 by White Star S.r.l. Via Candido Sassone, 24 Vercelli, Italy

Text copyright © 1999 White Star S.r.l.

First Edition
2 4 6 8 10 9 7 5 3 1

Library of Congress Cataloging-in-Publication Data

Gabbi, Giorgio.
  Shells: guide to the jewels of the sea / Giorgio Gabbi.
    p. cm.
  "First published in the UK in 1999 by Swan Hill Press"—T.p. verso.
  ISBN 0-7892-0631-5
    1. Shells. I. Title.

  QL403 .G32 2000
  591.47'7—dc21   99-055015

Printed in Italy

Consultant: James R. Cordeiro, American Museum of Natural History, Department of Invertebrates

Design: Anna Galliani

Drawings: Monica Falcone

Translation: S.T.V., Milan

Editorial Consultants: Valeria Manferto De Fabianis, Laura Accomazzo

American Editor: Richard Koss

Text Designer: Barbara Balch

Production Director: Louise Kurtz

1. The gastropod's foot permits all types of movement: reptation, lifting, covering with sand, or climbing. The photo shows a small trochid in the process of climbing.

2, 3. A giant clam from the Great Barrier Reef of Australia exposes its brightly colored mantle to the sunlight. This bivalve, which can reach gigantic proportions,

succeeds in feeding from the nutrient-poor waters of the reef through a symbiosis it has established with zooxanthellae, single-celled algae that live in its tissues.

INTRODUCTION

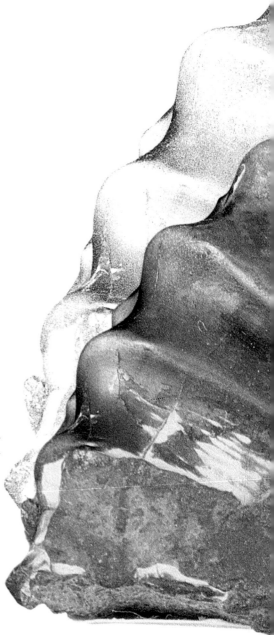

hells are beautiful, with elegant forms, surprising sculptures, refined designs and captivating colors. Shells remain intact for long periods of time, like precious metals and gems. And in fact, costly pearls are nothing more than a shell covering that the oyster builds around a foreign body that has entered its tissues. When man succeeded in producing that most noble of ceramic products, porcelain, he gave it the name of a shell, the marginella (*porcellana* in Italian), with its unparalleled glossy, smooth surface. And mother-of-pearl, an iridescent product from the humble abalone of our reefs, can provide an elegant touch to a simple button, and in its more precious forms provides the raw material for refined jewelry work.

Thus, it is no wonder that little shell treasures have been found with the remains of our most distant ancestors. It is yet another indication that the Paleolithic hunters and gatherers we commonly call cavemen had aesthetic tastes quite akin to our own, as we work and play at our computers. Archaeological excavations on sites that date back to classical antiquity have revealed collections of shells that came from thousands of miles away. In ancient Rome, they came from India, along with spices, gems, perfumes, and precious cloths. At the time of the great explorations, the dwellings of the rich and cultured of Europe were filled with spectacular, exotic shells. By that time, shell collecting was no longer just an aesthetic undertaking but an homage to the first conquests of modern science.

Thus, without knowing it, the child who stoops to collect a shell on the seashore is repeating a gesture that human beings have performed since the dawn of the evolution of our species. And why is the eye irresistibly attracted to the form of a shell? Perhaps because, while it is a part of nature, it is different from anything else found in creation. Certainly, a worm or a curled-up caterpillar takes on a spiral form, but the result is banal and arouses no curiosity. The snail's spiral is something unique, different, and only in modern times has science discovered its secret: it is a logarithmic spiral, a line that runs according to a rigorous mathematical relationship. No wonder it tantalizes the eye and mind.

But many of us do not ask such difficult questions. More simply, shells bring the sea to our homes. They remind us of beautiful sunny days, the salt air, and the enthusiasm we want to relive next year, perhaps on the same beach, or maybe in a completely different place—the tropics or the antipodes. For those who scuba dive, every shell evokes a particular seabed, the thrill of a new panorama discovered while exploring the blue depths. Even a simple bag of detritus, to be explored with a lens on a winter evening to reveal its little hidden treasures, takes us back to a magnificent, sheer wall, adorned with sea fans, or to a special grotto, dark as night but full of promise, or above the shining splendor of that coral formation, or into the green twilight of a forest of oarweed.

In this book, shells will be considered as travel companions, guides to exploring the marine environments that their makers, the mollusks, conquered well over 600 million years ago. To us, they will be much more than beautiful objects or alluring memories: they will help us understand and interpret the often enigmatic panoramas of the "sixth continent," which extends from the coastline where we feel the first sprays of water to the last horizon, where the blue of the sea merges with the sky. We will briefly consider the importance of mollusks and shells to man in both the past and the present, their unwitting role in the evolution of primitive society, and in trade, art, and science. Finally, we'll have some practical advice on producing a collection of shells that is beautiful to look at, helpful in understanding the sea, and respectful of nature.

6, 7. The highly elegant spiral of a fossil mollusk, a pyrite ammonite from the genus Pleuroceras, found in Germany. It dates back to the Jurassic period (from 180 to 135 million years ago), when these cephalopods underwent their greatest expansion. Like present-day nautiluses, they had a shell formed of chambers divided by septa.

A Resource for Humanity

Would our ancestors have survived without the protein supplied by the flesh of marine mollusks and the hard, sharp, easily worked material of their shells? Perhaps they would have, but prehistoric man's path would certainly have been more uncertain and difficult. Archaeologists have studied the enormous deposits of edible mollusk shells found along coasts throughout the world, from northern Europe to the most remote oceanic islands. Rather than the remains of gourmet shellfish banquets, they appear to be signs of a last-ditch resource of hunters and gatherers who found it difficult to locate other sources of food. Ancient Polynesian people did something unprecedented when they explored and colonized the immense Pacific Ocean, from Hawaii to the Easter Islands to New Zealand, using no navigational instruments as they crossed thousands of miles of open sea that separated one archipelago from another. The ancient conquerors of the ocean transformed the nacre of the pearl oyster into the fishhook, the primary tool of a population of fishermen and navigators. By fishing along the way, one could travel across the open sea for weeks or even months.

Scrapers, knives, arrowheads, and hoe blades are only a few examples of the vital tools that our Stone Age ancestors knew how to make from shells. But since the dawn of humankind, the most beautiful and curious shells have been used not only for utilitarian purposes but to satisfy spiritual needs. As early as the European Neolithic, it had been discovered that the trumpet shell (*Charonia tritonis*), with its truncated apex, could be used as a musical instrument, a tradition that

continued until classical antiquity. In Greece and Rome, a sea god, Triton, was depicted in the act of blowing the shell named after him. The people of pre-Columbian America used the shells of larger conches for the same purpose.

Universally used as amulets, symbols of authority, or ornaments to adorn belts, necklaces, hats, and clothes, shells have been traded among coastal and inland peoples since prehistoric times, and their two qualities, great durability and easily recognizable forms, transformed them from a trading object to a form of money. This probably took place in China as early as the second and first millennia before Christ, and lasted until metal money was introduced around A.D. 600.

But the financial success of *Cypraea moneta* and *C. annulus*, known as cowries, from *kauri*, the term that was used for them in South India, would last another 2,500 years. In the mid-tenth century the Arabian writer Ma'Sudi wrote in his book about the Maldive Islands, *The Golden Meadows*, "The queen knows no other money than the cowrie. When her treasure diminishes, she orders the islanders to cut fronds of the coconut palm and throw them onto the water. The cowries climb on, are gathered and placed on the sandy shore, where the sun consumes them and leaves only the empty shells. And these are delivered to the treasury."

Thousands and thousands of tons of these shells have traveled from archipelagoes and the coasts of the Indian Ocean to sub-Saharan West Africa. During centuries of slave trading, cowries were abundantly used by slave traders. In 1522, the price of a

slave in Benin was between 5,460 and 6,370 cowries.

Only at the end of the nineteenth century did colonial powers take cowries out of circulation as currency. Nevertheless, for the entire twentieth century, they continued to be used as small change in village markets. Other shells that made history in international trade even in ancient times include the pearl oyster (from the genus *Pinctada*) and murices, which were used to extract the famous purple dye of the Phoenicians. Almost everywhere, pearls of varying beauty and regularity from a number of marine and freshwater families had been used to make ornaments, but only those taken from *Pinctada*, with a perfect form and high gloss, acquired extremely high value. They were part of temple and royal treasures, adorned the crowns of queens and emperors, and shone around the necks or on the fingers of a very select number of privileged ladies. Their value peaked in ancient Rome. In his *Natural History*, Pliny the Elder wrote that they were the most precious thing in the world, and the historian Suetonius wrote that Aulus Vitellius, Roman emperor in

A. *From prehistoric times to the present, most people on the planet, including those who live far from the sea, have used shells for jewelry. One of the necklaces the dancer in this photo is wearing is made of large cowrie shells.*

B. *These little disks of mother-of-pearl and turquoise, used as earrings and clothing ornaments, look modern, but come from the Huari-Tihuanaco culture, which flourished in present-day Peru and Bolivia between the sixth and eleventh centuries.*

...the year 69, paid for a military campaign with revenues from the sale of a single pearl earring inherited from his mother.

Pearl fishing, which some young Arabs from wealthy families in oil sheikdoms practice for sport, was centered in the Persian Gulf, and the lives of pearl fishermen, who made free dives dozens of times a day, were extremely harsh. Disability and early death were quite common. Starting in the early nineteenth century, the button industry created great demand for mother-of-pearl, and pearl fishermen could thus enjoy a modest but secure living by gathering pearl oysters. Over-harvesting meant that finding a valuable pearl had become an increasingly remote possibility. The physiological mechanism that an oyster, a murex, a fan mussel, or a nautilus uses to produce a pearl was discovered. When a foreign body ends up in the mollusk's tissues, it reacts by wrapping it in concentric layers of mother-of-pearl and making a sort of appendage within the shell. In the late nineteenth century, three Japanese researchers independently discovered the secret of forcing an oyster to make a pearl to order, and one of the three, Kokichi Mikimoto, based a business empire on the discovery. The secret is a rather delicate surgical operation that transplants into the tissues of a pearl oyster raised in captivity a mother-of-pearl nucleus wrapped in a flap of tissue capable of producing mother-of-pearl, taken from another oyster.

The ancient Phoenicians were able to make the murex the basis of a flourishing industrial and commercial monopoly. Three species were utilized: the purple dye murex (*Bolinus brandaris*), the red-mouth purpura (*Thais lacera*), and the trunculus murex (*Hexaplex trunculus*): each mollusk secretes from a gland only a few drops of a yellowish mucus that quickly turned dark blue when exposed to the light.

In Ireland, piles of broken shells of the murex *Nucella lapillus* have been found. One thousand years before Christ, the ancient Irish used them to obtain a black-purple dye. Another luxury product provided by mollusks was taken from the byssus, the complex of filaments secreted by the glands of the foot and used by many species of bivalves to anchor to solid parts of the substratum. Processed and spun, the byssus takes on a silky texture. Today, an increasing number of countries limit the collection of mollusks.

for commercial use and encourage their cultivation. Thus, in tropical countries, mother-of-pearl is obtained from species that have proved easy to cultivate, like the topshell *Trochus niloticus* and the pearl oyster.

In 1972 one of the world's most authoritative associations of specialists in the field, Unitas Malacologica Europaea, recommended limiting the collection of live mollusks for both scientific and amateur purposes, to protect populations that in many cases were threatened by dangers like marine pollution or destruction of coastal habitats. In the following years, various international conventions compiled lists of threatened species or mollusk populations. An increasing number of countries have adopted measures to protect the marine environment, including bans and in some cases absolute bans on collecting shells, selling them, or taking them outside the country. A conscientious collector will in any case set clear ethical limits. You should consult specialized publications to find out which species are endangered, and always be sure to gather only very modest amounts. With this in mind, remember that, as illustrious scientists have noted, gathering shells for study or collection has never and could never endanger the survival of any species of mollusk. As one of the great malacologists of this century, the American R. Tucker Abbott, who passed away a few years ago, stated, "There seems among extreme conservationists a reluctance to encourage shell collecting as a science or as a worthwhile hobby. . . . However, an analysis of the fate of molluscan populations around the world indicates that the major cause of their reduction in most areas is due to pollution, man's destruction or major alteration of natural habitats, excessive commercial fishing, and finally the natural vagaries of mother nature herself." Nearly all species of mollusks produce thousands, or even millions, of young, in contrast to the small litters of mammals and limited broods of birds." "What marine scientists and shell collectors may harvest in their lifetimes has an effect on the size of the population of marine mollusks comparable to the contribution of the sound made by a ping-pong ball dropping at the foot of the roaring Niagara Falls." (*The Seashells of South East Asia*, ed. Graham Bash, Singapore, page 13).

So don't feel guilty about collecting shells, but always show respect for life. Thus, always try to collect shells of mollusks that have died of natural causes; often they are in perfect condition. When your search has an impact on the environment, like turning over rocks and pulling algae from the seabed, use the greatest discretion, always put the rocks back in their original position, and take only a small part of the vegetation you're interested in. If you want to collect a living mollusk (which you must do if you want to examine its behavior in an aquarium or dissect it to study its anatomy), only a minimal fraction of the local population should be sacrificed, to avoid changing the biological equilibrium. And when you find a species that through the fault of humans, collectors or not, has become rare or very rare in a certain area, for example *Pinna nobilis* or *Patella ferruginea* in Italy, if you find no empty shells, be happy with some notes in your notebook and a photograph. It will be a trophy of which you can be doubly proud: you found a rarity and you let it live.

10-11. The green and blue of the mother-of-pearl of an abalone (Haliotis iris) from New Zealand are due to a diet of brown algae.

C. The maker of this gilded silver saltshaker from Elizabethan England created a fighting cock from the shell of a nautilus (Nautilus pompilius).

C

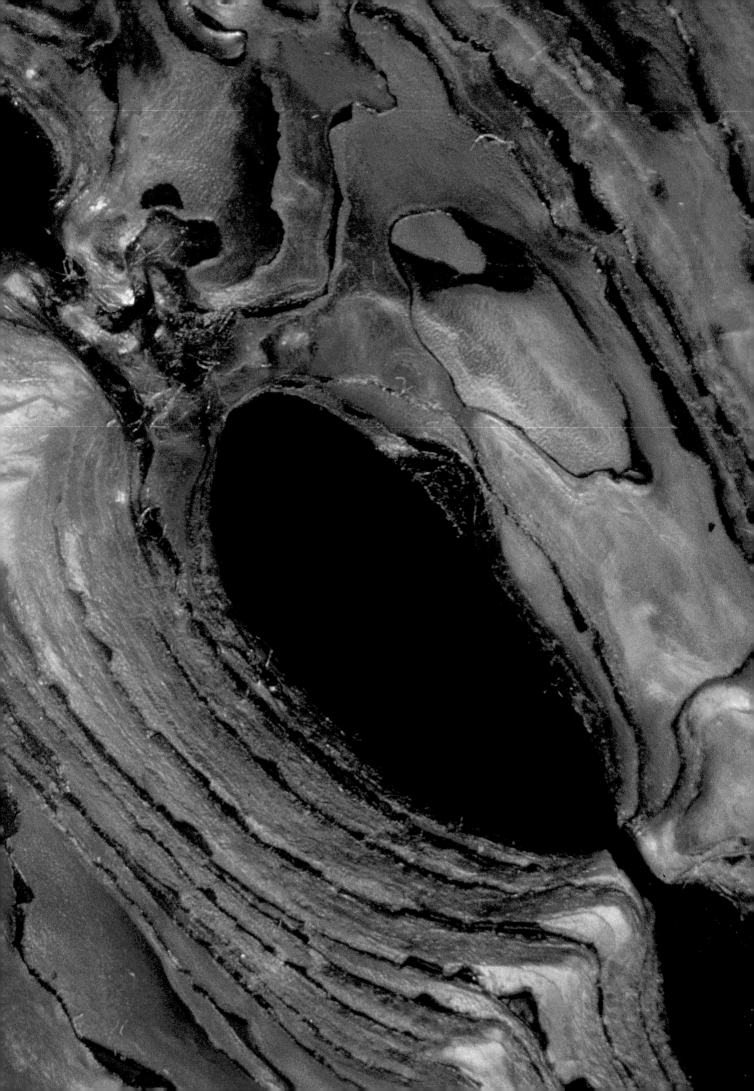

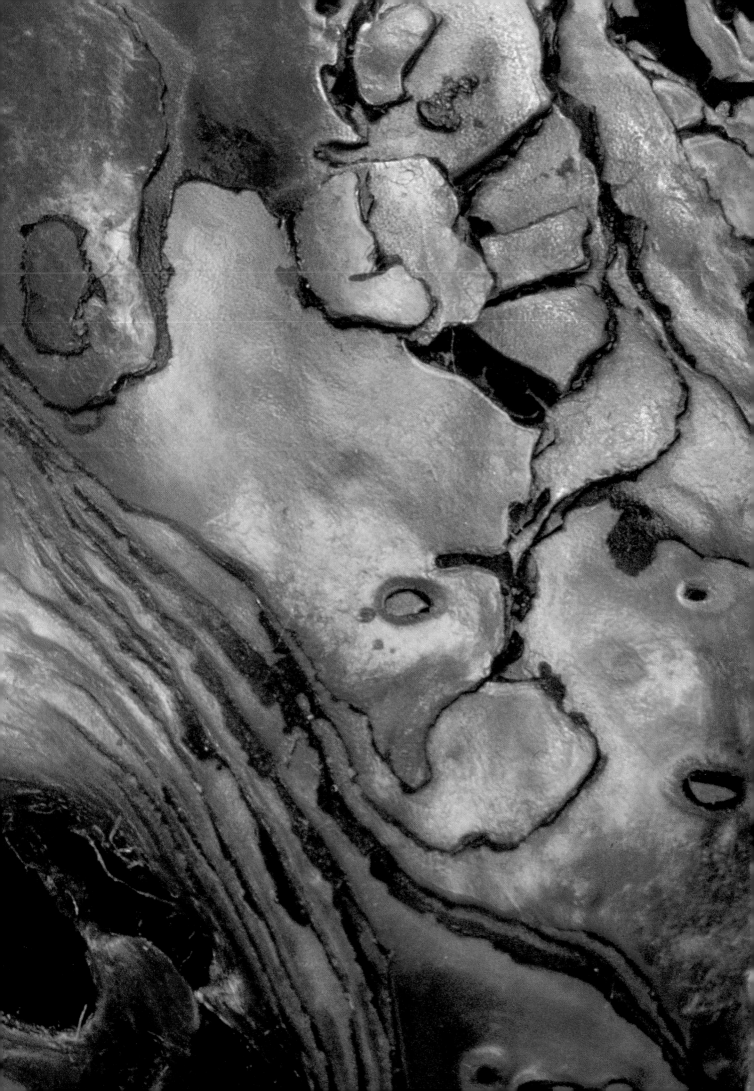

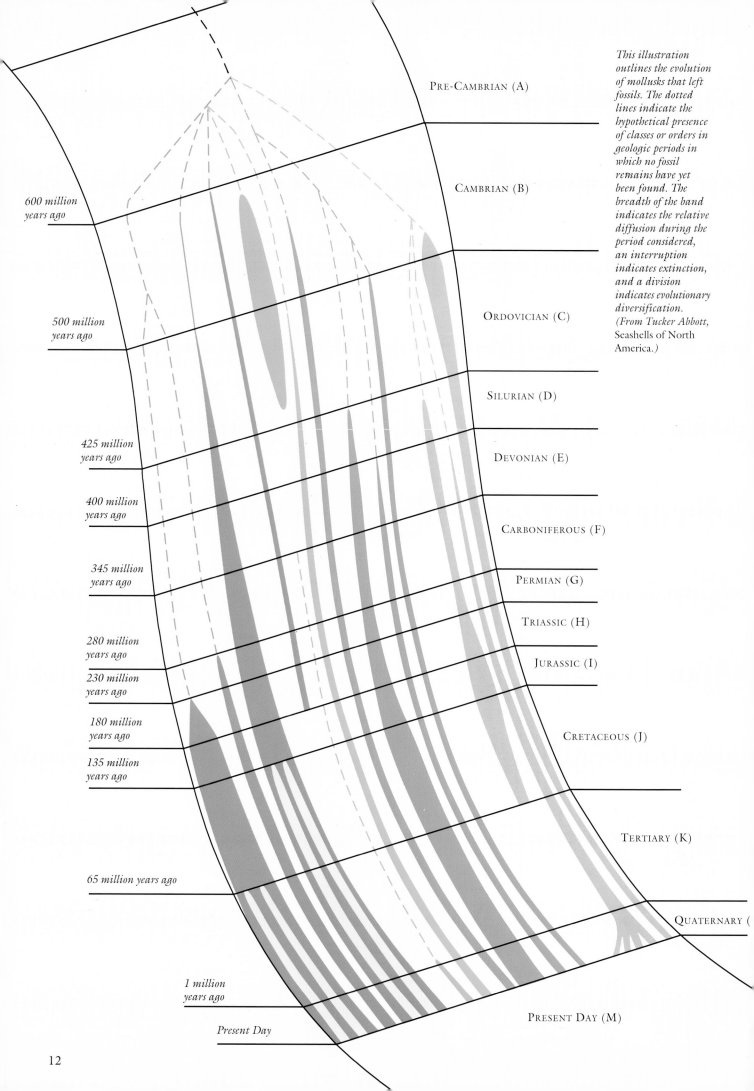

PRE-CAMBRIAN (A)

CAMBRIAN (B)

This illustration outlines the evolution of mollusks that left fossils. The dotted lines indicate the hypothetical presence of classes or orders in geologic periods in which no fossil remains have yet been found. The breadth of the band indicates the relative diffusion during the period considered, an interruption indicates extinction, and a division indicates evolutionary diversification. (From Tucker Abbott, Seashells of North America.)

600 million years ago

ORDOVICIAN (C)

500 million years ago

SILURIAN (D)

425 million years ago

DEVONIAN (E)

400 million years ago

CARBONIFEROUS (F)

345 million years ago

PERMIAN (G)

TRIASSIC (H)

280 million years ago

JURASSIC (I)

230 million years ago

180 million years ago

CRETACEOUS (J)

135 million years ago

TERTIARY (K)

65 million years ago

QUATERNARY (

1 million years ago

PRESENT DAY (M)

Present Day

A Family Tree 600 Million Years Old

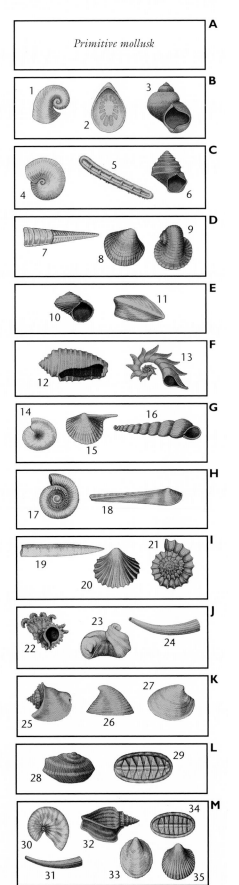

A

Primitive mollusk

	Gastropods
	Monoplacophores
	Polyplacophores
	Scaphopods
	Bivalves
	Cephalopods

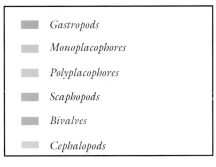

A

Pre-Cambrian (A)

Cambrian (B)
1. bellerophonts
2. monoplacophores
3. prosobranchs

Ordovician (C)
4. bellerophonts
5. amphineurans
6. prosobranchs

Silurian (D)
7. nautiloids
8. bivalves
9. prosobranchs

Devonian (E)
10. prosobranchs
11. bivalves

Carboniferous (F)
12. opisthobranchs
13. prosobranchs

Permian (G)
14. ammonites
15. bivalves
16. opisthobranchs

Triassic (H)
17. ammonites
18. bivalves

Jurassic (I)
19. nautiloids
20. bivalves

21. ammonites

Cretaceous (J)
22. prosobranchs
23. bivalves
24. scaphopods

Tertiary (K)
25. prosobranchs
26. prosobranchs
27. bivalves

Quaternary (L)
28. pulmonates
29. amphineurans

Present Day (M)
30. cephalopods
31. scaphopods
32. gastropods
33. monoplacophores
34. amphineurans
35. bivalves

A. The outer imprint of an ammonite, found in Italy on Monte Nerone in the Marchigiano Apennines. Fossils of this cephalopod are particularly abundant in soil from the Jurassic and Triassic.

F inding marine fossil shells high up in the mountains, hundreds of miles from the sea, is always a cause for wonder. Our ancestors invented fantastic explanations for such a strange event, until biblical tales set everyone straight by asserting that those petrified remains could be nothing other than traces of animal populations destroyed by the great flood—the antediluvians. To modern science, fossil shells were much more, and became an extraordinary aid to scholars in deciphering the earth's past. Geologists considered them the best fossil guides for dating sedimentary rocks, reconstructing climate changes in ancient seas, following the processes of land emergence and submersion, and many other kinds of research. Thanks to its calcareous hull, a shell leaves an always recognizable signature in the rock that imprisons it, even if the shell itself dissolves and comes to us only through the imprint of its interior.

The most ancient fossils date back to about 600 million years ago, the beginning of the Cambrian period, the earliest geologic period of the Paleozoic era. Before this period, scientists can only speculate as to how living beings evolved. In the Cambrian period, fossil mollusks already seem to have diversified into the classes that still survive today on the planet (the only one missing is the class of aplacophores, which has about 250 living species whose worm-like forms, with no shells, have left no fossils). The most remote finds, along with shells in surprising forms, show us snails and clams not very different from those of our days. Not to say that mollusks haven't evolved in half a billion years—far from it. Entire large families have become extinct, and others that once dominated the seas have been reduced to just a few species. New families have emerged. But mollusks had already developed their fundamental anatomical structures even before fish and reptiles appeared on the planet.

According to the most accredited hypothesis among scholars, the common ancestor of all mollusks was an organism with bilateral symmetry that had a shell with a depressed cone shape and moved by crawling on a fleshy foot. In outward appearance, at least, it was similar to present-day limpets (whose internal organization, however, is completely different). Of the six living classes of mollusks with a shell, the one considered most similar to this progenitor is the Monoplacophora class. This class had been considered extinct by the Paleozoic era; but on May 6, 1952, the Danish research vessel *Galathea* pulled up thirteen specimens, three empty shells and ten living ones, from a clayey seabed west of Panama, at a depth of 5,000 meters. For four years, these discoveries remained undisturbed in their glass bottles. Then, when malacologists Wingstrand and Lemche examined them, they realized that they were living fossils, practically identical to creatures that had been considered extinct for 400 million years. The discovery of *Neopilina galatheae* casts much light on the history of the first mollusks. Indeed, monoplacophores have at least a partially segmented body, a phenomenon known as metamerism. That is, they consist of parts (such as muscles, gills, and kidneys) that appear in repeating pairs for each segment.

This structure begins to give us answers to some old questions: Who are the mollusks' closest relatives? And who is their most remote ancestor? The organization of cuttlefish, snails, and mussels is so different from that of other invertebrates that any theory is hard to support. In the mid-eighteenth century, the great Linnaeus (Carl von Linné, the Swedish scientist who in 1758 laid the foundations for natural systematics in the tenth edition of his work, *Sistema Naturae*), had placed mollusks among the Vermes, following a tradition that dated back to classical antiquity and was based on a superficial evaluation of external features, such as the softness of the body and the lack of well-defined limbs. Linnaeus's successors were quick to understand that there is as much

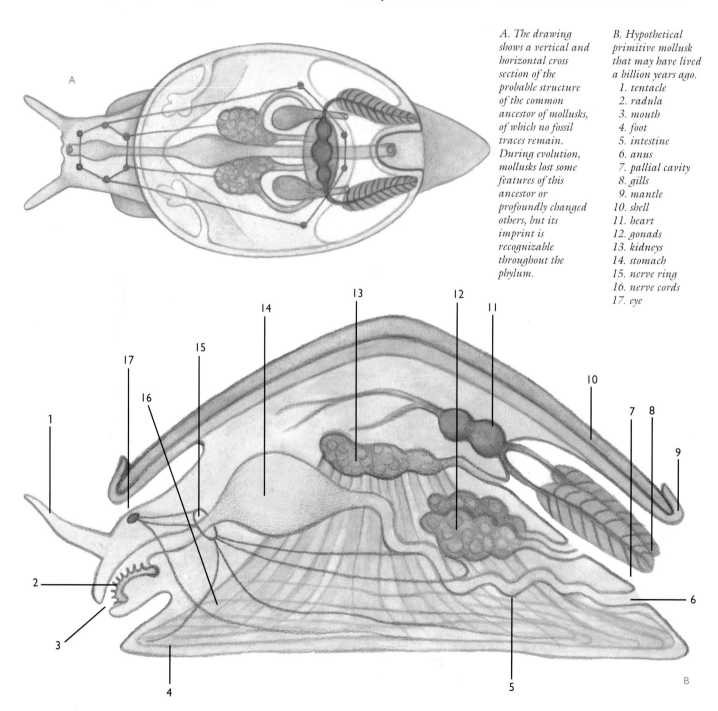

A. The drawing shows a vertical and horizontal cross section of the probable structure of the common ancestor of mollusks, of which no fossil traces remain. During evolution, mollusks lost some features of this ancestor or profoundly changed others, but its imprint is recognizable throughout the phylum.

B. Hypothetical primitive mollusk that may have lived a billion years ago.
  1. *tentacle*
  2. *radula*
  3. *mouth*
  4. *foot*
  5. *intestine*
  6. *anus*
  7. *pallial cavity*
  8. *gills*
  9. *mantle*
  10. *shell*
  11. *heart*
  12. *gonads*
  13. *kidneys*
  14. *stomach*
  15. *nerve ring*
  16. *nerve cords*
  17. *eye*

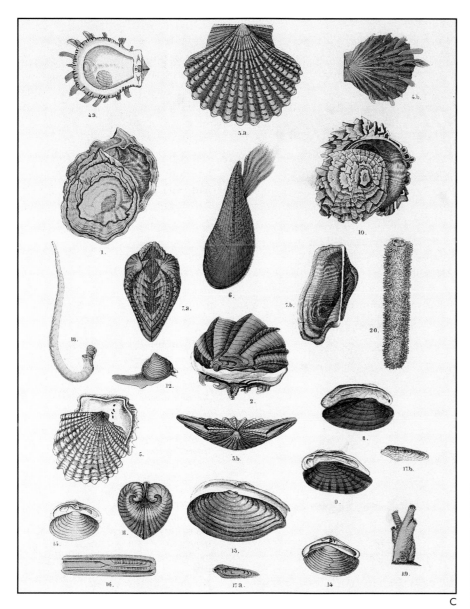

subspecies or even geographical races. Zoologists who study mollusks have always had significant differences of opinion on the validity of species and subspecies. In the past, when solely the external features of the shell were used to classify mollusks, an endless number of species was created, but this later proved to be inconsistent. Many species were attributed to genera or even families that were different from the original ones. In the meantime, many new species were found in nature. For someone who is not a professional zoologist, this makes it extremely difficult to consult texts that are more than fifteen or twenty years old. Anyone who is just beginning to collect shells should resign himself to the problem of nomenclature. With a bit of experience, you'll learn how to wade through old names, new names, and eliminated names. In the end, what counts is not so much the name, but the natural history that lies behind it.

C. This precious lithograph printed in Stuttgart in 1861 for the Systematische Atlas der Naturgeschichte *(Systematic Atlas of Natural History) by T. Bromme presents characteristic shells from some of the most common families of bivalves.*

D. The Swedish scientist Carl von Linné, in his catalogue of nature, Sistema Naturae, *had placed mollusks under "Vermes."*

difference between a snail and a leech as between a starfish and a poodle. Mollusks were then given their own group.

Modern science classifies living organisms based on their evolutionary history, i.e., their family tree. Within the animal kingdom, the organisms that have the same fundamental organization form a phylum (or type). Phyla (or types) include those of the mollusks, echinoderms, arthropods, and chordates. Within a phylum, organisms with a common ascendant are grouped into classes (for example, the phylum of chordates includes the classes of Mammalia, Reptilia, Aves, and so forth). Within each class, animals are grouped into orders (mammals, for example, include the orders of Carnivora, Rodentia, Insectivora, and so forth). Within each order, there are families (Carnivora is divided into Canidae, Felidae, Ursidae, and so on). Below the family, animals are classified into genus

(for example, the Canidae family includes the genera *Canis* and *Vulpes)* and the genera are divided into species (the genus *Canis* includes the species *lupus,* the wolf; *aureus,* the jackal; and *familiaris,* the domestic dog, while the genus *Vulpes* includes the species *vulpes,* the red fox; and *chama,* the African fox). We have used the example of mammals, which are the most familiar, to underline that, when we see two clams that look identical but have a different genus, they are actually as far apart on the family tree as a dog and a fox.

In zoology, the species is the fundamental group. Generally speaking, it indicates individuals that have a genetic heritage in common and can reproduce, generating fertile offspring. Particular environmental situations (such as isolation) can cause populations of the same species to have certain features that differentiate with regularity: We then speak of the formation of

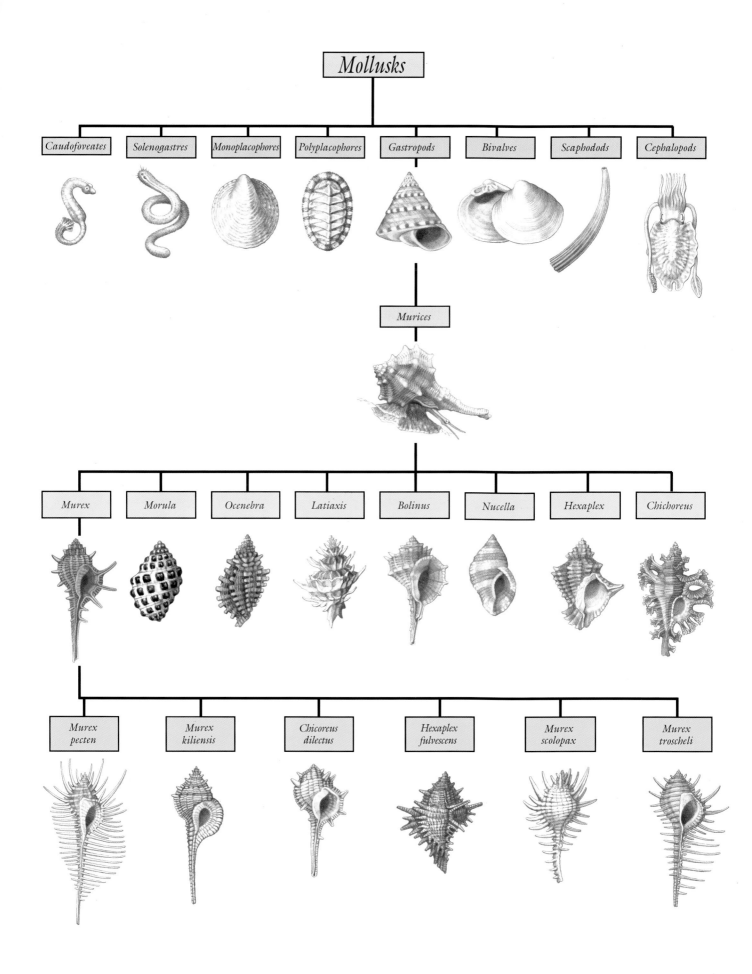

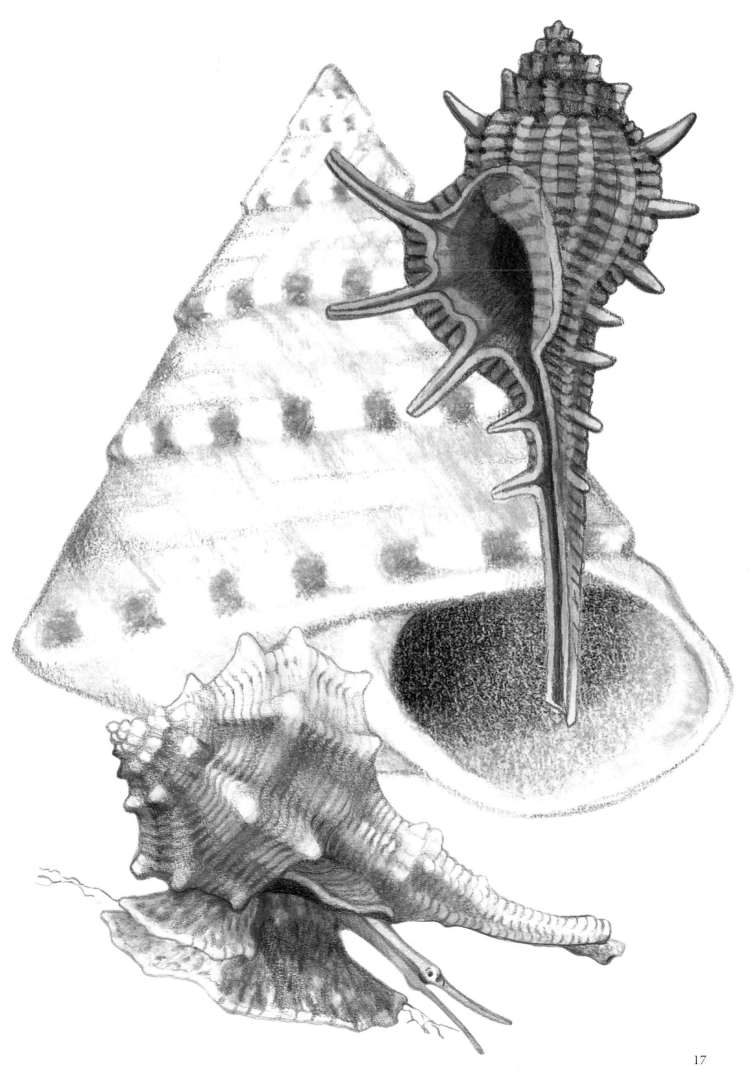

Questions of Kinship

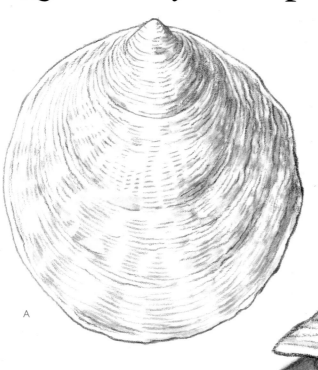

A

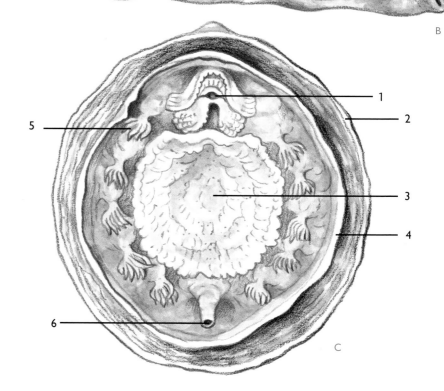

B

A, B, C. Considered to be living fossils, present-day monoplacophores have very primitive characteristics. In the drawing, a Neopilina *seen from above (A), from the side (B), and from the central area (C). The five pairs of gills could indicate that it is a descendant of a metameric ancestor, i.e., with a segmented body like that of anellids.*

1. mouth
2. shell
3. foot
4. mantle margin
5. gills
6. anus

D, E, F, G. *The drawings show a chiton (polyplacophore) as seen from above (D) and ventrally (E), as well as the scheme of its internal structure seen from the side (F) and the ventral portion (G).*

The shell, divided into eight imbricate plates (13), allows it to adhere firmly to rocky surfaces.

1. mouth
2. head
3. girdle
4. gills
5. intestine
6. gonads
7. excretory canals
8. kidney
9. heart
10. anus
11. radula
12. foot
13. shell with plates

G etting back to the phylum of mollusks and the problem of what could be their progenitor, monoplacophore metamerism, even if only partial, provides a first indicator. Two other phyla, the arthropods and the anellids, are characterized by metamerism. The larval forms of species in these phyla have significant similarities. The same hint of metamerism present in polyplacophores (see opposite) adds credence to this approach. Thus, the most accredited hypothesis today considers butterflies, earthworms, and snails as possible descendants of a common, albeit very distant, progenitor.

Let us now look at kinship issues within the phylum of mollusks with a shell, i.e., the path their evolution took and the classes it originated.

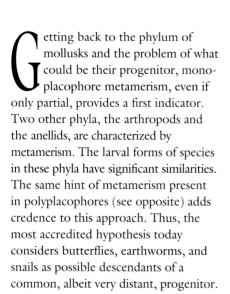

C

MONOPLACOPHORES

After the sensational find of *Neopilina galatheae,* in the second half of the twentieth century, another dozen species of these living fossils were found. They all live on seabeds, from depths of a few hundred yards to the abyss. They are all microphage detritivores. Their shells reach an inch or so in length.

H, I. *In the drawing, a tusk shell scaphopod (H), and a cross section (I) showing its internal structure. The animal is sedentary and lives attached to the* bottom. It feeds on detritus captured with its captacula, which also serve as gills. It has no eyes, and its nervous system is rudimentary.

1. captacula
2. foot
3. mouth
4. mantle
5. nerve ganglia
6. heart
7. stomach
8. kidney
9. hepatopancreas
10. gonads
11. mantle cavity
12. anus
13. back aperture
14. posterior

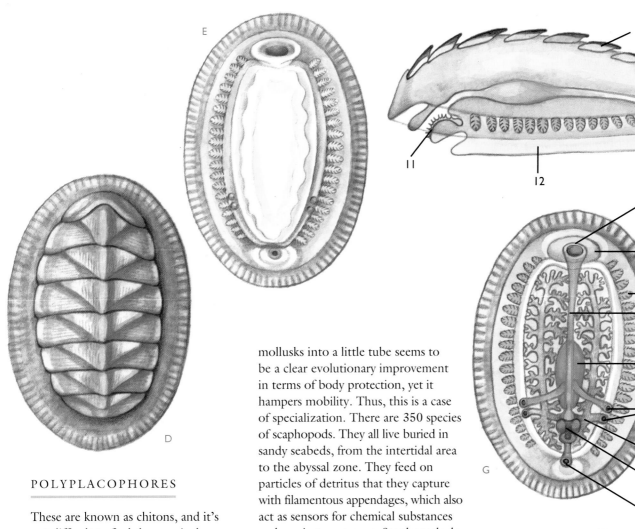

POLYPLACOPHORES

These are known as chitons, and it's not difficult to find them an inch or two below the water surface on reefs in intertidal areas, adhering to substrata like limpets. Their shell is formed of eight plates, usually imbricate, i.e., overlapping like the tiles of a roof, and they are a maximum of a foot (30 cm) long. Compared with the single shell of primitive mollusks, this transformation makes it much easier to adhere to the surface of a rock. The shell is permeated with pores, through which pass nerve endings with small sensory organs at the tips, both tactile and visual. This feature is similar to certain aspects of anellid anatomy. Today there are about 600 living species of polyplacophores. They are herbivores and detritivores, and live anchored to the seabed, from intertidal areas to the abyssal zone.

SCAPHOPODS

On sandy beaches you may find small, slightly curved, white tubes that somewhat resemble an elephant's tusk. These are tusk shells, members of the class of scaphopods. The transformation of the cone-shaped shell of primitive

mollusks into a little tube seems to be a clear evolutionary improvement in terms of body protection, yet it hampers mobility. Thus, this is a case of specialization. There are 350 species of scaphopods. They all live buried in sandy seabeds, from the intertidal area to the abyssal zone. They feed on particles of detritus that they capture with filamentous appendages, which also act as sensors for chemical substances and respiratory organs. Scaphopods do not exceed five inches (12 cm) in length, and have no head, eyes, or gills. Their digestive tracts and nervous systems are rudimentary. Their sedentary existence under the layer of sand on the seabed and the type of food they eat have made it unnecessary to develop the organs and functions required of animals just slightly more active.

CEPHALOPODS

On the other hand, cephalopods, the most evolved of the mollusks, are quite active. They are all carnivorous. They live in the open sea, as a part of the nekton or benthos. In this class of mollusks, the shell may appear as an outer hull, coiled around a single plane, with the inside divided into watertight compartments, like the nautilus. Much more frequently, the shell is internal, and may be a calcareous substance like cuttlebone, or a horny one like the squid's pen. But it may be completely absent, as in the octopus. There are about six hundred living species of cephalopods. With the giant squid, they reach record lengths of 65 feet (20 m).

A

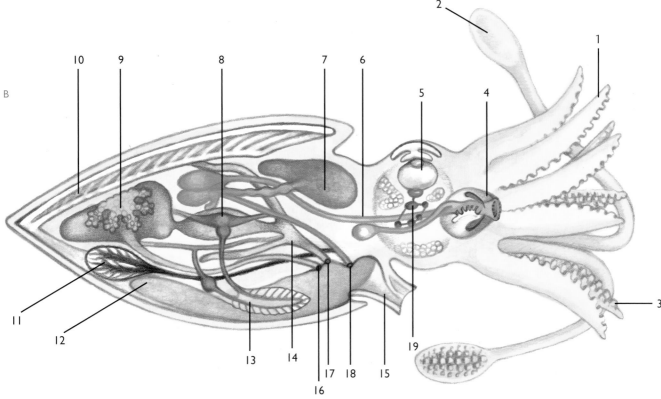

B

C

A. The octopus is a cephalopod completely lacking a shell, even an internal one. The example pictured in the photo is "walking" on the bottom, using its eight tentacles equipped with suckers. When it has to move more quickly, the octopus activates its "jet propulsion engine" by expelling an energetic blast of water from the siphon. Both the siphon and tentacles are evolutionary develop-

ments of the foot of the primitive mollusk.

B. The drawing shows the structure of a cephalopod from the subclass of coleoids, which includes decapods (spirulae, cuttlefish, and squid) and octopods (octopuses and argonauts). The pallial cavity (12) has become an organ for jet propulsion, regulated by the opening of the siphon (15).

1. tentacle arm
2. oral arm
3. sucker
4. mouth
5. eye
6. esophagus
7. hepatopancreas
8. heart
9. gonads
10. internal shell
11. ink sac
12. pallial cavity
13. gills
14. kidney
15. siphon
16. genital aperture
17. excretory aperture
18. anus
19. cerebral ganglion

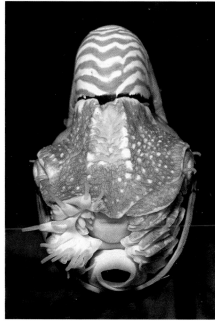

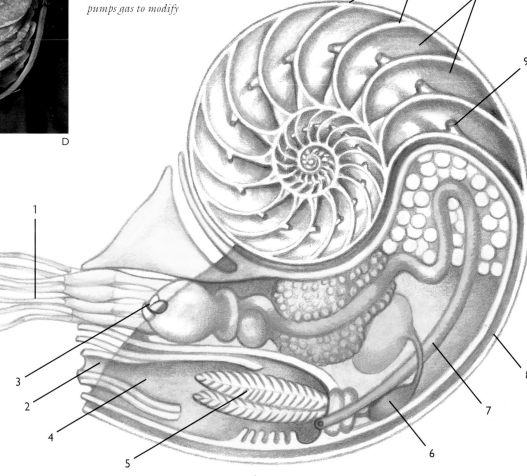

E. Internal structure of a nautilus. The spiral, symmetrical shell coiled around a single plane is divided into chambers (10) that the animal closes with a calcareous diaphragm (11) and abandons as it grows. The chambers connect to each other by means of a canal through which the nautilus pumps gas to modify its specific gravity and move vertically.

1. tentacles
2. siphon
3. mouth
4. pallial cavity
5. gills
6. heart
7. intestine
8. shell
9. canal
10. chambers
11. septa

G. A female Argonauta nodosa *from southern Australia. In this genus of cephalopods, the male is much smaller than the female. The female builds a false shell (ootheca, or egg case) in which it keeps the eggs.*

E

D

C. This long-fin squid (Loligo pealei) *lives in the northwest Atlantic. The largest member of the mollusk phylum is the giant squid, which can reach 65 feet (20 m) in length.*

D, F. The nautilus is a genus of cephalopods. It is a living fossil, the only representative that has survived of the subclass of nautiloids, which disappeared in the Paleozoic. Nautiloids were quite common and were sometimes gigantic; one fossil found in Germany was nearly eight feet (2.4 m) in diameter. Nautiluses are pelagic, and feed on crustaceans.

F

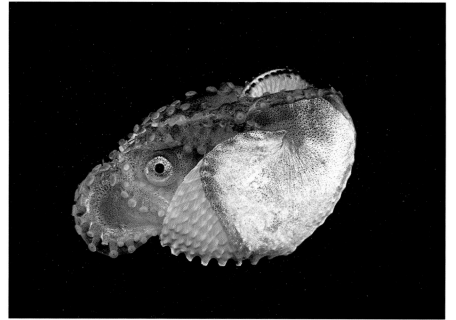

G

21

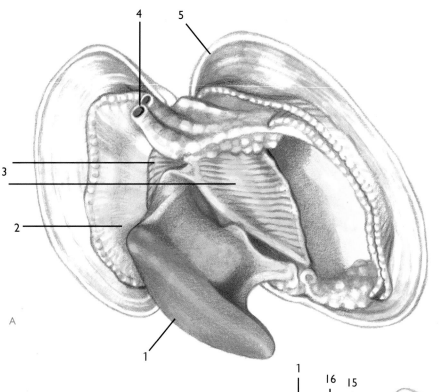

A

A. The structure of the body of a bivalve in the Veneridae family (clams) as it appears with its valves open.
1. foot
2. mantle
3. gills
4. siphons
5. shell

B. The drawing shows the structure of internal organs of a bivalve (Veneridae) in a longitudinal cross section.
1. adductor muscles
2. mouth
3. foot
4. visceral nerve ganglion
5. intestine
6. gonads
7. gills
8. pallial cavity
9. siphons
10. foot nerve ganglion
11. anus
12. kidney
13. heart
14. pericardium
15. hepatopancreas
16. stomach

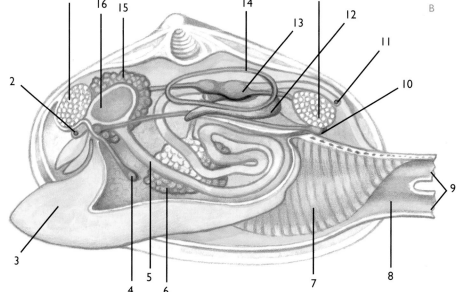

B

BIVALVES

This class of mollusks has solved the problem of fully protecting its body by dividing its ancestral shell in two, creating two hinged plates, the valves. It is believed that this process took place in the Cambrian or Ordovician period, when a monoplacophore evolved to adapt to life in a sandy environment. To better move through the grains of sand, the mollusk adopted a laterally compressed body form. The conical shell would have divided in two, as still occurs in the larval forms of bivalves,

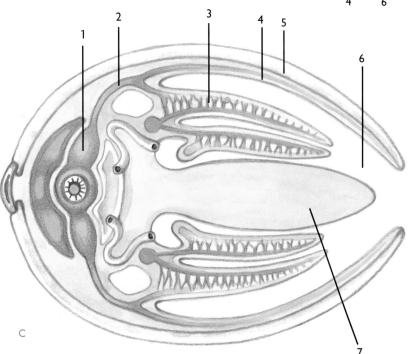

C

which have only one embryonic shell. The mollusk half-closes the valves to filter water and feed on the tiny organic particles in suspension, and to replenish its oxygen supply through the gills. Bivalves are animals that engage in little or no movement as adults. This sedentary nature has had important consequences on their evolution. Among other things, it has led to the disappearance of a head and true eyes. Unlike the classes discussed above, bivalves have successfully ventured beyond the marine environment, populating rivers, lakes, ponds, and streams. This class contains no fewer than 10,000 species, mostly marine and the rest freshwater. The largest bivalve, the giant clam, reaches 4.5 feet (137 cm) in length.

C. The drawing shows a cross section of the structure of a bivalve from the eulamellibranch order (clams, tellins, cockles), in particular the respiratory and circulatory system.

1. *heart*
2. *blood vessels*
3. *gills*
4. *mantle*
5. *shell*
6. *pallial cavity*
7. *foot*

D. The drawing shows the phases of natural pearl formation in a bivalve.
A: an irritating foreign object comes between the shell (1) and the epithelium of the mantle (2); the mollusk reacts by enveloping the foreign object with its mantle; the cells begin to secrete a thin layer of mother-of-pearl. Other layers are deposited (C and D) until a round pearl is formed.

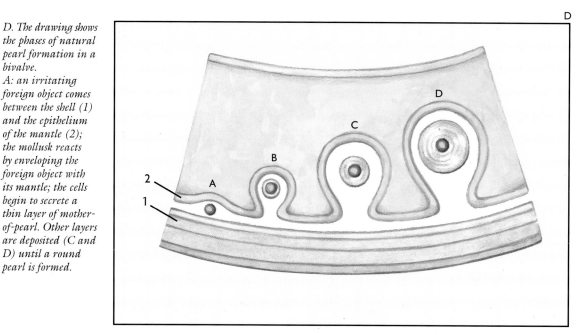

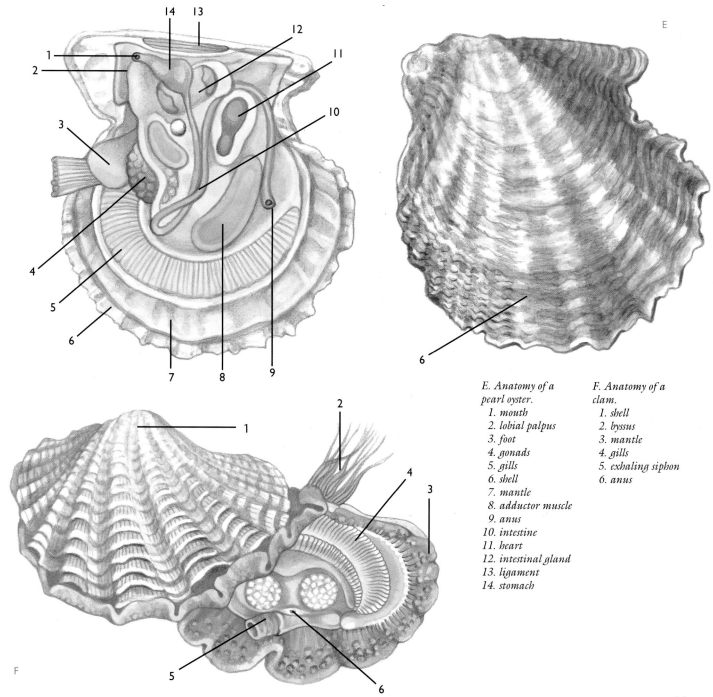

E. Anatomy of a pearl oyster.

1. *mouth*
2. *lobial palpus*
3. *foot*
4. *gonads*
5. *gills*
6. *shell*
7. *mantle*
8. *adductor muscle*
9. *anus*
10. *intestine*
11. *heart*
12. *intestinal gland*
13. *ligament*
14. *stomach*

F. Anatomy of a clam.

1. *shell*
2. *byssus*
3. *mantle*
4. *gills*
5. *exhaling siphon*
6. *anus*

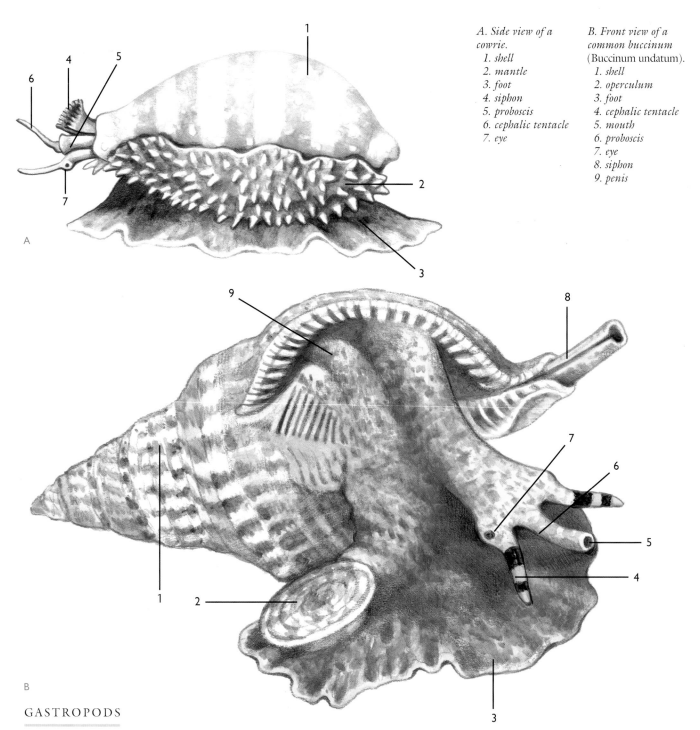

A

B

GASTROPODS

With the class of gastropods, mollusks conquered all environments on the planet—and captured the avid attention of collectors. Indeed, no other class of mollusks has such a wealth of species (more than 50,000) and shells prized for their beautiful forms, ornamentation, and color. After occupying every ecological niche, from the coastline to the open sea to the abyssal zone, gastropods colonized the fresh water (surface, underground, and even thermal areas), and finally extended to dry land, from tropical forests to deserts and the high mountains. They stopped only at lands permanently covered with ice. Compared with the hypothetical primitive mollusk,

the evolution of gastropods is marked by two fundamental developments: the first is the transformation of the shell from a shield to a spiral structure, i.e., a tube that gradually widens, coiling around an axis, and the second was the 180-degree counterclockwise torsion on a horizontal plane of the mollusk's visceral mass. As the shell evolved, the shield of the primitive mollusk that was the gastropod's ancestor probably grew in height until it assumed a pointed cone form, offering more volume and thus better protection, as the mollusk could retract its entire body inside it, leaving exposed only the part occupied by the base of the cone. But this kind of

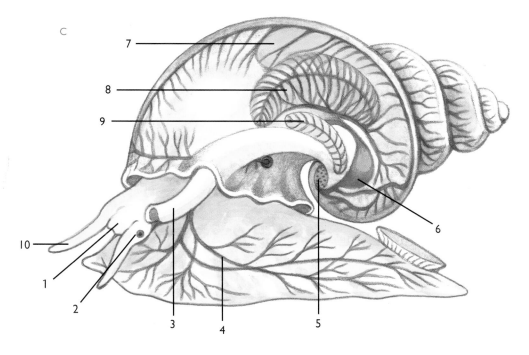

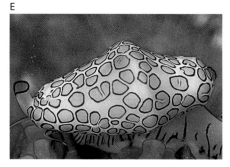

E. The spotted mantle of this ovulid from the Caribbean covers the shell entirely, as is common in families related to the cowries. Locally known as the flamingo tongue, Cyphoma gibbosum can reach 1 inch (2.5 cm) in length and prefers to live on gorgonians.

F. In marine gastropods, it is not uncommon to find animals equipped with a brightly colored foot, while the shell itself is dull, like the snail photographed on this page. The evolutionary significance of this phenomenon is not always clear.

G. A Patella ferruginea grazes on the film of seaweed covering coastal rock. The extraordinary force with which its foot clings to the rock is not due, as is commonly thought, to the action of a sucker, but to the structure of its cells, which are able to anchor to any slight irregularity.

H. Anatomical structure of a common buccinum (Buccinum undatum).
1. mouth
2. proboscis
3. cephalic tentacle
4. siphon
5. osphradium
6. gills
7. mantle margin
8. heart
9. kidney
10. digestive glands
11. gonads
12. anus
13. penis
14. proboscis muscles

structure created some problems in terms of locomotion. The evolution of that pointed, spiral cone into a snail form must have offered a clear advantage. Not only could the mollusk retract itself into the shell (and insulate itself from the outside environment by constructing a door, the operculum, that hermetically closed the opening), but at the same time the new snail-shaped shell was easier to transport than a long cone and did not compromise the animal's mobility.

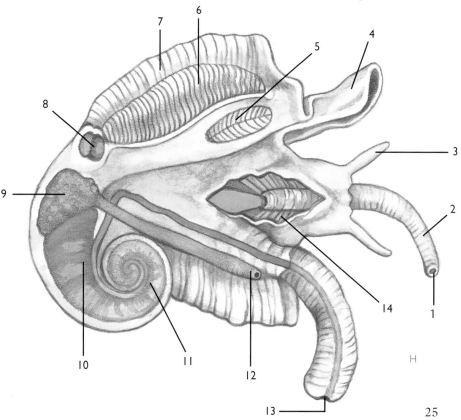

A. A prosobranch perfectly camouflaged in a colony of cnidarians. The form of the animal is confused with other forms in the environment, while its bright colors warn predators of the presence of stinging cells in the tissues.

A

It is not so simple to explain the other development in the evolution of gastropods, the dorsoventral torsion that rotated the group of organs consisting of the mantle, shell, and viscera 180 degrees away from the group formed by the head and foot. In this manner, the mantle cavity and the excretory canal of the kidneys and intestine moved to the front part of the animal, while the viscera and nerve fibers intersected to form an X. It has been hypothesized that this torsion was due to a mutation that occurred in the larval phase of a primitive gastropod, as the adult mollusk enjoyed no evolutionary advantage from the torsion. On the contrary, the little animal's excretory and reproductive organs ended up over its head, expelling their emissions into the current of water issuing from the mantle cavity very near its mouth. This obviously created serious hydraulic problems. In fossil gastropods and more primitive classes of living gastropods, the problem was resolved by opening a fissure or hole in the shell, in order to expel waste and anything else to the back, as far as possible from the mouth. In the next chapter, we will see how this torsion also resulted in profound anatomical changes.

B

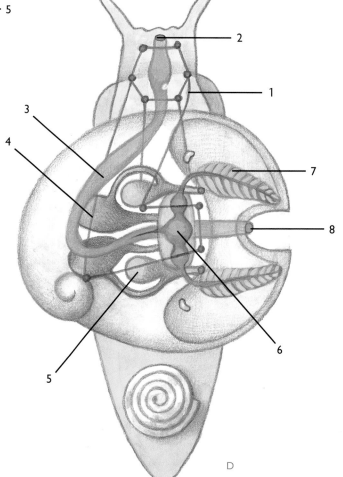

D

C

F

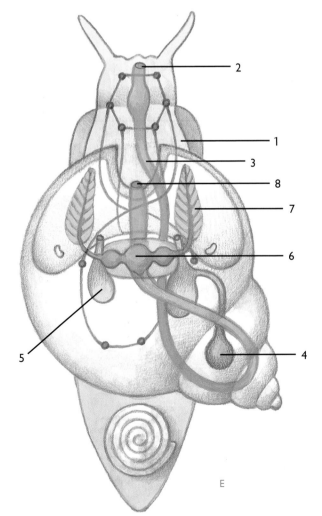

E

B, D, E. These illustrations reconstruct the evolutionary steps that have transformed the organization of a hypothetical primitive gastropod (B) into a present-day gastropod (E), through an intermediate phase (D) that is also hypothetical. The two decisive phenomena were the formation of the spiral shell and the 180-degree rotation of the organ group comprised of the shell, mantle, and viscera from the head-foot group.

1. nerve fibers
2. mouth
3. intestine
4. gonads
5. kidney
6. heart
7. gills
8. anus

G

C. A lovely photo of a triton, Charonia tritonis variegata, taken in Hawaii. It is present in most warm and temperate seas of the world. From ancient Rome to Polynesia, its shell has been used as a war trumpet or for religious ceremonies.

F. The ornamentation of this graceful gastropod mimics the coral polyps on which it feeds.

G. The surface of the tiger cowrie (Cypraea tigris) from the Indopacific is still quite common in most of its vast territory.

THE MOLLUSK:
ANATOMY OF A WINNER

A, B. The foot of
the ancestor of the
gastropods evolved
differently, depending
on the system of
locomotion the
animal adopted.
In A, we can see a
prosobranch with
a foot similar to
that of its ancestors,
adapted to sliding
along a substratum
(reptation). In B,
the foot of the

opisthobranch (a
Hydatina physis,
photographed in
Australia, where it
is commonly known
as the rose petal
bubble) allows the
animal to swim at
the water's surface.
Opisthobranchs
capable of swimming
have a very light
shell.

C. The drawing
shows the principal
elements of the
common northern
whelk (Buccinum
undatum), a
gastropod from the
Muricidae family,
a subfamily of the
Buccininae (which
other authors consider
a true family, the
Buccinidae). It feeds
primarily on dead
animals. The

relatively long siphon
allows it to withdraw
clean water from the
environment even
when it is on muddy
or slimy bottoms.
1. shell
2. operculum
3. inhaling siphon
4. tentacle
5. proboscis
6. mouth
7. foot
8. mantle edge
9. eye

These formless little creatures may be tasty when served as shellfish, but who knows how to explain their anatomy? And yet they produce shells, objects of extraordinary geometrical rigor, with a beautiful variety of forms, ornamentation, and colors. It is no coincidence that some collecting books mention only shells, while the organs of their builders are dismissed as soft parts. But if you want to take a look at the fascinating chapter of natural history written by these conquerors of every corner of the sea, you should at least have some idea of how they are made and function. This takes some attention, because in the eyes of us vertebrates, mollusks look like aliens. This is especially so for snails, whose anatomical structure is variable, because when they retract into their spiral shell, what happens to their bodies is a little like what happens to camping tents folded up into their bags: the parts that were on top end up on the bottom, and the things that were distant become close to each other; throughout the long period of evolution, this has caused great transformations.

But despite appearances and the extreme variety of forms in today's classes of mollusks, it has been possible to reconstruct a single original model of a mollusk. This model is only hypothetical, because, as we have seen in the preceding chapter, we will never know for certain what the progenitor of all mollusks really looked like; the metamorphosis of terrestrial rocks has destroyed all fossil traces. Its organization was reconstructed based on the anatomy of present-day mollusks and what we know of those fossils. During the course of evolution, some aspects of the mollusks's original structural model were lost or radically transformed, but the legacy left by the hypothetical progenitor can still be traced in all classes of the phylum.

A

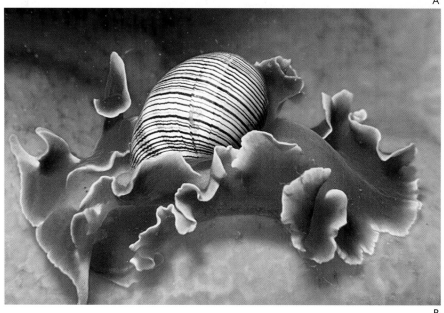

B

Basic mollusk organization includes five fundamental parts:

The foot, which is a fleshy, muscular organ used for locomotion. Its appearance may vary depending on the manner of movement. In species that move by crawling on a substratum, like most snails, the foot has essentially maintained its original appearance. It has changed greatly in species that have given up nearly all mobility, like clams, or which swim freely, like the nautilus or sea hare *(Aplysia)*.

The head, located in front of the foot. This is the area where the mouth opens, and the site of the cerebral

E

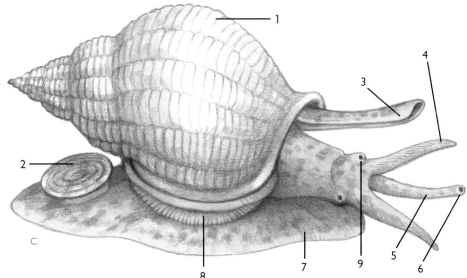

C

ganglia and sensory organs. Typically, the head of a snail has one or two pairs of tentacles, one of which has eyes at the base or the summit. In more sedentary species that do not move in search of food but filter nourishment suspended in the water, the head is reduced to a mouth and little more.

The visceral sac, located on the back in relation to the foot, includes the digestive tract and the excretory, circulatory, and reproductive systems (see below).

The mantle, a characteristic organ of mollusks, consists of an epidermal layer that covers the visceral sac and then descends to the base, forming a fold that surrounds the head and foot. The space that forms between the fold and the rest of the body is of particular importance, because a good part of exchanges with the outside environment occur in this cavity, known as the mantle cavity or pallial cavity (from *pallium*, "mantle" in Latin). Originally a respiratory organ, it has remained such for most mollusks. In almost all bivalves and in some gastropods, it also became an organ for taking in food, while in cephalopods and some bivalves, it was transformed into a sort of pump that allows the animal to move according to the principle of a hydraulic engine.

The shell, formed by a secretion of the mantle, was originally a simple oblong, depressed cone. During the course of evolution, many species lost their shells, or transformed them into an internal structure, or kept only vestiges of them—for example, in the form of cutaneous spicules in aplacophores—depending on the type of life they adopted. One of the following chapters will be devoted to the formation and different types of shells.

D, E. Two different ways to care for the outside of the shell. After the murex (E) builds its shell, it only repairs it in case of traumatic breaks, primarily due to attacks by predators. The husks of old shells that behave in this manner often show signs of wear, losing the periostracum and developing encrustations, with their shells furrowed by sponges and other animals. Like other cowries, Cypraea cervus *(D) behaves differently; it covers the outside of its shell with its mantle, thus keeping the surface of the shell extraordinarily shiny.*

D

In the Belly of a Marine Snail

Having defined the fundamental parts of mollusk organization, let us now look at some characteristic traits of the internal anatomy of the most interesting shell builders—gastropods. Their organization is the result of complex evolution. As we have seen above, a torsion of 180 degrees in the body mass containing the mantle, visceral sac, and shell from the head-foot mass deprived gastropods of bilateral symmetry. Consequently, the ganglia of the nervous system that ran along the two sides intersected to form a sort of X (a phenomenon known as chiastoneuria), and the organs that in

Here are some details on these organs.

Radula. Used to grasp and grind up food, this is a ribbon-shaped membrane armed with parallel rows of teeth, acting as a flexible rasp that slides along a sort of tongue, known as an odontophore. By extroflexing the odontophore and allowing the radula to slide, the snail scrapes away food even from very hard surfaces and conveys it, well-ground, to the esophagus. The rows of teeth and the radula itself wear out rather quickly, but the snail can produce new ones continuously through specialized cells known as odontoblasts. Each species has a radula with a

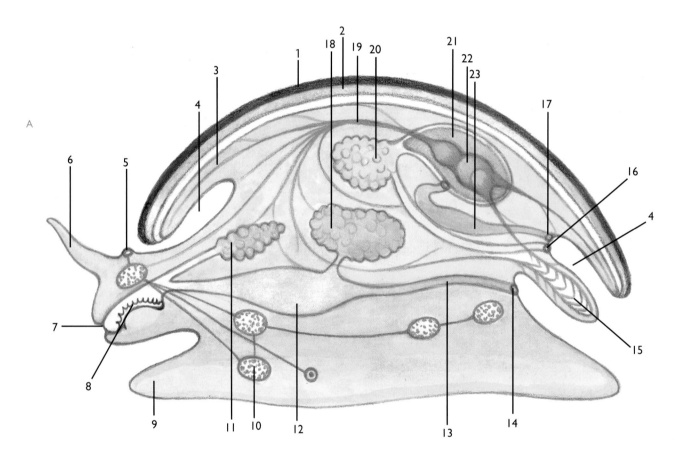

A. The drawing shows a general scheme of the internal anatomy of a mollusk.

1. periostracum
2. shell
3. mantle
4. pallial cavity
5. eye
6. cephalic tentacle
7. mouth
8. radula
9. foot
10. nerve ganglion
11. salivary gland
12. stomach
13. intestine
14. anus
15. gill
16. genital orifice
17. excretory orifice
18. hepatopancreas
19. blood vessel
20. gonads
21. pericardium
22. heart
23. kidney

an animal with a symmetrical structure normally appear in pairs, like kidneys, gills, atria of the heart, and gonads, have in most gastropods become a single organ.

Digestive tract. Begins with a mouth, in which cavity are two robust plates, the jaws, and continues with the crop, which includes an organ for taking in food, the radula, that is characteristic of the phylum of mollusks. The ducts of the salivary glands open up into the crop. The digestive tube then continues into the stomach and back intestine.

distinctive structure, depending on the type of food. When carefully observed under a scanning electron microscope, the radula allows malacologists to classify snails.

Salivary glands. These open into the gullet through two ducts. They produce the mucus snails need for digestion. In some families of carnivores, these transform into poison glands that can paralyze or kill prey.

Stomach. After the crop, the digestive tube continues into an esophagus, and then widens into a stomach. Food arrives here in the form of strings of particles bound together by mucus, and is partially digested through the activity of the crystalline style, which is located at the back of the stomach and releases enzymes for digesting glucides. Cilia on the stomach wall then carry the food to two large glands that form the spiral caecum.

Spiral caecum. This occupies a large part of the visceral sac. It both absorbs food particles and secretes enzymes. When you clean a shell by removing the soft parts, the spiral caecum looks like a dark spiral that occupies the innermost part of the shell.

Back intestine. This portion of the digestive tube runs in complex circumvolutions and ends in the anus, which opens into the mantle cavity. The current of water that runs within this organ removes catabolites from the body.

Circulatory system. The blood of mollusks is called hemolymph. Unlike the blood of vertebrates, which has numerous free cells (white corpuscles, red corpuscles, and so forth), hemolymph has only a small number of them. Oxygen is thus captured and released through two respiratory pigments dissolved within it: hemoglobin, which contains iron, and hemocyanin, which contains copper. Pumped by the heart, the hemolymph runs through circulatory vessels and gaps between the organs to reach the tissues. The hemolymph is purified by the nephridia (kidneys) and oxygenated by the ctenidia (gills), but often also by other vascularized tissues that play the same role in gas exchange.

Heart. This is composed of one or two atria that receive the hemolymph oxygenated by the gills and purified by the kidneys, and pump it into the single ventricle. Using an aorta, the ventricle distributes it to various organs. In mollusks, only oxygenated hemolymph, the equivalent of our arterial blood, passes through the heart.

Excretory system. This consists of one, or sometimes two, nephridia (or kidneys) located right behind the mantle cavity. The interior of a nephridium is like a spongy sac, as its walls consist of a tissue arranged in many intricate little folds, covered with cells that contain uric acid. Here the

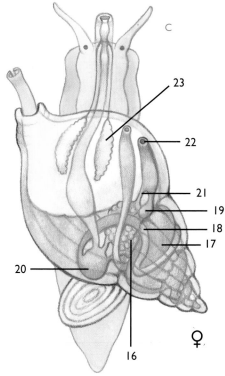

♂

hemolymph gives up its catabolites, urea, and other nitrogenous substances, and proceeds to the gills. The kidney expels the catabolites into the mantle cavity either through a simple orifice or through a conduit with cilia, the ureter.

Genital apparatus. This is different for each of the three subclasses of gastropods. With a few exceptions, prosobranchs have distinct sexes, while opisthobranchs and pulmonates are almost all hermaphrodites. In less evolved prosobranchs (like limpets and topshells) there is no internal fecundation (fertilization). Spermatozoa and ova from male and female gonads are released into the seawater, where fecundation takes place.

In more evolved prosobranchs (like periwinkles, cowries, and whelks) fecundation is internal, and the eggs are released into the marine environment either protected by a gelatinous mass or enclosed within egg capsules. The male has a gonad contiguous with the spiral caecum; the spermatozoa go through a prostate that runs along the bottom of the mantle cavity, parallel to the rectum. Fecundation occurs by means of a penis that may be quite large and emerges from the mollusk's head or neck, behind the right tentacle. The female genital apparatus is much

more complex. From the ovary, ova reach the albumen gland, which envelops them in a nourishing fluid, and then proceed to the capsule gland (in other species the gelatin gland), which produces the outer protection. The duct between the albumen gland and the capsule gland contains a side pocket, the spermatheca, where the male gametes are kept until used. The ovum is fertilized at the front end of the albumen gland. The female apparatus emerges just within the mantle cavity.

♀

B, C. The drawings provide a general outline of the main internal anatomical features of a male (to the left) and female (to the right) cenogastropod prosobranch.
1. mouth
2. proboscis
3. cephalic tentacle
4. eye
5. foot
6. siphon
7. gill
8. auricle
9. pericardium
10. ventricle
11. kidney
12. operculum
13. male gonads
14. anus
15. penis
16. female gonads
17. digestive gland
18. intestine
19. spermotheca
20. stomach
21. oviduct
22. female genital aperture
23. salivary glands

FEEDING, REPRODUCTION, DEFENSE: THE VITAL FUNCTIONS

Movement

A

When someone is moving too slowly, we say he's going at a snail's pace. Yet, without ever quickening their pace, snails have successfully made great strides over a half billion years. It's a sign that this is the best speed for them to meet the challenges of an aquatic environment. But just how does a snail's pace really function? In other words, how does a gastropod use its foot to crawl along a solid surface?

Experts discovered the secret of this form of locomotion, known as reptation, about 40 years ago. What moves the

the foot alternate in the movement: the portions that do not move adhere tenaciously to the substratum, so much so that a suction-cup action has been hypothesized. In reality, it is not an adhesion caused by a pneumatic depression, like a suction cup, but rather a very thorough adhesion of the foot cells, which are quite plastic and moistened with mucus, to every single irregularity of any surface they touch.

In bivalves, a class of mollusks much less mobile than gastropods, movement is by different means. For small movements on the surface of the seabed, the

B

C

A. Gastropods use a highly flexible foot for movement. This muscular, well-innervated organ not only allows the mollusk to slide forward through the mechanism of reptation, but also permits it to climb up slender supports, to lift its shell from the substratum, or to bury it in the sand or mud. The figure shows the trichotropid Torellia mirabilis *from the Antarctic coast.*

mollusk forward is a wave caused by muscular contractions that moves the foot in some species forward to backward, and vice versa in other species. In the first case, common to genera like *Haliotis, Trochus,* and *Littorina,* movement occurs when a small portion of the foot is raised, projected forward, and once again placed on the ground; its subsequent contraction moves the part behind the foot forward. If the wave travels the other way (as has been seen in the genera *Fissurella, Nerita,* and *Turbo*) the portion of the foot in contact with the substratum contracts, but the result is still the same—the gastropod moves forward. The parts of

D

B, C, D. A robber waits in ambush. Using its foot, the cone Conus textile of the Indopacific, which can kill small fish by paralyzing them with its poisonous dart, lies buried in the coral sand. It stays in contact with the surrounding environment through its siphon, which can be discerned by its alternately light- and dark-colored bands.

E, F, H, I. The photos show a large volute, Cymbiola imperialis, as it buries itself. Despite its massive shell, which can be as much as 25 centimeters long, the animal's large, relatively slender foot can perform the operation very quickly.

H

E

I

F

G. The drawing shows the system a bivalve, the cockle Acanthocardia echinata, uses to enter and exit the substratum. The red foot can alternately elongate and swell, pulling the animal into the seabed or out of it. The exhaling and inhaling siphons the mollusk uses to take in oxygen-rich water and food particles and expel catabolites are shown at the far left.

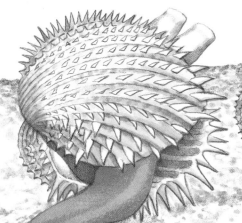

G

33

foot, alternating contractions and extensions and resting on the substratum, pushes the mollusk in the desired direction. On mobile seabeds of sand and mud, the foot can bury the mollusk in the substratum with a traction movement, achieved through a series of quick swellings followed by elongations, similar to the way certain earthworms move. But some species of bivalves use their shell and mantle to move at the water's surface with remarkable speed. Thus, scallops can jump at the water's surface by snapping the two valves shut (it takes only forty-six thousandths of a second for the muscle contraction). The mollusk

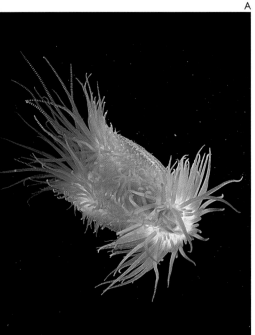

behaves in this manner when it becomes aware of an approaching predator. If this kind of emergency situation does not exist and such rapid, lengthy movement is not necessary, the scallop expels water from its shell in various ways, achieving movement in the opposite direction from the preceding one. In both cases, movement is based on the principle of a reaction engine. In an aquarium, if we provoke a bed of scallops into fleeing together, the effect is something similar to an underwater flight of butterflies.

A, C. The photos evidence two ways in which bivalves swim. Over a long period of evolution, a few families of this class of mollusks—which had originally given up mobility and sight to live an exclusively sedentary life, feeding on detritus suspended in the water—rediscovered the advantages of movement, and at the same time developed elementary eyes along the edges of the mantle. In C, a scallop from the Atlantic and Mediterranean, Aequipecten opercularis, *swims on the water's surface using a jet propulsion system that is activated by opening and closing its valves. In A, the file shell* Limaria hians *swims by opening its valves and moving its rich crown of filaments.*

B. The drawing shows the swimming scallop Pecten maximus *of the Atlantic. By alternately contracting and releasing its adductor muscles, the mollusk can rapidly open and close its valves, creating a strong jet of water that results in an elementary but efficient form of jet propulsion.*

D

D. Of all mollusks, the cephalopods, a class of predators, have found the most brilliant solution to the problem of locomotion. Thus, the giant Australian cuttlefish, while relying on the seabed for food, can move quite rapidly on the water's surface through the jet propulsion it achieves by expelling water through a siphon with an adjustable opening.

E. One gastropod, the Janthina, *relies on currents and wind for movement. It stays afloat using a raft that it builds by forming bubbles of mucus and gluing them together. Incapable of independent movement, it is part of the plankton and feeds by preying on planktonic cnidarians that it comes upon.*

The mollusks that have most highly refined the principle of reaction propulsion are the cephalopods: cuttlefish and squid are among the fastest of all marine animals.

They move using a very rapid muscular contraction (sixty-eight thousandths of a second) that expels the water in the animal's mantle through an appropriately placed siphon; by squeezing the siphon, the mollusk can regulate the speed of the water expelled and thus the speed at which its body moves. In this case, the principle of reaction propulsion is expressed by the formula "Mass of the animal multiplied by speed of the animal equals mass of the liquid multiplied by speed of the liquid," and as the two masses, the animal's and that of the liquid in its mantle sac, are fixed quantities, the speed of movement depends solely on the speed the water is expelled through the siphon.

Numerous species of gastropods and bivalves have completely given up movement as adults. In some cases they allow themselves to be carried by marine currents and become part of the plankton. This is the case of snails from the genus *Janthina*, who float on rafts of water bubbles held together by mucus. As we have noted, mussels anchor to the substratum with filaments of byssus. Common and thorny oysters cement a valve to the seabed. Vermetids have transformed their snail shell into a more or less wormlike tube cemented to the substratum. Date mussels *(Lithophaga lithophaga)* dig a tunnel in the calcareous rock and live there for their entire life, sheltered from predators, and shipworms *(Teredo navalis)* use the same strategy by boring wood. Dispersion of populations in these sedentary species takes place during their larval stage.

F

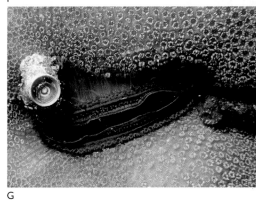

G

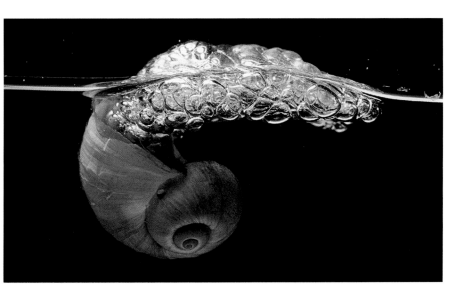

E

F. Two limpets buried among the cirripeds that cover the reef. In this case, they only appear to be immobile. When it is dark, the two limpets will leave their burrows to graze on the film of algae that covers the rock. When the meal is over, they will be able to return home with no problem.

G. Among the bivalves, the scallops are known for their mobility, but Pedum spondyloidum, *photographed here in the Arl Atoll of the Maldives, has adopted a life-style different from its relatives. Its larvae settle in a hollow of a coral formation and allow the coral colony to partially surround the shell. It has just enough room to close its valves and extroflex its siphons.*

Respiration

The exchange of gases with air dissolved in the water occurs in the mantle cavity through the ctenidia, gills with a lamellar structure that assume various forms, depending on the species. The water is circulated in the mantle cavity by cilia that create a current through their movement. In many species, the need to bury themselves in the sand or mud has led to the transformation of a flap of the mantle into an inhaling siphon, a proboscis-shaped appendage that inhales the oxygen-rich water from the substratum. In other species there is also an exhaling

A, B. Respiratory structure of a gastropod (A) and a bivalve (B). In A, the water rich in dissolved oxygen is sucked in by the siphon through the gills (1) and is subsequently returned to the environment through the shell cavity. In B, the water, after having been aspirated through the siphon (2) and having passed through the bivalve's bronchi, is expelled through the siphon (3).

1. gills
2. inhaling siphon
3. exhaling siphon
4. hypobranchial gland
5. osphradium
6. pallial cavity

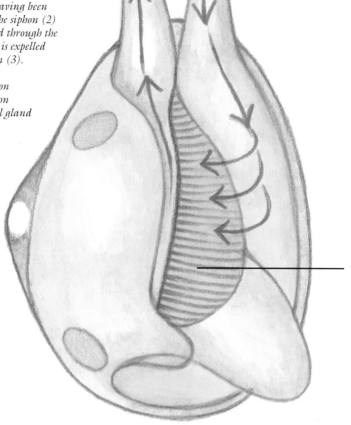

siphon that has the task of removing oxygen-poor water and catabolites from the mantle cavity.

Depending on the position of the gills relative to the heart, marine gastropods can be divided into two large subclasses: the prosobranchs, with gills in front of the heart, and opisthobranchs, whose gills are turned toward the caudal area. In opisthobranchs, the nerve ganglia do not intersect, perhaps because the original torsion of the body was followed by a straightening. The third subclass of gastropods, the pulmonates (of which only very few species are marine), have transformed the mantle cavity into a sort of lung that can take in oxygen directly from the atmosphere. There are also a few examples of mollusks with both gills and lungs, which can breathe either in or out of the water.

C. The movements of this gastropod on an uneven surface are controlled by the statolith, a minute calcareous formation that stimulates the nerve endings of the foot.

D. A strombus explores the environment with its eyes and antennae, whose chemical sensors supply the nervous system with vital information about the environment.

The Nervous System and Sensory Organs

Depending on the type of life they lead and the relationships they establish with their environment, mollusks have developed very diverse nervous systems. The more sedentary species, like the bivalves that feed by filtering particles suspended in the water, in general have elementary nervous systems, with nerve cells scattered along a few cords, connected to each other by simple ganglia that perform local functions. At the other extreme, we find more dynamic organisms, like carnivorous hunters who must identify, follow, and capture prey. It is no coincidence that these species have highly complex nervous structures and sensory organs, with ganglia that resemble the brain of vertebrates.

C

Sensory organs are also closely related to the animal's relationship with the environment. With regard to sight, the gamut runs from organisms with just a few photosensitive cells, capable of informing the animal of whether there is light and shadow in its environment and nothing more, all the way to species that have developed eyes with crystalline lenses that can focus on distant objects. The most evolved mollusk, the octopus, is capable of distinguishing various geometric forms. Aquarium experiments have shown that the octopus is capable of memorizing these geometric forms by associating them with pleasant or unpleasant sensations created by the experimenter.

In the great majority of mollusks, however, sight is not a primary sense, all the more so because much of the phylum prefers poorly illuminated or completely dark environments. Many species pass the daylight hours buried under the sand

or mud of the seabed and come out only at night. How do they orient themselves, and how, for example, do they find living prey or a fish carcass to devour? It is clear that marine mollusks have a complete battery of chemical sensors that permits them to sniff out currents of water and take advantage of the information they receive. It is much more challenging to identify in the laboratory which sensitive cells are used for which tasks in the chemical exploration of the environment.

Researchers are particularly interested in the osphradium, a plume-shaped organ traversed by a nerve that many gastropods have. Located at the base of the gills, an excellent position for analyzing the flow of water inhaled by the mollusk, the osphradium in effect seems to be a switchboard for detecting chemical substances, although it probably combines this function with testing the physical consistency of the solid particles suspended in the water, to prevent the gills from clogging.

With most of the body enclosed in a shell, many species of mollusks use various tactile appendages. Sometimes these are hairs or slender filaments, which in many cases seem to

E. The drawing shows the structure of a snail's nervous system. The process of cephalization (1), i.e., thickening of the ganglia in the head to form a brain, is still quite modest. Note in the digestive tract the x-shaped intersection of the nerve cords due to the torsion the snail underwent during the course of evolution. Neurons connect the cephalic ganglia to the eyes (2), the tactile and chemical sensors of the tentacles (3), the heart (4), the digestive tract (5), the gills (6) and the other organs.

D

be sensitive to both chemical and tactile stimulation. The edge of the mantle is the part of the body best equipped for this purpose, at least in most species. All species are also equipped with small organs that transmit information on the animal's position within its environment to the nervous system. At the base of the foot's nerve ganglia there are two pockets, the statocysts, within which moves a tiny calcareous formation, the statolith, which by stimulating the nerve endings orients the animal and gives it equilibrium.

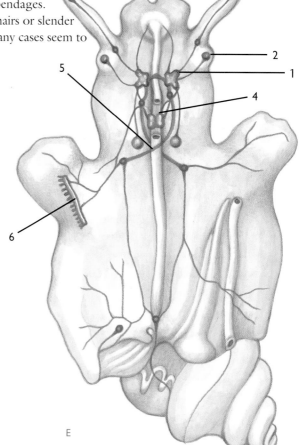

E

A

A, F. To a casual observer, marine gastropods seem to have no sight organs. But by focusing in closer, the underwater photographer was able to see the eyes of these two strombids from the Pacific, Strombus dentatus *(A) and* Lambis *(F).*

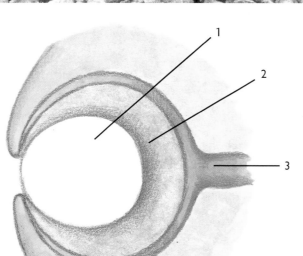

1
2
3

B

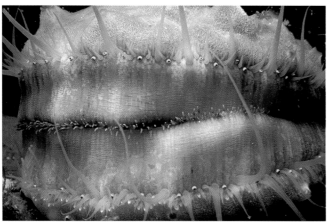

C

4

E

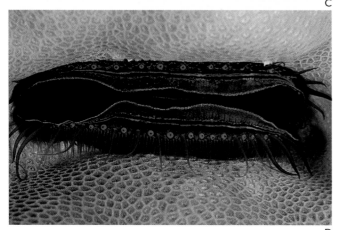

D

B, E, G. Mollusks who live in the dark or feed as parasites or detritivores have no sense of sight. Sight is quite poor in bivalves like the scallops, whose eyes are capable only of perceiving variations in the intensity of environmental light. In relatively primitive snails like the trochids, the eye (B), consisting of the vitreous chamber (1), retina (2), and optical nerve (3), is quite primitive and perceives only vague images. In more evolved mollusk predators like the murices, the eye (E) has a crystalline lens (4), and the images are more distinct. In *highly evolved cephalopods like squid, the eye (G) also has an iris (5) and optical ganglion (6). The images come into focus in essentially the same way as in vertebrates, not by modifying the form of the crystalline lens but by moving the lens away from or toward the retina.*

F

H, I, J. The striptease of a beautiful Cypraea pantherina from the Indopacific. When it is not disturbed, the cowrie (H) grazes peacefully on the algae from the seabed, with its shell wrapped in its semi-transparent mantle. As soon as it detects the presence of potential danger, it begins to retract its mantle, formed of very delicate tissue (I), which it then hides safely under its robust shell (J).

H

C, D. The evolutionary reconquest of the sense of sight has led to the development of a series of ocelli on the edge of the mantle of bivalves. These eyes have a very limited capacity, and act primarily in detecting the intensity of light in the environment, but are nonetheless sufficient to allow the animal to perceive the presence of danger and close its valves. This scallop from the Pacific Northwest coast (Chlamys hastata) (C), camouflages itself using a purple sponge encrusted on the upper valve, while a burying bivalve from the Red Sea (D) peeps out of the coral in which it has settled, showing off a spectacular series of red eyes.

I

G

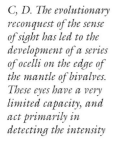

6

5

J

Feeding

During the course of their long evolution, mollusks have experimented with various feeding systems: there are herbivores, carnivores, and detritivores (which collect the particles of organic detritus that are continuously deposited on seabeds), suspension feeders (who capture organic particles that float at the water's surface), and parasites, which feed from the tissues of other animals by settling within them (endoparasites) or on them (ectoparasites). Among the carnivores, there are lazy species that feed on dead animals (necrophagia) or animals attached to the substratum. This is the case of murices, who graze on oysters, acorn barnacles, and mussels. There are also, however, active carnivores (for example, cephalopods like the cuttlefish and octopus) that can hunt moving prey due to their speed,

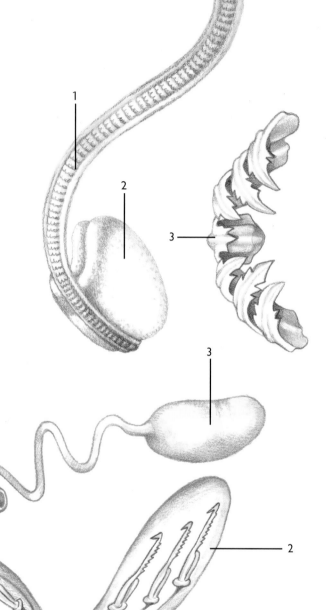

A

4

1

2

3

B

1

E

4

3

2

A. An example of a radula that is not highly specialized, used by less evolved snails like the cowries. The ribbon (1) is activated by a muscle (2) located behind the mouth. It has a great many rows of teeth armed with cusps (3) that can grind plant tissue. In the back portion (4), the rows of teeth are gradually produced by a special organ as the rows at the front wear out.

C

D

C, D, I, J. In this exceptional sequence, a Conus purpurascens of western Mexico shoots a dart into a small fish that has ventured near it, paralyzes it with a lightning injection of poison, and finally begins to swallow it. Cones like the one shown in the photo can be lethal to humans.

E. This image shows the dart protruding from the proboscis of a Conus striatus from the Indopacific. Cones inject their victims with a complex cocktail of toxic substances. The first to take effect create a tetanic contraction in the victim, to prevent any coordinated reaction; then other substances cause the vital systems to collapse and the organism to relax, allowing it to be ingested by the mollusk.

F, G, H. Cross-sections of a radula in a snail like a cowrie: Within the mouth (1), the ribbon of teeth (2) that makes up the radula slides back and forth, using a mechanical action just like a carpenter's rasp. It carries food particles (7) to the esophagus (6). The radula moves through the action of a muscle (4) anchored to a cartilage (5). The "radula pocket" (8) produces new teeth to replace those that wear out. In very primitive gastropods like the trochids, the radula consists of rows (3) containing dozens of teeth.

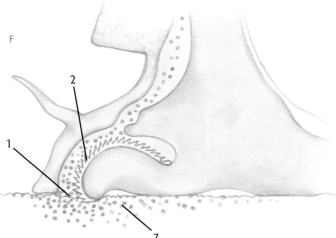

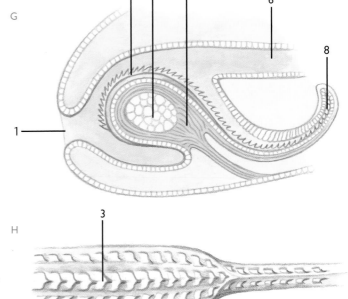

B. The drawing shows how the radula works in an evolved snail like the cone. The chitinous ribbon in herbivorous or perforating mollusks has become just one tooth (1) transformed into a poison-filled harpoon—essentially a syringe. Harpoons are produced (2) and continuously replaced, like the teeth of more conventional radulae. One by one, they descend into the proboscis (4), where they are filled with poison from a specially adapted salivary gland (3).

and carnivores that use ingenious methods of lying in ambush, like the cones, which are snails capable of striking their prey with a proboscis armed with a dart that injects a paralyzing poison. Each species of cone specializes in hunting other mollusks, worms, or even fish, but only the fish eaters have a poison powerful enough to pose a mortal threat to humans as well. Cones are one of the few families of mollusks whose close observation and collection require much experience and a great deal of caution.

We have seen that to capture and grind up food, mollusks have developed an organ unique in the animal world, the radula. Bivalves do not have a radula, but have developed ingenious systems to capture food particles from the water

A

B

D. The drawing shows a predator snail, a moon, attacking a bivalve. Its crucial weapon is its radula, which allows the attacker to drill the shell and suck out the tissues with its proboscis.

E. The radula is a fundamental invention in snails, and has been modified differently according to species. This chitinous rasp can scrape away food particles from vegetation, bore through the shell of prey, or even, paralyze prey by injecting a cocktail of refined poisons. In

A, through the enlarged opening of the mouth (1) of a predator snail (like the sand moon), we can see a portion of the radula, consisting of three rows of three teeth each (2), plus an auxiliary structure (3). By sliding the radula within the oral cavity and rotating the proboscis, the snail digs a perfectly circular furrow into the shell of the Cardium (4) that becomes a hole when the operation is completed (5). The predator then inserts its proboscis into its prey's shell and sucks out its tissues.

A, B, C. In this image captured in the Rangiroa Lagoon in Polynesia, the triton (Charonia tritonis) attacks a crown-of-thorns starfish (Acanthaster planci). Blocked by the triton's muscular foot (A, B), the starfish reacts and succeeds in making a counterattack against the aggressor, who then sprays it *with a white, poisonous substance (C), which kills it. The triton takes six hours to devour it. Acanthaster. planci feeds on coral polyps and is a danger to the integrity of the reef; the triton is thus a protected species in many countries precisely because it prevents this star-fish's uncontrolled proliferation.*

C

they inhale as they breathe through the gills, killing two birds with one stone, so to speak. The vibrating motion of a system of cilia forces water from the outside to the gills, located in the mantle cavity. For bivalves who live embedded in the substratum, the water flows through an inhaling siphon that may be even longer than the rest of the body. The gills are very developed and have complex forms. While their well-vascularized tissue captures oxygen dissolved in the water, special cilia systems, often equipped with mucus, dispose of inedible particles and convey useful particles to the mouth. The water utilized is expelled from the mantle cavity at the back end of the animal (through an exhaling siphon, for bivalves who live buried) along with catabolites, feces, and renal excretions.

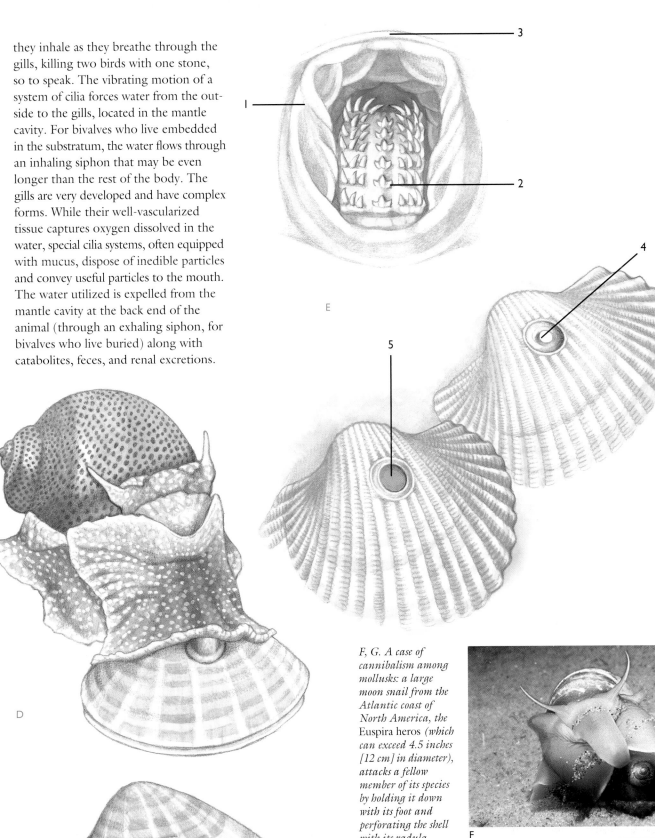

F, G. A case of cannibalism among mollusks: a large moon snail from the Atlantic coast of North America, the Euspira heros *(which can exceed 4.5 inches [12 cm] in diameter)*, attacks a fellow member of its species by holding it down with its foot and perforating the shell with its radula. When the hole is complete, the attacking snail inserts its proboscis into the flesh of its victim and devours its tissues. Usually, however, Euspira heros *hunts by moving under the sand of the seabed and attacking the bivalves that lie buried there.*

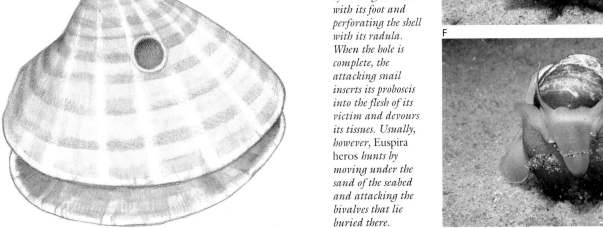

F

G

A. A Colubraria *explores a shark's scar in an attempt to reach the fish's internal tissues and suck its blood.*

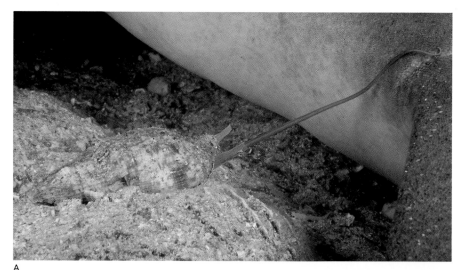

A

B

B. Three tiny wentletraps from the species Epitonium billeeanum *feed on the tissues of coral polyps from the genus* Tubastrea, *at Richelieu Rock in the Andaman Sea (Thailand).*

C. A predator turning into prey: in the sea of the Galapagos Islands in the East Pacific, a large fasciolariid, Pleuroploca princeps, *successfully attacks a murex, an active predator of bivalves.*

C

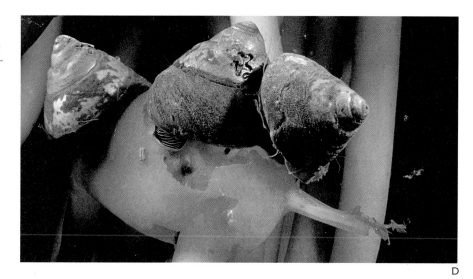

D. Three specimens of the turbinid Tegula *graze on the tissues of a large sea-tangle along the coast of California.*

D

E

E. An example of parasitic and vampire-type behavior: the gastropod at the center of the photo, a Colubraria obscura *from the Fasciolariidae family, has climbed onto the bubble of mucus that the parrotfish* Scarus soridus, *from the coral reefs of Thailand, has used to wrap around itself for protection. The mollusk has penetrated the mucus with its long, thin proboscis, which it inserts into the mouth of the sleeping fish to suck blood from its tissues.*

Reproduction

The reproductive strategies of mollusks vary from species to species. Less-developed representatives of the phylum use external fecundation: males and females discharge gametes into the water simultaneously, and the chance encounter of an ovum with a spermatozoon creates the larva of a new individual. Clearly, this is an enormously expensive strategy in terms of energy, because only a tiny fraction of the gametes hit the mark. Obviously, it is practiced only by aquatic mollusks.

More evolved species use internal fecundation, which occurs when individuals of different sexes or hermaphrodites mate. Internal fecundation permits high rates of reproduction using a relatively small number of gametes. It also permits the female reproductive system to protect the eggs from the outside environment by giving them a shell. In numerous species, the eggs are further

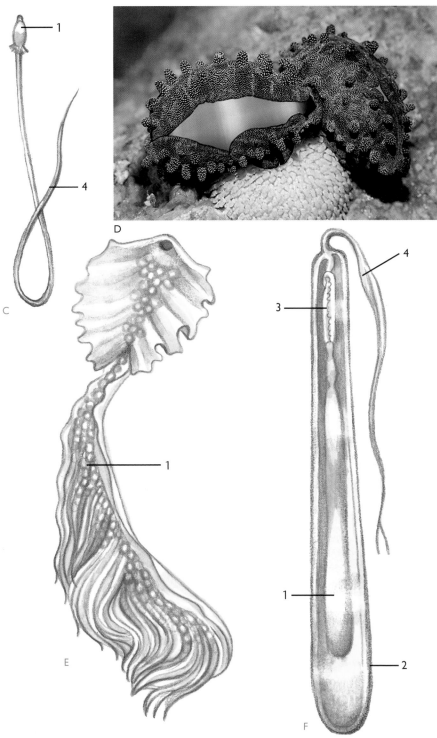

A. A limpet from the Antarctic province, Nacella concinna, from the South Orkney Islands, is releasing zygotes into the open water.

B. A Tridacna gigas, the largest bivalve in the world, emits a little cloud of ova into the water. Fecundation will take place in the open water, when ova encounter spermatozoa from the same species. The success of this

external reproduction is based on the immense number of zygotes released into the sea—hundreds of millions from each individual reproducer.

C, E, F. During the course of evolution, mollusks have used many reproductive strategies. Within the phylum, there are forms of external reproduction, with ova and spermatozoa released into the sea,

and internal fecundation of the ova, where individuals of the opposite sex or hermaphrodites mate directly or at a distance. There are also forms of panthenogenesis (fecundation without the male). Here, we see three systems mollusks use to bring the sperm to the ovum:
C. A trochid spermatozoon (1) moves by itself, using a flagellum (4).
E. The spermatozoa (1) travel in packs

(spermatozeugmae) within particular cells specialized in movement: the one illustrated is a spermatozeugma from Ceritiopsidae.
F. In cephalopods like the squid, the mass of spermatozoa (1) travels protected by a tunic (2) within a complex organ, the spermatophore. This tunic has an ejaculating organ (3) and a flagellum (4) for propulsion in open water.

G

H

protected by wrapping them in egg capsules. On the other hand, growth of the egg within the female system and the production of already formed individuals (viviparism) is quite rare among mollusks.

We have seen that hermaphroditism is the rule among opisthobranchs and pulmonates. The anatomical details of the reproductive organs normally prevent self-fecundation; for fecundation to occur, two hermaphroditic individuals must meet, and the male organ of each must fecundate the female organ of the other. A hypothesis advanced for the advantage of this strategy is this: snails move quite slowly, and encounters among individuals are relatively rare. If the sexes were separate, the probability that these encounters would occur between males and females would be no more than 50 percent. With both sexes in the same individual, however, .probabilities of encounters at least theoretically useful for reproduction rise to 100 percent.

I. An unfertilized ovum of a mollusk. We can see the nucleus (1) with the chromosomes (2).

J. The embryos can be seen forming through the transparent egg capsules of Nucella lapillus.

K. This image shows hatching Littorina *eggs. Most of the species of this genus of gastropods, which live in the supralittoral or tidal zone, do not form larva capable of swimming in the open water, but directly develop little snails that crawl away on the substratum after birth.*

D. Two Cypraea talpa *deposit eggs in the waters of Isla del Cocos in Costa Rica.*

G. Egg capsules deposited by two Conus scalaris, *a species from the more primitive family of conids, in western Mexico.*

H. Egg being deposited by the Bulla gouldiana *of California, the largest bullid in existence (its shell is up to 4.3 inches [6.4 cm] long). As is* usual for opisthobranchs, individuals of this species are hermaphrodites. The eggs are released in long, thin, gelatinous strings that form tangled masses.*

J

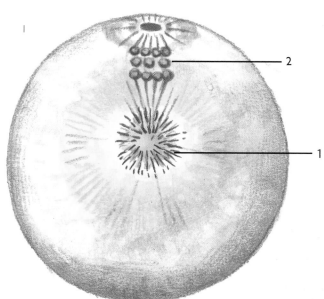

I

1

2

K

A

F

B, C, G, H, I, J, M, N.
B. The spermatozoon (3) enters the ovum and reaches the nucleus (2) (the polar bodies of the ovum are indicated under 1).
C. The union of the gametes forms the first cell of the new individual, the zygote (the egg sac in 4).
G. Two-cell development stage.
H. Four-cell development stage.

I. Multicell development stage.
J. Embryo (trochophore) at 22 hours of development (5, apical cilia).
M. Trochophore at 30 hours.
N. Trochophore at 44 hours, enlarged approximately 300 times:
  6. apical tuft;
  7. velum;
  8. larval mouth.

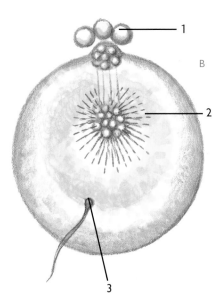

B

1

2

3

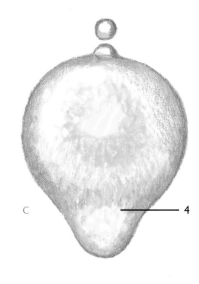

C

4

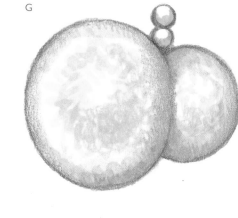

G

D

E

A. Three egg capsules of Nassarius reticulatus. This common snail of European seas deposits about a hundred of these capsules at a time.

D. Strange necklaces are not uncommon on sandy or muddy seabeds: these are the eggs of the moon snail, which we see in this photo as it deposits its eggs.

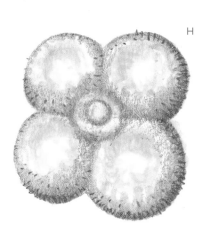

H

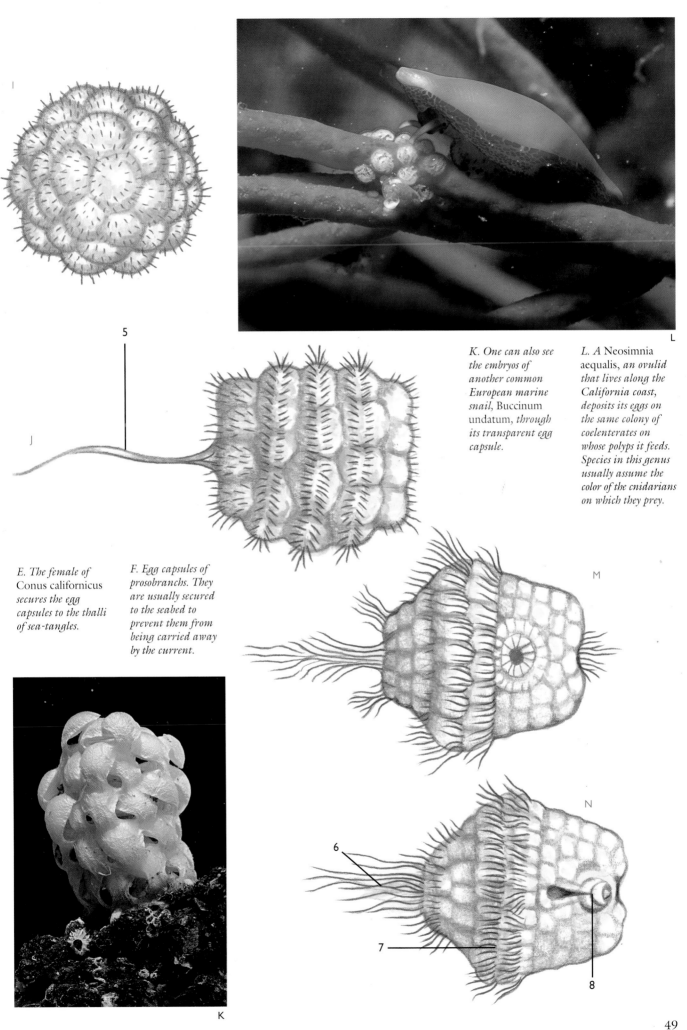

I

5

J

K. One can also see the embryos of another common European marine snail, Buccinum undatum, *through its transparent egg capsule.*

L. *A* Neosimnia aequalis, *an ovulid that lives along the California coast, deposits its eggs on the same colony of coelenterates on whose polyps it feeds. Species in this genus usually assume the color of the cnidarians on which they prey.*

L

E. *The female of* Conus californicus *secures the egg capsules to the thalli of sea-tangles.*

F. *Egg capsules of prosobranchs. They are usually secured to the seabed to prevent them from being carried away by the current.*

M

N

6

7

8

K

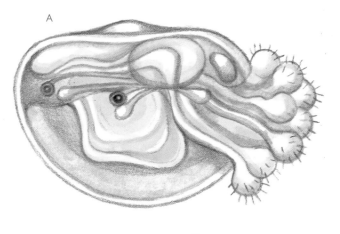

A

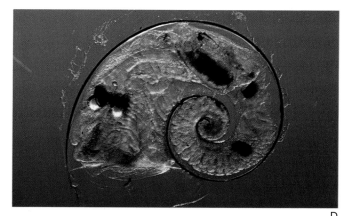

D

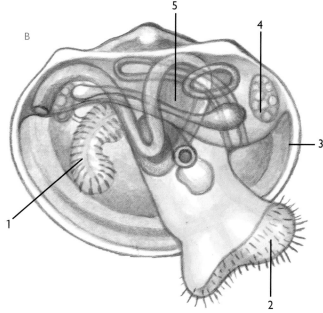

5

4

3

1

2

B

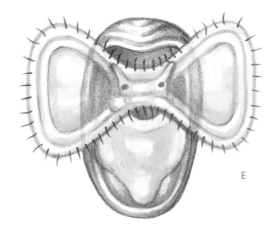

E

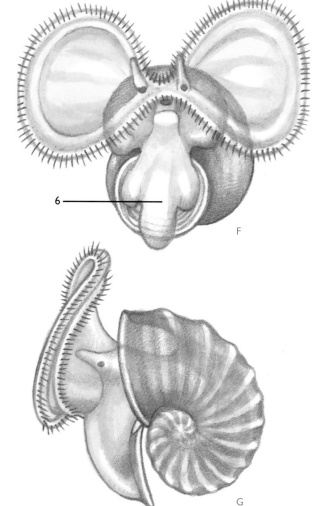

6

F

A, B. The develop-
ment of veliger larva
in a bivalve.
A. The structure of a
5-day-old embryo.
B. The veliger at
15 days. One can
distinguish the gills
(1), the foot (2), the
embryonic shell (3),
the adductor muscle
(4), and the stomach
(5).

C, H. Two veligers of
littoral mollusks from
Australia's Great
Barrier Reef. The
shell, already at the
embryonic stage, and
part of the digestive
tract are visible in both.
In C, the operculum
has also already
formed. The length of
larval life varies
greatly from species to
species. When it is
prolonged for entire
months, as for the

triton, it encourages
the dispersion of the
species over vast areas.

D, K. Pictured are
two pelagic mollusks,
an Atlanta (D) and
a Carinaria cristata
(K), prosobranch
gastropods that are
part of the plankton
even as adults. Most
mollusks in this sub-
class flow with the
plankton only during
their larval existence.

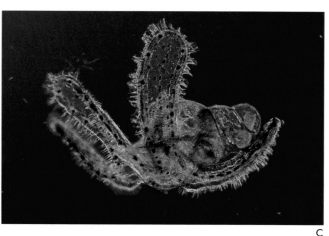

C

G

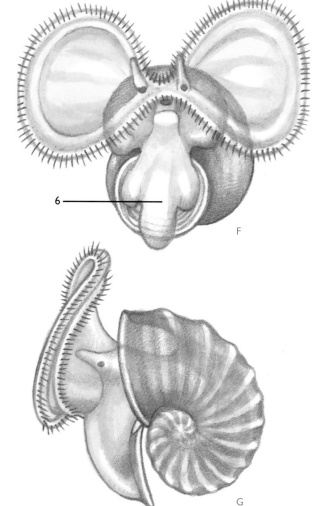

50

H

E, F, G, I, J. Some phases in veliger larval development of gastropods. This is a more evolved larval form than the trochophore, and is characteristic of the phylum of mollusks. In families that have veliger-type embryos, the trochophore form is only a stage of development within the egg. The velum, which allows the veliger to move freely through the water (although the movement is limited, within the plankton carried by sea currents), may take different forms: two lobes as in E and F, four lobes as in I (larva of Comormondia gracilis) or six lobes as in J (larva of Aporrhais pespelecani). In this phase of their development, gastropods have a distinct head, equipped with eyes and tentacles, a larval shell, and an early development of the foot (F-6).

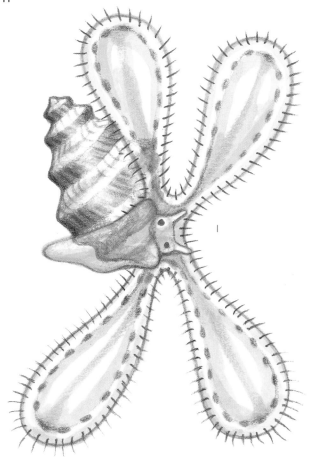

J

In marine mollusks, when the egg hatches, a larva generally appears that will float with the currents as part of the plankton. The larva may have a trochophore form (that is, a simple ciliated top, similar to the larva of other phyla of invertebrates) or a veliger form, which is a more evolved larva, characteristic of mollusks. The individual is already able to form a little shell, generally different in appearance from the adult shell, and has wing-shaped growths (the velum), equipped with cilia it uses to move through the water and obtain food. At the end of the larval period, the mollusk allows itself to fall to the seabed: if it finds the right

L. A group of immature Conus anemone, a very common cone along the southwestern coasts of Australia. Often, a number of females in this species will gather in groups to lay their eggs in the same area.

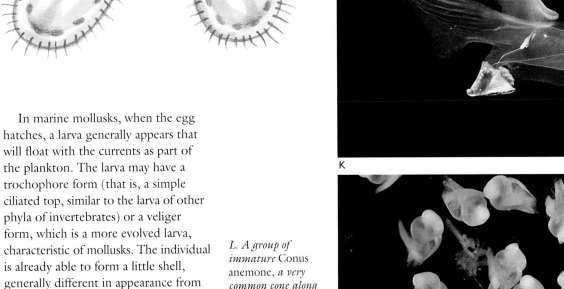

K

L

51

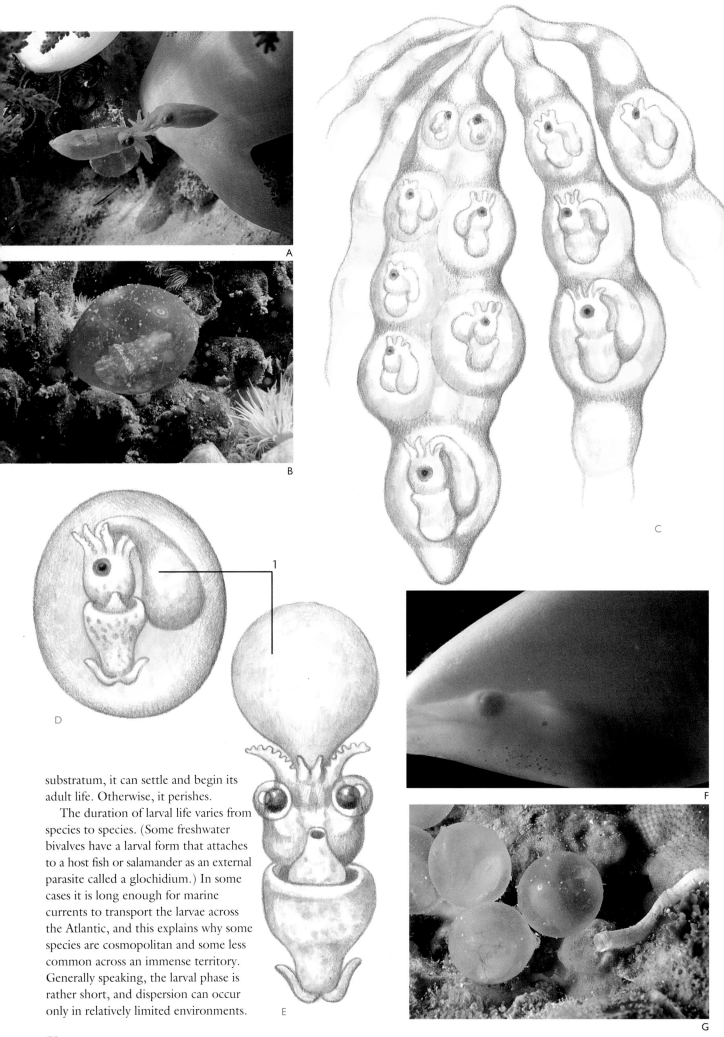

A

B

C

D

1

E

F

G

substratum, it can settle and begin its adult life. Otherwise, it perishes.

The duration of larval life varies from species to species. (Some freshwater bivalves have a larval form that attaches to a host fish or salamander as an external parasite called a glochidium.) In some cases it is long enough for marine currents to transport the larvae across the Atlantic, and this explains why some species are cosmopolitan and some less common across an immense territory. Generally speaking, the larval phase is rather short, and dispersion can occur only in relatively limited environments.

A. Cuttlefish mating. The cephalopods have developed a variety of very effective systems to avoid the loss of spermatozoa in the marine environment. Mating sometimes takes place at close quarters, while on

other occasions organs released from the male's body swim toward the female.

B. The formation of a mollusk larva seen through the translucent membrane of the egg.

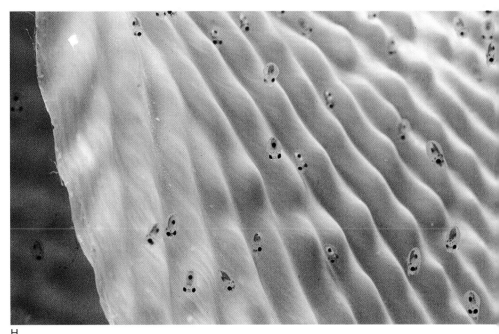

H

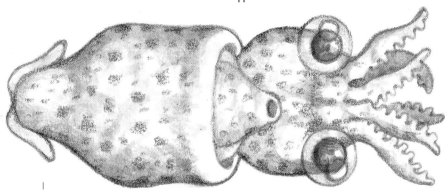

I

C, D, E, I. The stages of development of a squid. In the cluster of egg capsules (C), about 4 inches (10 cm) high, each embryo develops by assuming the basic structure of the adult individual (D) and gradually absorbing the yolk in the sac (1). When it

hatches from the egg, the little squid continues to empty the yolk sac (E) until it completely disappears. At this stage (I), the squid begins its life as a pelagic hunter. Its first food will be tiny forms of planktonic life.

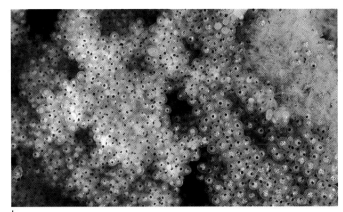

J

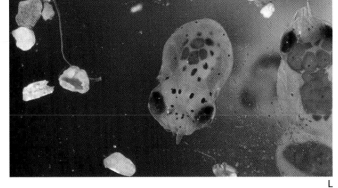

L

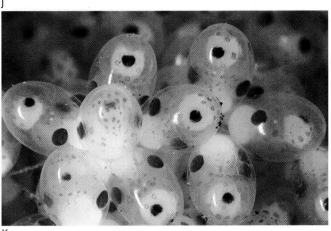

K

F. A giant of the sea takes shape: the embryo of an Australian giant cuttlefish (Sepia apama) inside its egg.

G. Cuttlefish eggs photographed on a detrital seabed in Yemen.

H. The female argonaut has always elicited the interest of natural history experts because it builds a unique, elegant pseudoshell that it carries with it in the high sea just to hold its eggs. The picture shows the birth of argonauts before the walls of the mother's pseudoshell.

J, K, L. A mass of Argonauta nodosa eggs almost ready to hatch. In L a newborn argonaut faces a perilous period of life in the plankton.

THE MOTHER-OF-PEARL FACTORY

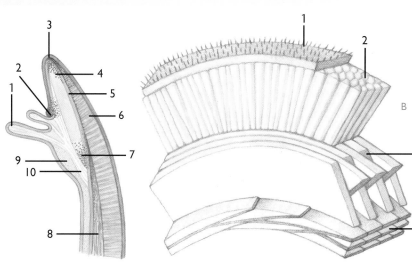

A. The illustration outlines the process of shell formation in a bivalve. The outer pallial epithelium (1) produces the periostracum (3) in the periostracal fold (2). The cells of the inner pallial epithelium (5) produce (4) the kaleite prisms of the ostracum (6), while the innermost area (7) produces crystals of aragonite that are used to build the hypostracum (8). The mantle (9) has a retractor muscle (10) that can pull it back into the shell.

Marine mollusks build their shells with the calcium carbonate they find in food and seawater. Specialized cells found at the edge of the mantle crystallize calcium carbonate into two fundamental forms: calcite, with prism-shaped crystals, or aragonite, with lamellar crystals. The shell is built by imprisoning the crystals within the weave of a network of organic material, the conchiolin, which, chemically speaking, is a polysaccharide similar to the chitin that forms the exoskeleton of insects. A small quantity of water is also imprisoned within the shell's structure. This explains why a shell, which may at first sight seem only a piece of limestone, is actually a "living rock," which may deteriorate with time and through the effect of light rays.

A shell has three layers: outermost is the periostracum, a covering of conchiolin

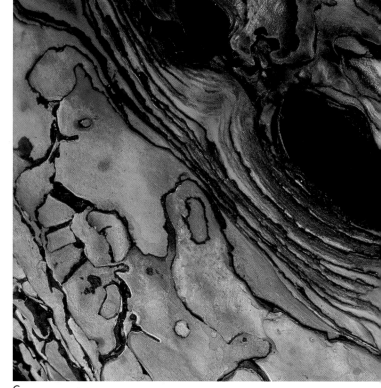

only that is often brown or blackish in color. It is absent in some families, like cowries, and often appears eroded even when the mollusk is living, dissolving quite rapidly after the shell is empty and exposed to the elements. Souvenir shell vendors frequently eliminate it to improve the shell's appearance, while specialized sellers and demanding collectors are careful not to destroy it. In fact, every collection should have at least one specimen that is as close as possible to how nature made it. The next layer is the ostracum: formed of calcite crystals, it is the hard and

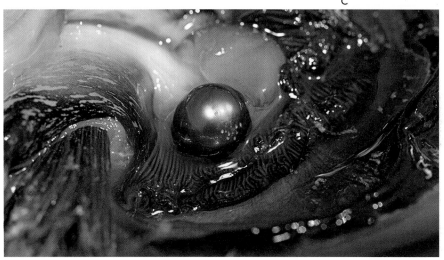

C

D

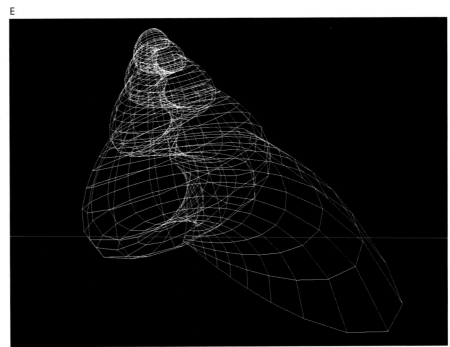

permanent part of the shell. Within this is the hypostracum, which is rather thin, formed of lamellar, unbroken aragonite. In some families, these hexagonal lamellae, cemented together in overlapping layers like the rows of bricks in walls, take the form of mother-of-pearl, a substance that is not only beautifully iridescent but also hard—two times harder than industrially produced synthetic ceramic.

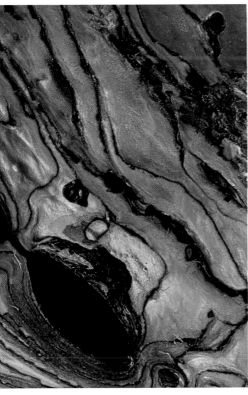

C. The extraordinary iridescence of the mother-of-pearl of the paua, an abalone from New Zealand (Haliotis iris). *This is the innermost layer of the shell, formed by sheets of crystallized calcium in the form of aragonite.*

D. A precious black pearl from Tahiti, produced by a Polynesian subspecies of the pearl oyster, Pinctada margaritifera cumingi. *Having become impossible to find in the natural state (in 1970, not one pearl was found in the 300,000 oysters collected in the Takapoto lagoon), it is now produced in cultivated pearl beds.*

E, F. In nature, the instructions for building a logarithmic spiral shell are written in the mollusk's genes. But we can ask a computer to emulate nature by providing an appropriate mathematical function. The polygonal outline of the electronically invented shell structure (E). The computer coverage of the polygons creates a shell that is extraordinarily similar to what can be found on a beach (F).

The part of the mollusk that builds the shell is the edge of the mantle. We have seen that the mantle cavity is an extremely important organ for the animal's relationship with the outside environment.

We can thus see how the evolution of the shell may reflect the transformation of the mantle and its cavity. For example, when a gastropod equips itself with siphons to pump water in or out of the mantle cavity, its shell acquires siphonal canals. This is a very important aspect in identifying the systematic position of a shell and the family to which it belongs.

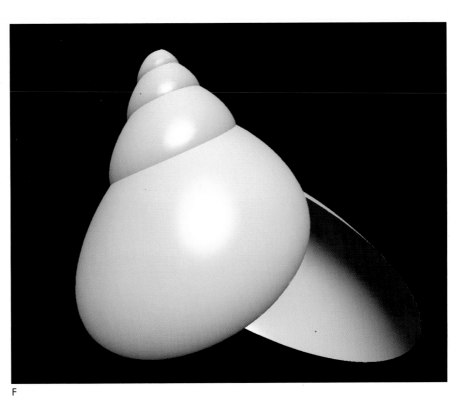

A, C. When X-rayed, shells with an elongated spire like the Fasciolaria lignaria *pictured in A often exhibit the type of coiling shown in the radiograph (C). Here, the coil axis, the columella, is sinuous.*

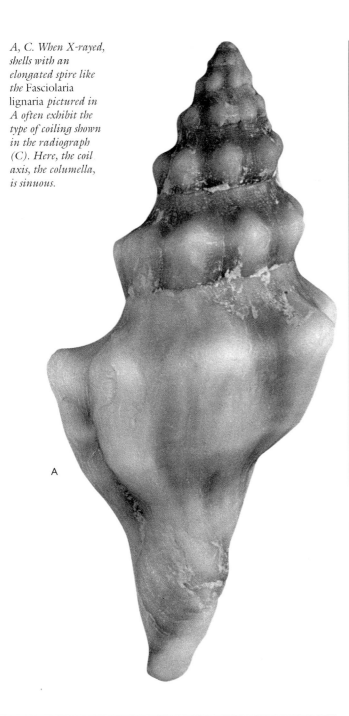

A

C

B

56

B, D. The X-ray image reveals the extraordinary elegance of the internal structure of the globular shell of Tonna galea, *a giant tun from the European seas.*

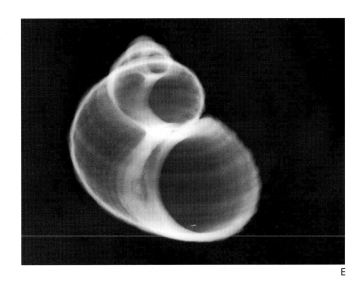

E

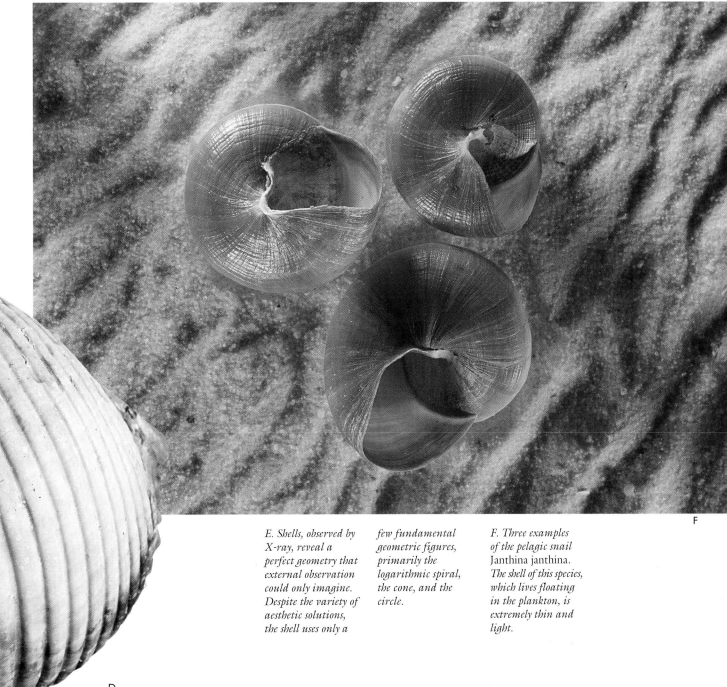

F

D

E. Shells, observed by X-ray, reveal a perfect geometry that external observation could only imagine. Despite the variety of aesthetic solutions, the shell uses only a few fundamental geometric figures, primarily the logarithmic spiral, the cone, and the circle.

F. Three examples of the pelagic snail Janthina janthina. *The shell of this species, which lives floating in the plankton, is extremely thin and light.*

A, C, D. A side (C), front (D), and cross-section (A) view of the shell of Nautilus pompilius. *This cephalopod, which lives in the Southwest Pacific, has four gills (other cephalopods have only two) and a symmetrical flat shell. The shell is also convoluted, as the last whorl covers all the other whorls. The cross section reveals another peculiarity of the nautilus shell that makes it different from all other gastropods: it is divided into chambers, which the nautilus gradually abandons as it grows. Divided by septa, the chambers connect through a series of small holes that run through the entire spiral. The mollusk, which can take in or expel gas from the chambers, uses its shell to move vertically in the water, as a fish does with its air bladder, changing its specific gravity.*

B

A

C

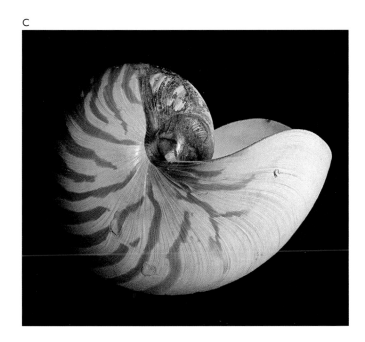

D

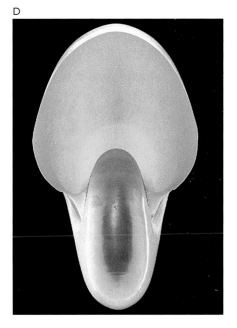

B, E. A side view (B) and a front view (E) of the nautilus shell, photographed using X-rays: the internal structure shows how the shell is formed, through the construction of cells abandoned by the mollusk as it grows. The result possesses a geometrical purity, an essential elegance and a fluidity of form which even an artist would find difficult to match.

E

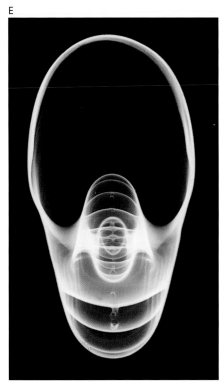

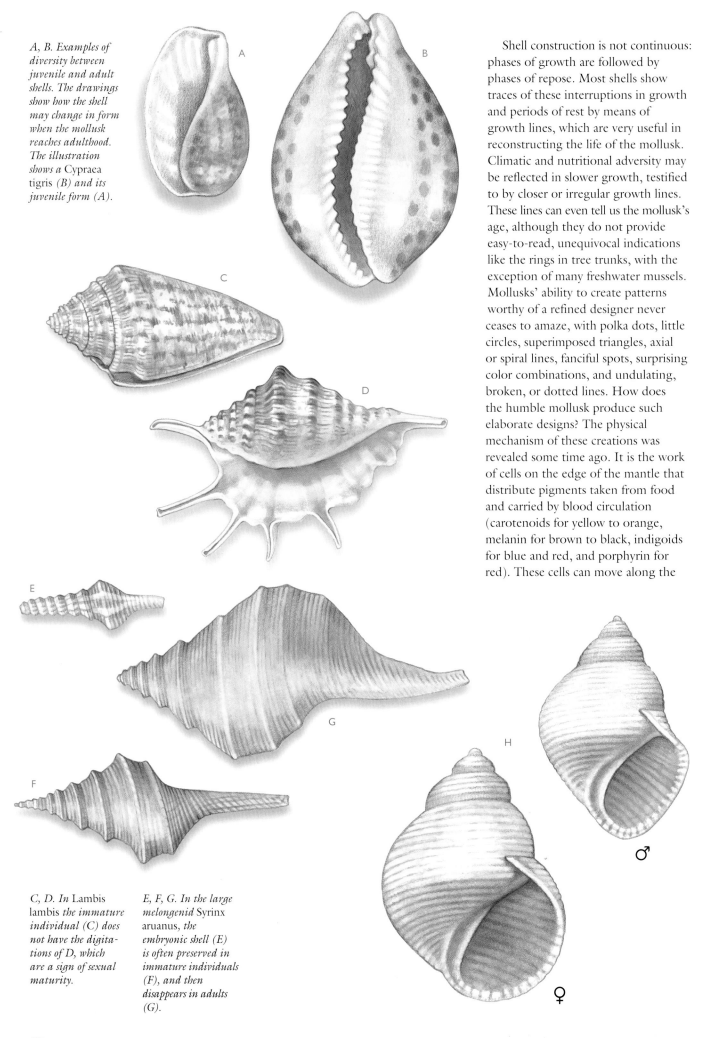

A, B. Examples of
diversity between
juvenile and adult
shells. The drawings
show how the shell
may change in form
when the mollusk
reaches adulthood.
The illustration
shows a Cypraea
tigris (B) and its
juvenile form (A).

Shell construction is not continuous:
phases of growth are followed by
phases of repose. Most shells show
traces of these interruptions in growth
and periods of rest by means of
growth lines, which are very useful in
reconstructing the life of the mollusk.
Climatic and nutritional adversity may
be reflected in slower growth, testified
to by closer or irregular growth lines.
These lines can even tell us the mollusk's
age, although they do not provide
easy-to-read, unequivocal indications
like the rings in tree trunks, with the
exception of many freshwater mussels.
Mollusks' ability to create patterns
worthy of a refined designer never
ceases to amaze, with polka dots, little
circles, superimposed triangles, axial
or spiral lines, fanciful spots, surprising
color combinations, and undulating,
broken, or dotted lines. How does
the humble mollusk produce such
elaborate designs? The physical
mechanism of these creations was
revealed some time ago. It is the work
of cells on the edge of the mantle that
distribute pigments taken from food
and carried by blood circulation
(carotenoids for yellow to orange,
melanin for brown to black, indigoids
for blue and red, and porphyrin for
red). These cells can move along the

C, D. In Lambis
lambis the immature
individual (C) does
not have the digita-
tions of D, which
are a sign of sexual
maturity.

E, F, G. In the large
melongenid Syrinx
aruanus, the
embryonic shell (E)
is often preserved in
immature individuals
(F), and then
disappears in adults
(G).

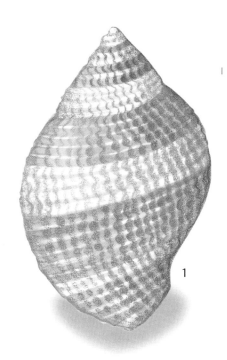

1

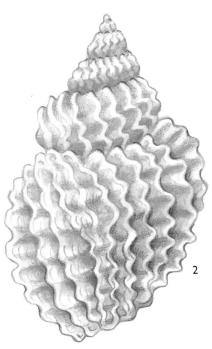

2

J, K. In these illustrations, we see the formation of sculptures and designs on the surface of a shell (K). To make the protuberance (4), the mantle edge first forms a small fold (1), which is then accentuated (2 and 3). The protuberance is complete when the mantle gradually reduces the fold, finally becoming flat again. The colorful designs are formed through two distinct phenomena. In the first, pigment cells migrate along the edge of the mantle. When they distance themselves at regular intervals, a semi-

K

H, I. Besides age, other factors disguise the fact that two seemingly different shells are members of the same species. In H (Littorina pintado), we see an example of sexual dimorphism. The female has a larger and more bulging shell, to allow for the internal development of the eggs. In I, the Nucella lapillus *of calm waters (1) has less and brighter colors than the more robust shell with more pronounced ribs of a member of the same species (2) exposed to the movement of the waves.*

edge of the mantle in one or another direction, oscillate around the starting position, or interrupt their work and begin again later. The movements, which are at right angles from the direction of advancement and pauses in constructing the shell, explain how designs and colors are created. The colors can change with the growth of the mollusk or a dietary or environmental change, for example a variation in marine salinity, a rather frequent occurrence in closed bodies of water into which large rivers flow. It is

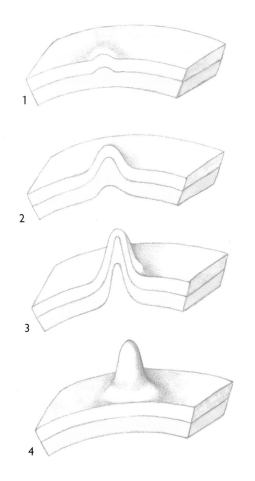

1

2

3

4

J

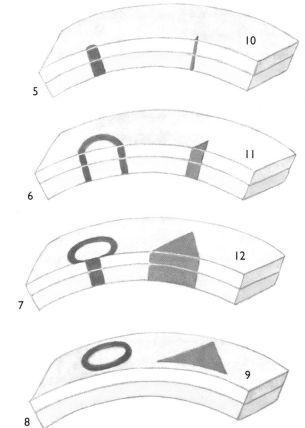

5

6

7

8

10

11

12

9

circle is formed (phases 5 and 6), and when they draw closer together again (phase 7), the circle closes (8) and the cells cease their activity. Intermittent pigment cells (the second type of phenomenon) create a triangle (9). The cells begin activity in (10), activate other symmetrical cells (11 and 12), and then cease activity. The phenomena of migration and intermittence, often combined, explain the fantastic creative ability of mollusks.

A

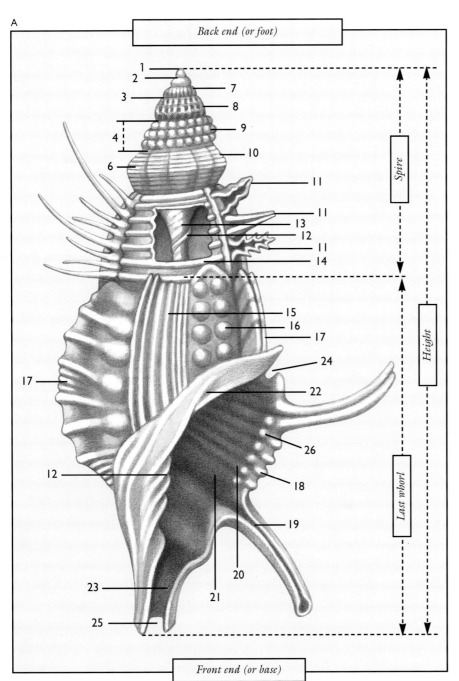

Back end (or foot)

Spire

Height

Last whorl

Front end (or base)

1
2
7
3
8
9
4
10
6
11
11
13
12
11
14
15
16
17
17
24
22
12
26
18
19
20
23
21
25

D

E

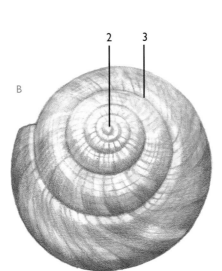

5

2   3

B

C

A, B, C.
Nomenclature for
a shell and its
ornamentation.
  1. apex
  2. protoshell
  3. suture
  4. indentation (or
  *   whorl)*
  5. umbilicus
  6. shoulder
  7. axial striae
  8. reticular sculpture
  9. mammillary
  *   sculpture*
  10. spiral striae

11. spines
12. columellar fold
13. columella
14. spiral ribs
15. axial ribs
16. tubercle
17. varix
18. outer lip
19. digitation
20. labial folds
21. aperture
22. inner lip
23. siphonal canal
24. back cavity
25. front cavity
26. teeth

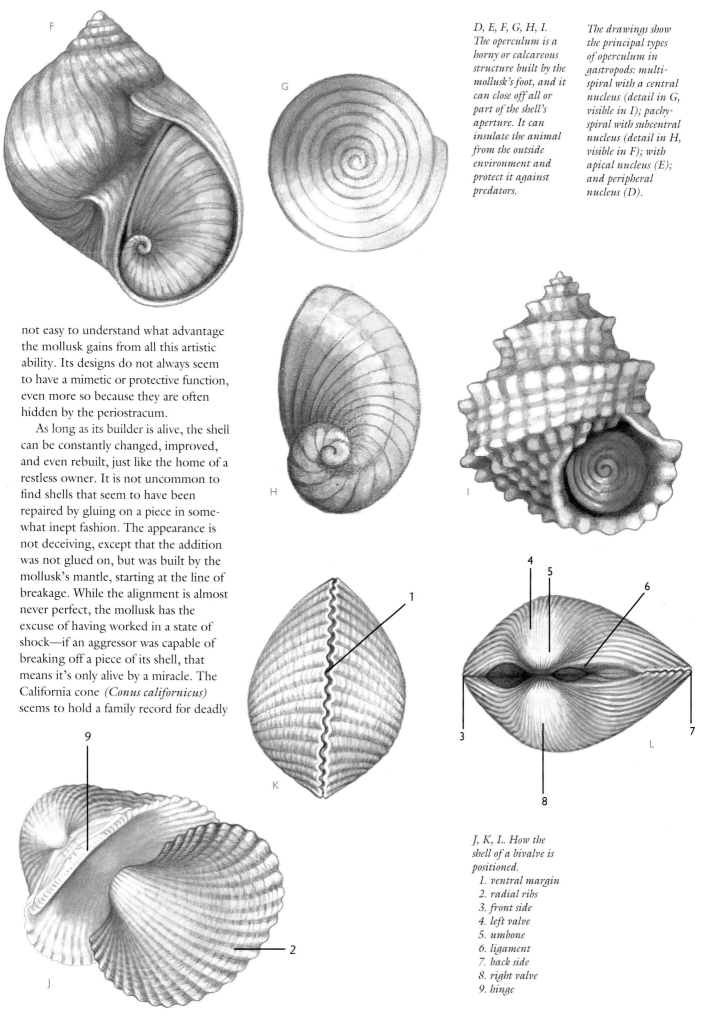

F

G

D, E, F, G, H, I.
The operculum is a
horny or calcareous
structure built by the
mollusk's foot, and it
can close off all or
part of the shell's
aperture. It can
insulate the animal
from the outside
environment and
protect it against
predators.

The drawings show
the principal types
of operculum in
gastropods: multi-
spiral with a central
nucleus (detail in G,
visible in I); pachy-
spiral with subcentral
nucleus (detail in H,
visible in F); with
apical nucleus (E);
and peripheral
nucleus (D).

not easy to understand what advantage
the mollusk gains from all this artistic
ability. Its designs do not always seem
to have a mimetic or protective function,
even more so because they are often
hidden by the periostracum.

As long as its builder is alive, the shell
can be constantly changed, improved,
and even rebuilt, just like the home of a
restless owner. It is not uncommon to
find shells that seem to have been
repaired by gluing on a piece in somewhat inept fashion. The appearance is
not deceiving, except that the addition
was not glued on, but was built by the
mollusk's mantle, starting at the line of
breakage. While the alignment is almost
never perfect, the mollusk has the
excuse of having worked in a state of
shock—if an aggressor was capable of
breaking off a piece of its shell, that
means it's only alive by a miracle. The
California cone *(Conus californicus)*
seems to hold a family record for deadly

J, K, L. How the
shell of a bivalve is
positioned.
  1. ventral margin
  2. radial ribs
  3. front side
  4. left valve
  5. umbone
  6. ligament
  7. back side
  8. right valve
  9. hinge

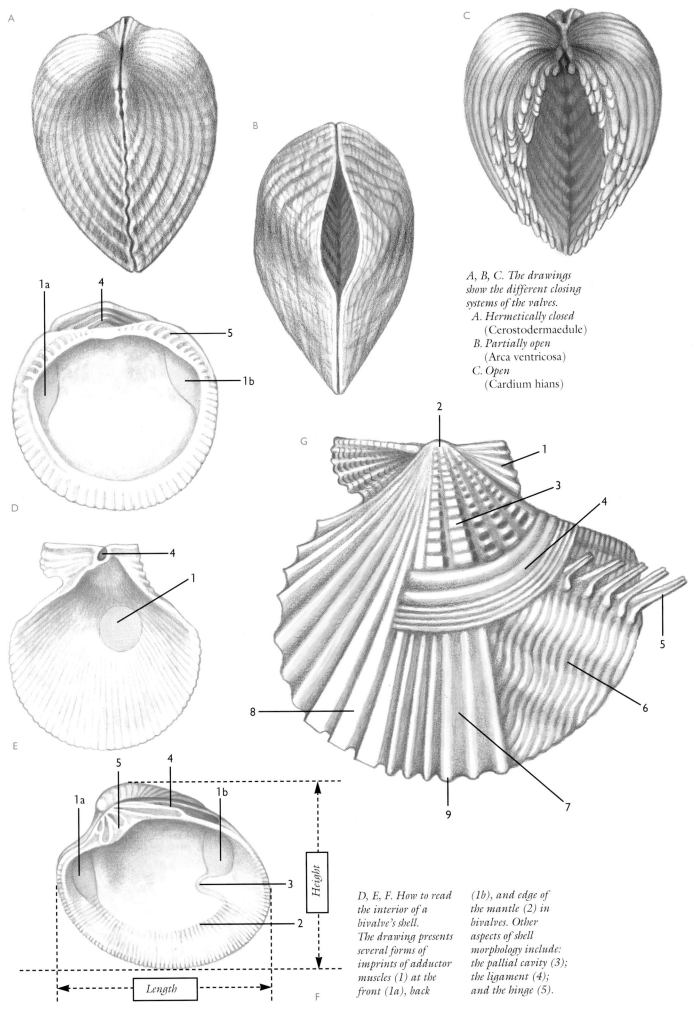

A

B

C

A, B, C. *The drawings show the different closing systems of the valves.*
   A. Hermetically closed (Cerostodermaedule)
   B. Partially open (Arca ventricosa)
   C. Open (Cardium hians)

G

D

E

F

Height

Length

D, E, F. *How to read the interior of a bivalve's shell. The drawing presents several forms of imprints of adductor muscles (1) at the front (1a), back (1b), and edge of the mantle (2) in bivalves. Other aspects of shell morphology include: the pallial cavity (3); the ligament (4); and the hinge (5).*

encounters that ended well: of a
sample of 195 shells collected on six
different sites, repairs were found on
154 of them. One cone in the sample
had fully six scars. The aggression was
attributed to large brachyuran crabs in
the cone's territory, whose claws are
tough enough to break its shell. In
this case the mollusk saved itself by
retracting far back into the shell in
time, and the crab's claw found only
a piece of inedible rock.

G. Ornamentation
in hypothetical
bivalve shell.
  1. auricle
  2. umbo
  3. radial ribs with
     scales
  4. concentric ribs
     and stripes
  5. spines
  6. oblique ornamentation
  7. radial furrows
  8. radial ribs
  9. ventral margin

H. A chiton shell
(nomenclature of
a hypothetical
polyplacophore).
  1. girdle
  2. cephalic plate
  3. posterior plate
  4. tuft of bristles
  5. median plate
  6. calcareous spines
  7. scales
  8. radial granules
  9. bristles
  10. radial ribs
  11. longitudinal ribs
  12. transverse ribs
  13. median area
  14. lateral area
  15. granules

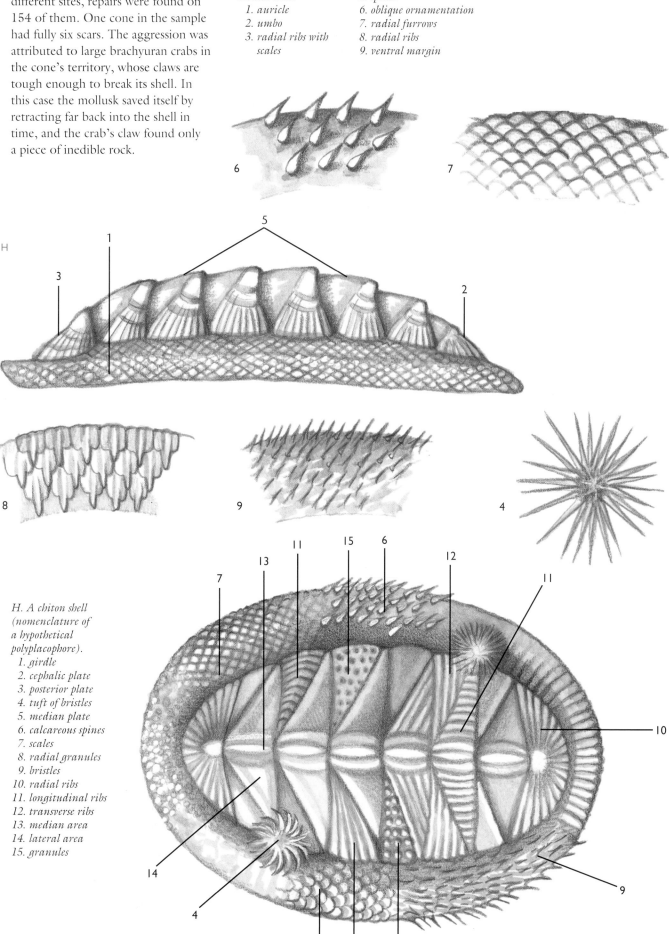

WHERE SHELLS ARE FOUND

Geography of Marine Mollusks

There are very few species of mollusks that can be considered cosmopolitan, i.e., found in all or nearly all seas of the world. *Atlanta peroni,* an atlantid that lives a pelagic life and swims to depths of 10,000 feet (3,000 m), has been found everywhere. *Janthina janthina,* a purple snail that floats, allowing itself to be carried by the currents with plankton across the oceans, is ubiquitous, except for Arctic and Antarctic seas. A few benthic mollusks have a near planetary distribution due to the very long life of their larvae, which can cross the oceans, carried by currents. This is the case of the great trumpet shell *(Charonia tritonis),* which lives on rocky seabeds in all warm seas of the planet. The giant tun *(Tonna galea)* also has a vast

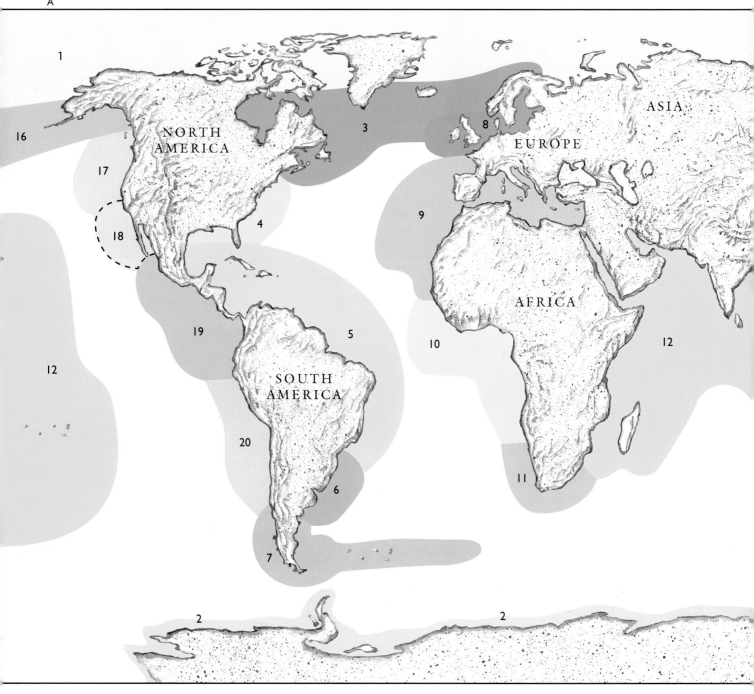

distribution, from the Mediterranean to the American coasts of the Atlantic, where it can be found from the Caribbean to the Argentine port of Mar del Plata.

Infinitely more numerous are species with a very limited geographical distribution, like an island or a small secluded body of water. These species are known as endemisms, and are the result of the well-known evolutionary phenomenon of the formation of new species under conditions of geographical isolation. Thus, the island of Malta has a little topshell all its own, *Gibbula nivosa*, an elegant little snail .3 inch (9 mm) in diameter. In Polynesia, the Marquesas Islands, which have rather few shell species (170 in all) have fully

thirteen endemic species, from six different families.

Between the extreme cases of cosmopolitanism and endemism, the overwhelming majority of species of marine mollusks have a distribution that encompasses vast coastal areas, either delimited by geographical barriers like continental masses, or by oceans, or by diversity in surface water temperatures. It is not so much the average annual temperature of the water that limits distribution of a species as the seasonal highs and lows. Variations in climate periodically shift these extreme values, and consequently also a particular species' limits of distribution. For example, the common northern whelk *(Buccinum undatum)*, an Arctic and Atlantic species, entered the Mediterranean and spread there as the sea was going through cold periods. Today its shells are found almost exclusively in the subfossil state, although a few small relic populations survive in cool, deep areas of the northwest Mediterranean.

Biogeographers have divided coastal areas of the world into twenty malacological provinces, which are defined in such a way that no less than half the species present in each one live exclusively within its confines. In a biogeographical province, we can distinguish a center of dispersion, the area from where the majority of the species originally spread, and a metropolis, which is the area where most species currently live. The two areas may or may not be the same, depending on past environmental and biological events. Despite everything that has been said about the boundaries between one province and another, they can be nothing but very vague and temporary. There are overlapping areas, and different writers use subdivisions that differ at least in part. Subject to these special cases, we should note that most shell species are quite stable over time. In fossiliferous coastal areas, we find essentially the same fauna that live in the nearby seas.

For each species, the area of diffusion, or geographical distribution, is the result of events occurring over many hundreds of thousands of years, during which environmental conditions evolved and the biological capacity of the species developed to adapt to new conditions and occupy new territories. In the last

century and a half, man has greatly interfered with this natural process, both voluntarily, by cultivating mollusks from distant seas, and involuntarily, by accidentally transporting larvae and adults while fishing and in maritime traffic. Perhaps the most notorious case was opening the Suez Canal, which caused a flow of mollusks from the Red Sea to the Mediterranean that has increased over recent years, following the decreased salinity of the Bitter Lakes halfway up the canal, which had until then constituted a biological barrier. Today there are many dozens of these so-called lessepsian species, named after the man who built the canal, the Frenchman Ferdinand de Lesseps.

B

A. The drawing shows the twenty malacological provinces.
1. Arctic
2. Antarctic
3. Boreal
4. Transatlantic (or Carolinian)
5. Caribbean
6. Patagonian (or Argentinian)
7. Magellanic
8. Celtic
9. Mediterranean
10. African
11. South African
12. Indopacific
13. Australian
14. New Zealand

15. Japanese
16. Aleutian
17. Oregonian
18. Californian
19. Panamic
20. Peruvian

B. Reefs, which can only form in the clear waters of the intertropical zone, are home to a wide range of shell species.

C. The cameo shell, Cypraeacassis rufa, lives near reefs across most of the Indopacific province.

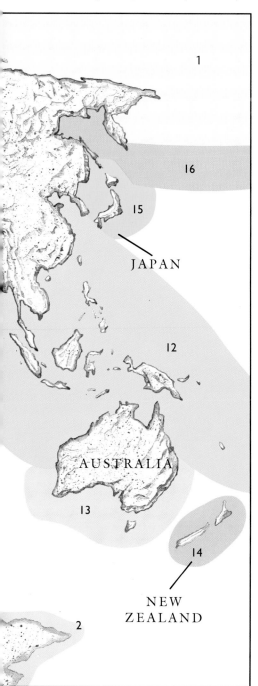

C

A. The coastline of the tropical malacological provinces have characteristics similar to the coasts of temperate provinces, with two important exceptions: the coral reef and its immediate surroundings, and the mangrove forest. The photo shows Tahiti, a high island of volcanic origins, with its coast rimmed by the coral reef. It is part of the Indopacific province.

B. The white beach of the island of Sipadan. It is part of Sarawak, in northern Borneo, under Malaysian governance. It too is in the Indopacific province.

A

B

C

D

E

Particularly beautiful are the Strombidae, with the especially elegant and uncommon *Strombus gallus*.

Panamic. Extending from the Gulf of California to Ecuador, including the Galapagos Islands, this stretch of the Pacific American coast only has a few species in common with the Indopacific province: a few have reached the Galapagos or remote Clipperton Island, but they have not yet landed on the continent. Panamic shells do, however, have ancestors in common with species in the Caribbean province, because during the Tertiary period, before the beginning of the Pliocene, the Isthmus of Panama was open and the Gulf of Mexico and the Pacific Ocean were connected. Various shells from the two provinces are thus paired, like the two cowries, the Panamic *Cypraea zebra* and the Caribbean *Cypraea cervinetta*.

E. The coast of Guadalupe Island at Pointe des Chateaux. Caribbean province.

F. Kauai, an island in the Hawaiian archipelago, of volcanic origin. Indopacific province.

G. The emerged land is desert, but the sea along it is rich in life. This is the coast of Shadwan Island, in the Red Sea. Indopacific province.

H. Coast with mangrove vegetation on Grand Comoro Island in the Indopacific.

C. The Maldive Islands, a true paradise for divers. Their clear waters are home to a rich shell population. Indopacific province.

D. Sand Island in Key West, the southern tip of Florida. Caribbean province.

Indopacific. This is one of the largest provinces, and has the greatest wealth of species: it extends for three-quarters of the equator, from the west coast of Africa to the Hawaiian Islands, going through southern Asia and northern Australia. It is also the most popular among collectors throughout the world, due to the wealth of beautiful, colorful shells. The metropolis of the Indopacific province is the Indonesian archipelago, while the center of dispersion is considered the Philippine archipelago (which at present has no fewer than 5,000 species), along with the whole band of archipelagoes running from the Ryukyu Islands in the far south of Japan to the Great Barrier Reef of Australia.

West Africa. This province has relatively few species for several reasons, including the fact that the Atlantic coast of Africa does not have a great variety of biotopes, and is lacking in areas sheltered from sea storms. Nevertheless, its exploration is by no means complete, and probably new species will be found in the future. It is delimited to the north by Cape Blanc, Mauritania, and to the south by Namibe (formerly Moçâmedes), Angola, and thus has a rather limited extension due to the cold currents and rising deep waters. Two families are particularly well represented: the margin shells, or marginellas, with dozens of beautiful species, and the volutes, with about a dozen species from the genus *Cymbium*.

Caribbean. Runs from the Florida Keys to Rio de Janeiro. Its environments vary greatly (from coral reefs to mangrove swamps, to vast sandy areas in sheltered environments), and it has a wealth of species that, distributed over a wide expanse of territory, also include a multitude of subspecies, races, and varieties. The Pleurotomariidae family is well represented, with about a dozen species of these primitive gastropods.

F

G

H

A, B. The Norwegian coast, seen here in the Kvaenangen Fjord (A) and the Lofoten Islands (B), has a temperate shell fauna despite its latitude, due to the moderating influence of the Gulf Stream. Its Atlantic coast is part of the Boreal province, while the southern coast is part of the Celtic province.

A

C

THE TEMPERATE PROVINCES

Japanese. Includes the Japanese archipelago (except for the southern-most minor islands) and the east coast of Korea, plus a short stretch of the east coast of Russia. It has a wealth of species (over 5,000) and many extremely fascinating shells. It includes rare slit shells, two turbinids, *Guildfordia triumphans* and *Guildfordia yoka*, with their lovely appendages, and the great deep water turrid *Thatcheria mirabilis*, known as the Japanese wonder shell, with an extraordinary ladderlike form

B

that makes it one of the most coveted shells of all.

Aleutian. Runs across the Pacific, from the northwest coast of America and the northeast coast of Asia, including the Aleutian archipelago and Sakhalin Island. Here there is an abundance of species from the genera *Trophon*, *Littorina*, and *Patinopecten*. A characteristic species is the abalone *Haliotis kamtschatkana*, with its thin shell that may be over 6 inches (15 cm) long. It is hunted by the sea otter, which uses rocks to break its shell. The bivalves include a gigantic hiatellid, *Panopea generosa*, which may weigh 9 pounds (4 kg) and has a shell up to 9 inches (23 cm) long. It buries itself over a yard deep in the substratum. Its very long siphons, which make up about half the animal's weight, cannot be retracted.

Mediterranean. Includes the Atlantic coast from Brittany to Cape Blanc, the Azores, the Canary Islands, Madeira, and the entire Mediterranean, including the Black Sea. Shells are of the warm temperate and in part subtropical type in the Atlantic south of the Strait of Gibraltar (known as the Mauritanian region) and cold temperate with a few northern features to the north (the Portuguese region). Depending on the climate phase, the Mediterranean basin has been populated by Atlantic fauna from one or the other of these two regions. When, as in the current phase, temperate-warm conditions prevailed, cold-water shells became extinct or took refuge in deep areas.

The Mediterranean is full of endemisms. Among the most characteristic shells are the cowrie *Luria lurida*, the purple dye murex *Bolinus brandaris*,

from which the Phoenicians obtained their famous purple dye, the pilgrim's clam or common scallop *Pecten jacobaeus*, the pelican's foot shell *Aporrhais pespelecani* (also common in the North Atlantic), and the Mediterranean rugose (spiny) bonnet, *Cassidaria echinophora*.

Celtic. Includes the British Isles and continental coasts along the English Channel, the North Sea, and the Baltic. Some of the more characteristic and frequent shells include the common periwinkle (*Littorina littorea*), which is gathered for food, the whelks *Buccinum undatum* and *Neptunea antiqua*, and the murices *Nucella lapillus* and *Patella vulgata*. In the fjords, we may find the acmeid *Tatura testudinalis*. On muddy seabeds the tellin *Macoma balthica* is extremely common.

Boreal. Straddles the North Atlantic, extending from the western coast of Norway to the southern coast of Iceland and Greenland to the northeast coast of America that runs from Cape Cod to Labrador. Generally speaking, cold-

C. The seas of Sardinia, in the center of the western basin of the Mediterranean, are home to a vast number of shells from the Mediterranean province.

D. Aerial view of the vast beaches in the region of Cape Cod, in Massachusetts.

water shells are not as brightly colored, and for a long time collectors ignored them, but in the far north of the Atlantic there are also large species with elegant shells, like the wentletrap *Epitonium greenlandicum,* beautiful turrids from the genus *Bela,* lovely murices from the genus *Trophon,* and large whelks like *Colus islandicus.*

Transatlantic (or Carolinian). Includes the coast of North America from Cape Cod to South Florida. Common among the bivalves are the large, thick-shelled venerids known as quahogs from the genus *Mercenaria,* which are gathered for food, the pholadid *Cyrtopleura costata,* and the hiatellid *Panopea bitruncata.* The gastropods include the melongenid *Busycon carica* and the whelk *Neptunea lyrata decemcostata.*

Californian. Encompasses the American Pacific coast from British Columbia in Canada to the Baja California peninsula. Some writers recognize a separate Oregonian province

between the Californian and the Aleutian provinces. The most noteworthy shells in the area are certainly the large haliotids or abalones, with their amazing iridescence. After indiscriminate fishing for food purposes threatened their populations, their harvesting was limited by law. There are also more than fifty species of chitons and a good variety of murices.

New Zealand. Despite its relative proximity to Australia, the New Zealand archipelago has few species of mollusks in common with the coast of the

continent. Of the fifty or so species of chitons, the most noteworthy is *Eudoxochiton nobilis,* which may be 3 inches (8 cm) long, and the strange butterfly chiton, *Cryptoconchus porosus,* 6 inches (15 cm) long. Among the most beautiful and sought-after gastropods of New Zealand are about twenty species of volutids. Along with the precious mother-of-pearl of the abalone (paua), with its particularly bright green iridescence, they are used to make costume jewelry.

E. A spectacular rocky formation at the southern tip of Baja California in Mexico. This is where the temperate Californian and the tropical Panamic provinces meet.

Australian. The northern part of the continent is part of the Indopacific tropical province. The southern coast, running from Brisbane in Queensland to Geraldton in Western Australia and the island of Tasmania, is bathed by temperate waters, with a wealth of beautiful shell species. Some of the most characteristic include the potamidid *Pyrazus ebeninus,* which populates the muddy expanses of estuaries in incredible numbers, and a living fossil, the great cerithid *Campanile symbolicum,* which vanished in Europe and Asia millions of years ago and now is found there in the fossil state.

South African. Includes all of South Africa except Natal and including Namibia. Despite the relatively cool water, there is a wealth of beautiful cowries. One of the rarer finds is the slit shell *Pleurotomaria africana.* There are over twenty species of limpets, including some large and highly prized cones and turbos.

Patagonian (or Argentinian). Extends from Rio de Janeiro to the northern coasts of Tierra del Fuego. It has only rather recently been explored for shells, and research is far from complete. Only now are books being published for shell collectors in this area, who have had very little material available in the past. Large volutes live in the circumlittoral areas, and are occasionally collected by Russian trawl fishing boats. Among these are the rare *Pachycymbola ferussacii,* up to 4 inches (10 cm) long, and the even rarer and more coveted *Provocator palliata,* 3.5 inches (9 cm) long.

Peruvian. Runs from Ecuador to southern Chile. One of its murices, *Concholepas concholepas,* is very well known, with a strange form that makes it look like an abalone. It lives in the intertidal area. It is a protected species: overharvesting for food purposes (it was sold as a delicacy known as *loco*) caused its disappearance from large stretches of coast. Some of the most interesting shells in the area include a large triton, *Fusitriton magellanicus.*

Magellanic. Forms various subregions, with the southern tip of South America, the island of Chiloé, Tierra del Fuego, the Falkland Islands, southern Georgia, and the subantarctic archipelagoes. The intertidal areas of the ice-free coasts are home to mussels like *Brachidontes purpuratus* and *Mytilus edulis platensis,* and farther down *Aulacomya aler,* which may be over 6 inches (16 cm) in length. In the infralittoral band, mollusk fauna diversifies, with representatives from numerous families.

A

B

A. In the image we can see a stretch of the rocky coast of Tasmania. Rich in life, the coastal waters of this large island are part of the Australian province.

B. A sickle of beach across from the shallow seabed of an inlet in the Falkland Islands. Along with the extreme south of the South American continent and other subantarctic islands, the archipelago is part of the Magellanic province of cool waters.

C

D

C, D, E. Three views of the Alaskan coast near the Bering Strait. The mechanical action of the glaciers makes a permanent settlement of mollusks impossible in the tidal area. Nevertheless, some species live in the infralittoral zone and migrate higher up when the coast is temporarily freed of its icy mantle. At greater depths, there are few species of shells, although in some areas the populations are quite dense. This is the Arctic malaco-logical province.

F. The waters of Port Lockroy in Antarctica, still locked in by ice. The Antarctic malacological province has been studied over recent decades and is not yet well known. The waters around the continent of ice are nevertheless very abundant in life, and mollusks are also represented with more species than was once thought.

E

F

THE COLD WATER PROVINCES

Arctic. The Canadian, Northern European, and Siberian coasts bathed by the Arctic Ocean have no mollusks in the midlittoral band due to the abrasive action of ice. In the infralittoral and circumlittoral, there are species with brownish or whitish shells, generally covered by a thick dark periostracum. The predominant bivalves include species from the genera *Yoldia, Nuculana, Hiatella* and *Mya*, while the most frequent gastropods are from the genera *Buccinum, Colus, Margarites* and *Trophon.* Of all malacological provinces, this is considered the most impoverished, with less than 400 known species.

Antarctica. It is difficult to imagine how the coasts of the continent of ice could be home to populations of fragile mollusks. Yet about eighty conchiferous mollusks have been found along the coasts of Adelaide Island alone. The limpet *Laevilitorina antarctica* is a summer resident in the midlittoral band, invaded by glaciers for ten months a year. Farther below, in the upper infra-littoral band, there is the eatoniellid *Eatoniella kerguelensis.* Thirty feet (10 m) below is the muricid *Neobuccinun eatoni.* In the circumlittoral band, below 80–100 feet (25–30 m) in depth, there are still herbivore species who feed on rhodoficious algae, with little need of light; farther down are carnivorous and necrophagous species who extend to hundreds of yards in depth.

The Saltwater Realms

High tide

Low tide

1

2

3

W here there's sea there are shells: there is no coast, abyss, or stretch of open sea that does not include a population of mollusks, with two exceptions: the band of polar coasts regularly occupied by permanent glaciers, and pebbly, wave-swept beaches. In both these cases, mechanical forces prevent larvae from settling and adults from surviving. But in polar regions where glaciers are seasonal, mollusks occupy stretches of coast that are temporarily ice-free; and bold little snails come to pebbly beaches during periods of great summer calm, ready to flee as soon as the sea grows rough.

Marine biology breaks the sea down into various environments: a fundamental distinction is between the benthos and the pelagos. Organisms that live in close connection with the seabed, either buried or firmly adhered, or depend on it for food and crawl over it or swim just above it, without ever going far from it, are part of the benthos, and are referred to as benthic. The overwhelming majority of mollusks with shells are benthic.

Organisms that live in open water and do not depend on the seabed or the organisms that populate it for their

A. Clusters of mytilids (this is the subspecies chilensis *from the cosmopolitan* Mytilus edulis, *the Atlantic mussel), left high and dry by the low tide, at West Falkland Island in*

the Falklands archipelago. We know that the shell with its hermetic seal allows the mussel to spend many days underwater, especially if the temperature is cool as in this subantarctic region.

A

B

vital functions are known as pelagic. In its turn, the pelagos can be broken down into plankton, organisms that move with the masses of water, and nekton, the group of animals capable of moving freely even against the movement of the water.

Anyone studying shells needs to have a clear idea of the various areas into which the benthic domain can be broken down. The first distinction is between the littoral system, which involves the seabeds where chlorophyll-producing plants can grow, and the deep system, which extends beyond the limit of chlorophyll-producing vegetation.

B. The coral reef at low tide at Vava'u, on Tongo Island in the South Pacific. In this situation, the mollusks that live at the midlittoral level escape the direct rays of the sun and take shelter under the branches or coral or in crevices in the reef.

D. Four aspects of the upper levels of the littoral system. The abundance of light and oxygen-rich water encourages settlement of numerous forms of life, despite the disadvantages of fluctuations in temperature and salinity, of wave action, and, in too many areas, of the presence of pollutants due to human activity. Hundreds of species of mollusks have made it their exclusive habitat, or visit it from deeper habitats.

C

D

4

C. The breakers of the Atlantic Ocean crash against the reef of the Iles de Glénans Islands in Brittany. The colonies of mussels, firmly anchored to the rock with very strong filaments of byssus, are not affected by these waves in the slightest. In fact, the mussels offer shelter to other species of mollusks and various little animals who could not otherwise withstand the waves.

5

1. Supralittoral zone. Bathed by sea spray.
2. Midlittoral zone. Between the normal high and low tide levels.
3. Infralittoral zone. From the normal low tide level to the limits of growth of marine phanerogams.
4. Circumlittoral level. Runs from the lower phanerogam limit to the chlorophyll algae limit.
5. Deep system. Runs from the chlorophyll algae limit to the bottom.

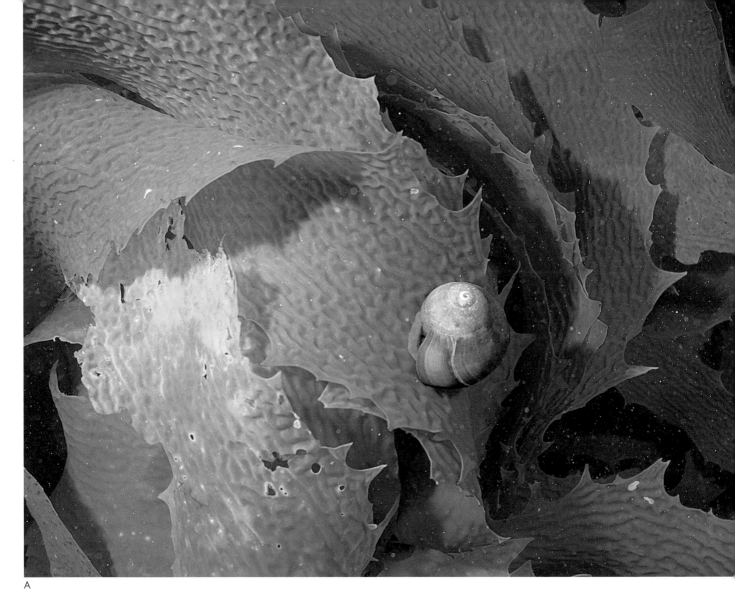

A

A. The photophilic algae of the infralittoral zone host populations of little snails in every sea of the world. It's difficult to spot them by day, because they take refuge at the base of the vegetation.

B. Competition for space is quite fierce in the infralittoral zone. A shipwreck is rapidly covered with bivalves, as seen in the photo, in addition to algae, sponges, cnidarians, and other forms of life.

In its turn, the littoral system is divided into four levels. Going from top to bottom, the first level is the supra-littoral band, whose upper limit is where ocean spray regularly reaches, with a lower limit marked by wave movement of normal intensity during high tide. Lower down is the midlittoral band, also known as the intertidal or tidal area. Its upper limit is marked by the line that waves regularly reach during high tide, while the lower limit is the average low tide mark for normal tides.

The third level of the littoral system is known as the infralittoral band: it runs from the lower edge of the midlittoral to the lowest point where phanerogamic marine plants can grow. Along the coasts of Europe, these are meadows of *Zostera*, and, in the Mediterranean in particular, *Posidonia oceanica*, the deepest-growing saltwater plant. On average, *Zostera* grows to 80–100 feet (25–30 m) deep, but much depends on the transparency of the water. Where it is extremely clear, there is enough

B

C

D

light to support plant growth even at 150 feet (45 m) deep, while in murky water the limit is 25–33 feet (8–10 m). Finally, the lowest level of the littoral system is the circumlittoral, which, as we have noted, descends to the lowest point where chlorophyll-producing algae can still grow.

Almost all shells of interest to collectors come from these four levels of the littoral system, which can be explored without too much difficulty. Exploration of the first two requires truly minimal equipment, and the third can be examined during normal scuba diving expeditions, while the fourth level, the circumlittoral, would require very difficult dives, and thus shells must be collected by professional fishermen with trawls.

The deep sea, where there is no light or chlorophyll-producing plants and organisms depend almost entirely on the snow of organic material from the pelagic domain, is the realm of scientific research. The system can be broken down into three levels. The first is the bathyal, which generally corresponds to the continental slope, which runs from the edge of the continental shelf, at an average depth of 650 feet (200 m), and drops rather abruptly to 5,000–8,000 feet (1,500–2,500 m). The next level is the abyssal, formed of vast, rather flat areas, which may nevertheless be interrupted by underwater peaks and mountain ranges, gradually descending to about 20,000 feet (6,000 m) from the continental slope. Finally, there is the hadal level, which includes oceanic trenches that can reach depths of 36,000 feet (11,000 m) or so.

In the benthic domain, the physical nature of the substratum is of vital ecological importance. In fact, it plays a major role in the formation of particular biocenoses, i.e., groups of living organisms bound by reciprocal dependence. Almost all mollusks are restricted to a particular type of substratum. In other words, it makes no sense to look for sandy or muddy seabed shells in a rocky environment (the case is a little different for washed-up shells: the currents and waves that carry them to shore may have taken them from various environments and then mixed them).

Later on, we will examine in detail some interesting environments for the study of shells. For now, we'll make one important distinction, between fixed and mobile substrata. Of course, this distinction should be considered in relationship to what animal organisms need to live. For mollusks, this includes fixed substrata, not only rocks and towers of large masses, but also objects that seem mobile to us, like the chains of anchors, the hulls of boats, and the shells of various animals, while mobile substrata include sand, mud, organic detritus, and shingles, including large pebbles, in areas where the wave action rolls them. In a very sheltered cavity, those same pebbles could become a hard substratum and could become home to fauna similar to that found on reefs.

C. The Posidonia oceanica *meadow environment marks the lower limit of the infralittoral zone in the Mediterranean. The most visible mollusks are the beautiful nacres* (Pinna nobilis) *shown in the photo, which use their byssus to anchor to solid parts of the seabed. In recent years, fishing with trawl nets and indiscriminate harvesting of these mollusks have gradually reduced populations over vast areas.*

D. The spectacular camouflage of the common Lopha cristagalli *bivalve, which lives in the shallow waters of the Indopacific province.*

E. Large topshells in shallow water, in a Polynesian lagoon. This environment has been repopulated relatively recently; the last glaciation caused the total extinction of its malacofauna.

E

On Coastal Rocks

The breakers crash against the rock wall, columns of foam fly skyward with the roar of thunder. Under these hammer strokes, even the hardest rock is eroded, and in time even the hugest cliffs crumble. We humans look on fearfully. Even the strongest swimmer would have to struggle to come out alive from that white inferno. Yet this environment, seemingly so hostile to life, is populated by an extraordinary quantity of animal and plant species and is preferred by many species of mollusks. In fact, it may be the environment in which primitive mollusks evolved. But what elements of coastal rock are favorable to marine life? There are many—many more than we would expect. Protrusions and crevices, cracks and caves, create alternating areas of bright light and shadow, exposed areas and sheltered areas. Where there is light there is vegetation, and thus food, from a thin blackish pellicle of lichens above, to rich meadows of algae below, in areas less exposed to wave motion. Shade, on

A

A. A lovely view of dusk on the emerging reef at Point Pinos near Pacific Grove, California.

B. In the Venice Lagoon the tidal range is about 3 feet (1 m). The drawing shows in a schematic form (for illustrative purposes, the proportions are not accurate) the population of a platform above the high tide (HT) level, in the midlittoral, and under the low tide (LT) level.
1. Melaraphe neritoides
2. Liyia
3. crab (Pachygrapsus)
4. barnacle (Chtalamus)
5. Patella
6. Littorina saxatilis
7. chiton
8. barnacle (Balanus)
9. oyster (Ostrea edulis)
10. mussel (Mytilus galloprovincialis)
11. crab (Carcinus)
12. prawn (Palaemon elegans)
13. alga (Enteromorpha)
14. alga (Porphyria)
16. alga (Ulva)
17. alga (Ceramium)
18. alga (Gracilaria)

C. Tidal pools on the Crozon Peninsula in Brittany are frequented by many mollusk species.

D. This colony of Mytilus californianus has settled along the northwest coast of the United States. Appearances can be deceiving: hidden by the mass of bivalves, a deep fissure furrows the rock.

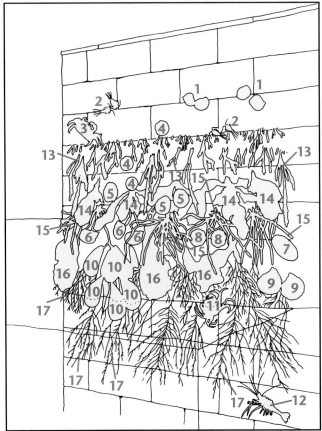

B

C

D

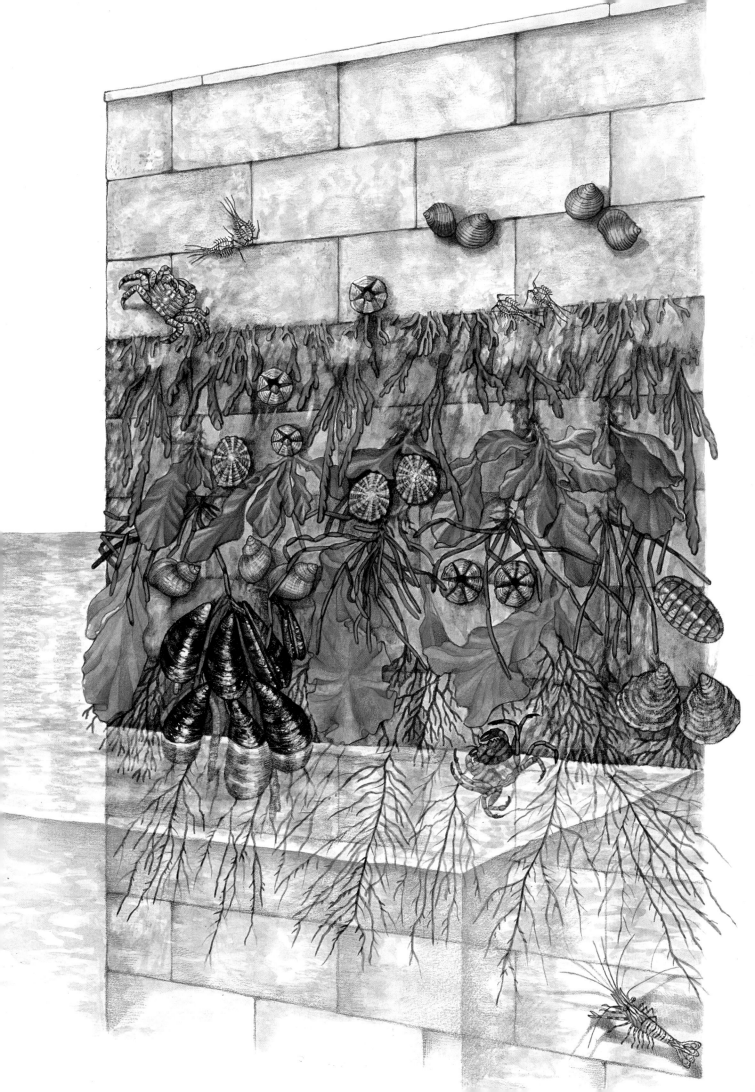

the other hand, offers protection from predators.

Another gift of the rocky coast is the abundance of oxygen, which wave motion continuously dissolves in the water. There is also a great deal of suspended organic material, as all detritus that floats on the sea is tossed here, and a variety of dissolved salts, including those of terrestrial origin, carried by the rainwater that flows into the sea. Finally, there is the rock itself. Don't be deceived by its forbidding appearance; it helps those who can help themselves. First of all, it provides a solid anchorage. And when it is calcareous, it even allows some species of mollusks to dig tunnels where they can live a completely tranquil, albeit highly cloistered, life.

The reef area that is subject to alternating tides and wave motion has seen the evolution of species capable of firmly adhering themselves. Limpets, chitons, abalone, and even, in the cold waters of Chile and Peru, the murex *Concholepas concholepas* do this through a sort of temporary sticking action that resembles a suction cup but is not. This ability to anchor themselves allows properly equipped gastropod mollusks to alternate periods of immobility, especially when the sea is rough, with movement in search of food, especially at night. Other means of anchoring include the byssus, a bundle of robust horny or chitinous threads secreted by

A

B

the mollusk's foot and affixed to the rock. The most familiar example is the mussel. The extreme solution is to adhere to the reef using a sort of cement, as do the vermetids, gastropod mollusks that have transformed their snail-like shell into a tube similar to sedentary polychete worms, and who feed by using long, filamentous appendages to capture detritus suspended in the water. Cirriped crustaceans use the same method.

On the rocky coasts, there is a great difference between populations that inhabit various levels. The supralittoral is occasionally battered by violent waves,

C

A. Competition for a place in the sun: limpets and acorn barnacles contend for space on a reef off the coast of Devon, England. Nevertheless, the mollusks are not in competition for food with these arthopods. In fact, limpets graze on the pellicle of algae that grows on rocks, while acorn barnacles use their tufts to capture food particles suspended in the water.

but normally the rock is only moistened by ocean spray, which collects in fissures and cracks in particular. Very few marine mollusks live permanently on this level, which is actually more aerial than aquatic, and seems better for creatures with lungs that can take in oxygen directly from the air. Most species of mollusks in this environment use their gills to breathe the oxygen dissolved in the little water that arrives with the spray, which they can conserve for long periods within their shell. The environment is also subject to great fluctuations in temperature and salinity, depending on the time of day and the season. For this reason, it is a practical habitat only for highly adaptable species.

The first living beings that spring into view, however, are not mollusks but immobile cirripeds, commonly called barnacles *(Chthamalus stellatus)*, which encrust vast areas with their little cones cemented to the rock. No one would call them even distant relatives of another crustacean that frequents this level, the highly mobile runner or marbled crab *(Pachygrapsus marmoraturs)*. With a little attention, we can see, especially along fissures on European reefs, massive populations of a very dark, tiny snail, hardly more than .1 inch (3–4 mm) in height, the *Littorina neritoides*. It can live in a dry environment for long periods, because its branchial chamber also acts as a very simplified lung. Still, it needs to deposit its eggs in water. The eggs are enclosed in planktonic egg capsules, which produce swimming veliger larvae. The snail keeps the egg capsule in the oviduct until the sea rises to the level of the rock it inhabits, which in the Atlantic occurs twice a year, during the great equinox tides. On the African shore of the Mediterranean and in Sicily, the lighter *Littorina punctata* is common, up to just over .5 inch (15 mm) in

height and adorned with little bands of white and brown dots. *Littorina saxatilis*, up to .6 inch (16 mm) high, can be seen on the Atlantic coast of Europe in the supralittoral band but is usually more common on the lower level. This little snail also tolerates a dry environment quite well, and as it is viviparous, it does not need to immerse itself in water to deposit its eggs. On the coasts of the supralittoral band of the Mediterranean, you may sometimes see the Portuguese limpet *(Patella rustica)*, only in very sheltered areas, as well as a trochid, the common trumpet *(Monodonta turbinata)*, which lives only in the fissures, and a chiton, *Chiton olivaceus*. All these mollusks feed by grazing on the algae that forms on the reefs.

In the supralittoral band, the reef pool environment is very interesting. Reef pools are small or large cavities that form where the slope and nature of the rock allow, and are periodically filled with salt water by the more violent waves. During sunny periods when the sea is calm, the pools dry out, becoming a salty crust, while during heavy rains and over time the salt is washed away and the pools become fresh or brackish water. In the Mediterranean, the only mollusks that frequent this very changeable micro-environment are periwinkles, while in

B. The low tide reveals a rich colony of oysters in these tidal pools on Monte Bellos Island in western Australia.

C. A tidal pool in the Pacific Rim National Park in British Columbia. The shallow seabeds of this coast are extraordinarily rich in life, so much so that it is difficult to spot open patches of substratum.

D. In the midlittoral zone of this reef in the American Northwest, mussels (Mytilus californianus) *and* acorn barnacles (Semibalanus cariosus) *compete for room and to some extent food, as the two species feed on suspended particles. Nevertheless, these waters are rich in nutrients.*

D

ones). In the Mediterranean, this is the favorite area of two very common trochids, the common trumpet *(Monodonta turbinatus)*, more frequent on rocks exposed to waves, and the tessellate trumpet *(Monodonta articulata)*, which prefers more sheltered environments. Vast populations of these snails can be seen in just a few square yards of reef. Here we begin to see a few limpets, especially the China limpet *(Patella rustica)*, which is distinguished from other limpets primarily because it is less flat and is adorned by little black dots. Actually the giant limpet *(Patella ferruginea)* is most characteristic of the midlittoral band. It is larger, with a beautiful pattern of radial, rust-colored ribs, sometimes so accentuated that it

boats, and anywhere they can anchor with their byssus. This characteristic adaptability has permitted large-scale commercial cultivation. As early as Roman times, the common mussel *(Mytilus galloprovincialis)* and the Atlantic mussel *(Mytilus edulis)* were cultivated. Mussels are filterers, and although they colonize large stretches of reef when the sea is clean, they prefer polluted environments with a wealth of suspended organic material. This is an excellent reason to avoid gathering them in nature for food purposes (which is also prohibited by Italian law). On the Atlantic coasts of Europe and North America, mussels and cirripeds are the prey of a murex, *Nucella lapillus,* which in the past was harvested for its indelible

the tropics there may also be nerites, dove shells, and purpuras.

The next level, the midlittoral, is much richer in life. Where tides are modest, this band only has an average height of 1 to 2 feet (30–60 cm), but this may increase to many yards along coasts with heavy tides. Its surface area obviously depends on the slope of the rocks. If the slope is gentle, and the surface of the rock is rough, tidal pools form, which are a much more stable and lively environment than the rock pools described above.

There are a great many mollusks at this level, both in species and in individuals. In addition, because this area can be easily explored with minimal equipment when the sea is calm, it is one of the most profitable in terms of observing and collecting shells. It is not a homogenous area, even where it is very shallow. There is an upper area, bathed primarily by wave motion, and a lower area, which is almost always submerged, at least for part of the day. The upper band is frequented by periwinkles characteristic of the supralittoral band, which periodically descend to damper environments. In Atlantic Europe, this is the preferred foraging ground for *Littorina saxatilis* (which also lives along the coasts of North America from Seattle to New Jersey, with an isolated population in the Venice Lagoon as well); there is also *Littorina littorea,* large and edible (up to 1 inch [26 mm] high, it is known as *bigorneau* in French restaurants and periwinkle in English

appears stellate. But overharvesting has caused it to virtually disappear from the coast of continental Italy and made it very rare even in the few areas where it survives, in the islands of the Tuscan archipelago and Sardinia. Fortunately, it is still numerous along the coasts of Algeria and Morocco. Along the American coast of the Pacific, the midlittoral band is frequented by the large black abalone *(Haliotis cracherodi)*, which was also overharvested for a long time and is now protected, as are other abalones of the California province.

For vast areas of coast throughout the world, especially in cold seas, the lower midlittoral rock level is inhabited by large populations of mussels. Mussels colonize any solid substratum, even artificial, like wharves, piers, hulls of

purple dye, used in laundries to mark fabrics. In warmer waters, midlittoral rocks are home to populations of elegant cones like *Conus californicus,* from central California to Mexico.

Among the most interesting facies (associations of living beings characterized by an individual dominant species) of the lower midlittoral band is the *trottoir* (literally "sidewalk") formed by a very solid mass of calcareous algae, primarily from the genus *Lithophyllum,* that has a shelf form up to a yard thick and two yards wide. Full of cracks and perforated in every direction, the trottoir retains moisture even at low tide, and its mollusk population is quite varied. In the Mediterranean this is one of the favorite habitats of the Portuguese limpet *(Patella ulyssiponensis)* and a chiton, *Lepidochitona corrugata*, which can easily be observed living on the surface of the *trottoir*. Within the concretions is the fragile, whitish, and rather rare little snail, *Fossarus ambiguus*, of the Fossaridae family, the little *Trimusculus mammillaris*, which looks like a limpet but is very distant in evolutionary terms (it was considered a marine pulmonate until the 1975 creation of the Divasibranchs subclass, to which it was ascribed along with another limpet-shaped former pulmonate from the Mediterranean, the false limpet *Siphonaria pectinata)*, and another tiny, pink-toned bivalve no more than .125 inch (3 mm) high, *Lasaea rubra* (Laseidae family), which has the peculiarity of being ovoviviparous: the young leave the mother's shell when they are about half her size. The above are small shells that experts in nomenclature have had to study a great deal, often changing their names. For collectors, it is difficult to keep track of these changes, but it's necessary if we want to use drawings and photos in books that may be somewhat dated to identify our finds.

In different environments of the lower midlittoral level, various species usually prefer the infralittoral band, which is always underwater unless there is an exceptionally low tide. The common limpet *(Patella caerulea)*, very common in the Mediterranean, is one of the most interesting in its variety of forms and iridescent shell. In calm water, the shell is thin, with a very regular oval form and narrow radial ribs, while in rougher water, the shell becomes sturdier and the ribs become sparser and more accentuated, giving the shell a stellate form. In the past, malacologists believed these forms were distinct species, and even gave the shell about fifty different scientific names. A collector can put together an elegant series of *caerulea* without detaching even one, just by going to the edge of the rocks and collecting those that died naturally and were cleaned by fish and other necrophagous animals. *Patella vulgata* is quite common in this environment in the Atlantic; it is larger (up to a diameter of 2.75 inches [70 mm]), more clearly conical, and much less variable in form and color. If you want to examine a living limpet, you must detach it from

A. The limestone rock in the midlittoral level to about a hundred yards deep is home to perforating mollusks like the date mussels (Lithophaga lithophaga) *in the photo, present in the Mediterranean, the Atlantic Ocean and the Red Sea.*

B. Examples of Trochus niloticus *on a shallow seabed on Sunday Island in the Kimberley region of western Australia.*

C. A ventral view of the limpet, a gastropod perfectly adapted to life on rocky, *wave-battered surfaces. Visible are the broad, disk-shaped foot, which guarantees the animal very strong adhesion to the substratum, the head, the mouth, and the head and lateral tentacles.*

D. A population of periwinkles in a fissure of a reed in Cornwall. Some species of this family spend much of their lives underwater. They feed on the film of algae and lichens that the sea spray forms on the rocks in the supralittoral band.

D

C

the rock without hurting it. This operation requires some skill; wait until the mollusk lifts the edge of the shell slightly from the rock, and then insert a thin blade and press it with a quick rotating movement, which will prevent the limpet from reacting and adhering to the substratum.

The limpet is a mollusk with archaic features. One that probably lived about 400 million years ago, known as *Damilina*, was found in a fossil state in Bohemia. At first glance, it might seem similar to primitive monoplacophores. But appearances are deceiving: the limpet's seeming bilateral symmetry, visible in its horseshoelike muscular system, proves false if you anatomically examine its internal organs. These reveal its past history as a true snail, which like others underwent a torsion of the viscera. Its return to a shield-shaped shell is an evolutionary adaptation to the reef habitat.

The reef is one of the marine environments most sensitive to the activity of man. The indiscriminate collection of animal species certainly plays a significant role. Another worrisome element is pollution from hydrocarbons dumped into the sea either through carelessness or as a result of oil tanker spills; controls on this high-environmental-risk activity are far from effective. Port structures, shoreline reclamation, and even the construction of beach resorts directly on the reef upset or even destroy the fundamental prerequisites for life in the coastal environment.

Descent into the Shadows

A

A, C. Even at a modest depth of 30–60 feet (10–20 m), among the walls and below the spurs of rock, and even more so within caves, the quantity of light decreases quite rapidly. The species of algae change. In these environments, we may see mollusks that normally settle at greater depths in the coral environment.

Anyone who likes to snorkel prefers rocky seabeds that are always underwater or only rarely emerge during especially low tides.

Whether you snorkel from the surface, free dive, or use scuba gear, the infra-littoral band offers the greatest number of species. The most spectacular show is in tropical coral reefs (discussed below), but there is no dearth of thrills in temperate-water environments either.

Your gaze will be captured by fish as they elegantly glide or swiftly dart, or by less active creatures who are just as distinctive in form and color, like starfish, sea urchins, and colorful sponges. Mollusks with shells are elusive, and

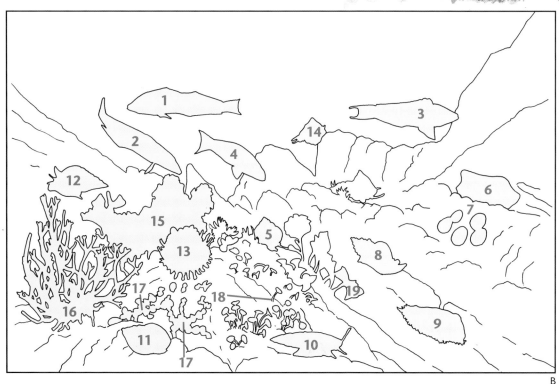

B

many are masters of mimicry. Sometimes, as you begin exploring a rocky seabed in the infralittoral band, you may see only limpets and mussels. This is certainly deceiving, and gradually, as your eyes grow accustomed to the peculiarities of the underwater landscape, you may note that a small sponge is hiding the shell of the thorny oyster *(Spondylus)*, firmly anchored to the rock, or what seemed to be a greenish clump of algae turns out to be the shell of a well-disguised murex. Not to mention the snails that play hide-and-seek among the algae and fissures in the rock. In this environment, experience will play an important role in what you see.

Where wave action is not particularly powerful, the underwater reef is covered with photophilic, or light-loving, algae.

B. The illustration shows an example of a rocky infracoastal environment (European coastline). The elements of the coastline, for illustrative purposes, are not in true proportions.

1. Coris julis *(male)*
2. Coris julis *female*
3. Thalassoma pavo *(female)*
4. Thalassoma pavo *(male)*
5. Gibbula varia
6. Arca noae
7. Patella caerulea
8. Hexaplex trunculus
9. Haliotis tuberculata lamellosa
10. Mitra zonata
11. Thais lacera
12. Buccinulum corneum
13. Spondylus gaederopus
14. Calliostoma laugieri
15. *alga* (Ulva)
16. *alga* (Codium)
17. *alga* (Halimeda)
18. *alga* (Acetabularia)
19. *alga* (Udotea)

C

Ocinebrina edwardsi, the red-mouth purpura *(Cymia lacera)*, the horn nassa *(Nassarius corniculum)*, the common whelk *(Buccinulum corneum)*, the trunculus murex *(Hexaplex trunculus)*, the sting winkle *(Ocenebra erinaceus)*, the knotty tulip *(Fasciolaria lignaria)*, the cone *(Conus mediterraneus)*, the mother-of-pearl top *(Gibbula richardi)*, the variegated top *(Gibbula varia)* and the concave top *(Gibbula rarilineata)*, the rock cerith *(Cerithium rupestre)*, and the beautiful rough turbo *(Astraea rugosa)*, whose calcareous operculum has been called St. Lucy's eye and is considered a good luck charm by fishermen. A number of gastropods live

A

B

A. The turbinid Turbo petholatus *in the coral reef of New Guinea. It is fairly common and is harvested to make ornamental objects.*

B. Two specimens of the turbinid Lithopoma, *encrusted with seaweed, on a cliff in British Columbia.*

C. A large abalone from California, Haliotis corrugata. *It may reach 10 inches (25 cm) in diameter and lives primarily at depths of from 20 to 33 feet (6–10 m).*

D. A Spondylus gaederopus *is camouflaged among the algae on a rocky seabed on Malta.*

E. The murex Urosalpinx cinerea, *1.5 inches (4 cm) long, hunting on a seabed in California.*

In this environment, populations of mobile mollusks can be broken down into three groups. The first includes mollusks that are in general quite small and prefer living on the thalli of algae (we'll talk about them in the chapter on mollusks of underwater meadows), dropping to the sea floor and seeking shelter in the cracks of the rock only when disturbed. The second includes those who graze on the rocks, even during broad daylight, while the third group comprises those who stay in the shadows during the day and move to open areas only at night.

An extraordinary number of shell species live in these seas. As an example, in well-lighted environments in the Mediterranean province, you will see murices like *Muricopsis cristatus* and

cemented to the substratum in this environment, including the vermetids *Vermetus cristatus, Petaloconchus glomeratus,* and *Serpulorbis arenaria,* who during the course of evolution lost their spiral-shaped shell and took on the wormlike appearance that gives the family its name. Limpets, who also live in the midlittoral band, inhabit this environment as well. The common limpet *(Patella caerulea)* lives up to 16 or 20 feet (5–6 m) in depth, while the China limpet *(Patella ulyssiponensis)* lives higher up and rarely descends below 10 feet (3 m). Among the bivalves, the common mussel *(Mytilus galloprovincialis)* can be found as deep as about 10 feet (3 m), especially in waters rich in organic substances; the Noah's ark *(Arca noae)* often inhabits

C

E

small cracks; and there are also large beds of flat oysters *(Ostrea edulis)*.

There are shadowy areas even just a few yards deep, where you will see species that prefer to take refuge from direct light. Some examples are the abalone *(Haliotis tuberulata lamellosa)*, many trochids, including the elegant members of the *Clanculus* genus, *Clanculus cruciatus* and *Clanculus jusseui*, the murex *Engina bicolor*, the striate cantharus *(Pisania striata)* and *Fusinus rudis*, and the little horny miter *(Mitra cornicula)*. But there are also ubiquitous species in the rocky environment that can be found on various detrital seabeds and in meadows of algae or Posidonia.

It is thrilling to enter an underwater cave for the first time. You may feel euphoric as well as a bit anxious, as the twilight of the cave is full of mystery. It's a completely different world from the bright waters just a few yards away. And this is a completely justified sensation. In fact, at just a few yards deep, the lack of light radically changes the plant and animal environment. Just

D

10 to 16 feet (3–5 m) below the surface, all that's needed is a wide rocky roof or large masses in close proximity to create plant and animal associations that are very different from the reef in full light. But in a cave, if light is dramatically less than at the surface, you will find yourself in a true deep-sea environment. As the darkness gradually increases, algae grow scarce, those below the tide level vanish, and the fanlike thalli of *Udotea petiolata*, the prickly-pear-like thalli of *Halimeda tuna*, and the calcareous little rods of *Pseudolithophillum expansum* appear among the soft algae. This environment is a precursor to the coral habitat, which normally begins at a few dozen yards deep, where the green meadows of marine phanerogams can no longer grow.

Light, which the various species of algae need to grow, cuts and breaks up the infralittoral band, creating deep-sea niches in relatively shallow water, depending on the play of light and shadow created by rock formations. In this environment, a dive at a constant depth, let's say about 30 feet (10 m), will allow you to explore a good variety of environments that would otherwise require much deeper dives. Mobile mollusks are less dependent than algae on changes in light, but have a marked preference for a particular environment, although it is not uncommon to see them in adjacent environments as well. Thus, the abalone *Haliotis lamellosa*, the murex *Fusinus rudis,* and the bivalve *Cardita calcyculata* prefer the infralittoral environment sheltered from direct light, but they also live in niches within the coral environment.

A very interesting association is that of mollusks with cnidarians growing in the infralittoral band. In all seas of the world, but in particular in the Caribbean and Panamic provinces, this ecological niche contains most representatives of the Epitoniidae family, the wentletraps—over two hundred species of shells, sculptured with unrivaled elegance. Wentletraps feed primarily on cnidarians, whose tissues they suck, wherever they find them, including various substrata at any number of depths.

In the Mediterranean, there are over thirty species. The largest wentletrap is *Amaea magnificum* from Japan, which

reaches 4.9 inches (12.5 cm) in size. Only half as big, but much more famous in the history of shell collecting, is the lovely, pale pink precious wentletrap, *Epitonium scalare,* found from southern China to the coast of Queensland, Australia. In the eighteenth century this shell was so prestigious that it was manufactured and sold by various Chinese counterfeiters, who were able to reproduce it using rice paste. The most coveted wentletrap in America (it lives from North Carolina to the Caribbean) is the noble wentletrap, *Sthenorhytis pernobilis,* whose habitat is also quite deep. From Florida to England to the Mediterranean we find *Epitonium lamellosa*, which is rather common on sandy seabeds, where the cnidarian *Anemonia sulcata* lives. Many species of wentletraps are difficult for collectors, because they are quite hard to identify. There are two ovulids in the Indopacific: the large *Ovula ovum,* white with a brown aperture, and very popular with collectors, and the small *Calpurnus verrucosus*, which both live in the infralittoral band. At greater depths, and associated with red coral, is the ovulid *Pseudosimnia carnea* from the Mediterranean and Caribbean provinces; its shell ranges from pale pink to brick red. In all warm and temperate waters of the world associated with gorgonians, there are ovulids from the subfamily Simniinae, which generally assume the color of the cnidarians on which they feed. These are tiny shells like the graceful orange *Cyphoma gibbosum* from the Caribbean, less than 1.2 inches (3 cm) in length.

On and Under the Sand and Mud

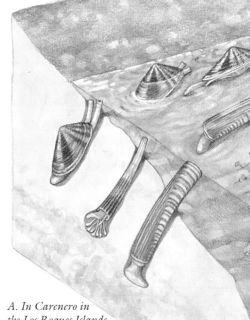

A

B

A. *In Carenero in the Los Roques Islands of Venezuela, the sea has tossed an incredible number of strombid shells on the beach; these shells are abundant on shallow, sandy beds throughout the Caribbean.*

B. *Its sturdy foot allows this Australian moon from the genus* Polinices *to plow the shallow sandy bed near Wooli. Like all naticids, this snail also attacks bivalves buried in the sand by perforating their shells with its radula and then inserting its proboscis into the hole.*

C. *This drawing represents schematically the population of a sandy bed of the Indo-pacific province.*

1. Donax cuneatus
2. Dentalium elephantinum
3. Solen truncata
4. Natica onca
5. Neritopsis radula
6. Terebra affinis
7. Polinices melanostomus
8. Phalium areola
9. Natica aracnoidea
10. Epitonium scalare
11. Casmaria ponderosa
12. Lambis chiragra
13. Conus striatus
14. Cypraea lamarckii
15. Cypraea pantherina
16. Strombus
17. Xenophora solarioides
18. Strombus variabilis
19. Nassarius conoidalus
20. Architectonica perspectiva
21. Conus geographus *(devouring a fish)*

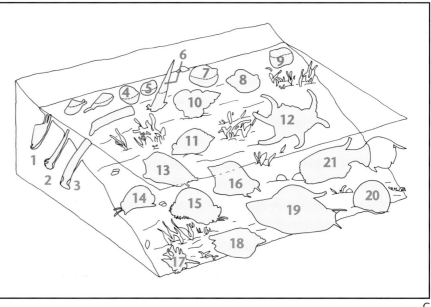

C

Beaches are the first place that comes to mind when we think of gathering shells, but they are not necessarily ideal. Of course, in the winter, after a strong sea storm has turned the coastal seabeds upside down, you may gather a good collection of specimens that are still fresh and intact, but normally, above the high tide mark you will only find single valves of common bivalves and a few gastropod shells, broken or made chalky by the sun. Of course, while these modest finds have no place in a collection, they are useful indicators of the environment on the underlying seabeds unless they are leftover food or garbage abandoned by fishing boats. At any rate, it is worthwhile to carefully observe the detritus washed up on shore, because there are areas where the currents, tides, and waves bring in enormous quantities of microshells,

especially if the nearby seabeds are made up of meadows of algae and phanerogams. In a sample of a liter of sand from the beach at Sfax, Tunisia, a total of 174,286 microshells was counted! In some quite particular environments, there are beaches formed only of shells, such as Shell Beach at Shark Bay Natural Park in western Australia, where you can walk for miles on a layer of shells up to 33 feet (10 m) deep. The beach is made up solely of the valves of the little cardiid *Afrocardium erugatum,* which inhabits the bed of the opposite lagoon. The shells are blown to the beach by the wind after the surf carries them, dead and empty, to the shore.

When you go from a stretch of reef, or from various solid substrata, like a pier or wharf, to a sandy beach, you will see completely different species of shells.

On beaches formed of materials that dry out quickly, like sand and shingles, no mollusks live above the high tide mark. The case is different if the materials dry out slowly, like earth mixed with rocks and decomposing plant material, found along the shores of brackish marshes, or in canals and estuary areas sheltered from wave motion. Here the humidity lasts long enough to allow mollusks to live within the crevices in the material. Of course, only mollusks with very small shells can move through this environment. In the Mediterranean these include *Truncatella subcylindrica, Ovatella myosotis, Assiminea littorina,* and a few others. The fine sand on the portion of beach periodically inundated by the tide is home to a certain number of mollusk species, but there are far fewer where there is coarse sand or shingles. In the

Mediterranean (but not in the Adriatic), it is not difficult to find specimens of the wedge shell *Donacilla cornea* by digging with your hands into the sand at the water's edge, provided the sand in the area is siliceous and not calcareous. In the intertidal area of the Adriatic, you will find the chicken venus *(Chamelea gallina)*, two species of coquina *(Donax trunculus* and *Donax semistriatus)*, known locally, and improperly, as tellins, and, since the late 1960s, an immigrant from the Indopacific region, the ark clam *(Anadara inaequivalvis)*.

But where the tide is much broader and uncovers sandy seabeds dozens or even hundreds of yards wide, as occurs along vast stretches of the French Atlantic coast, collecting mollusks,

A

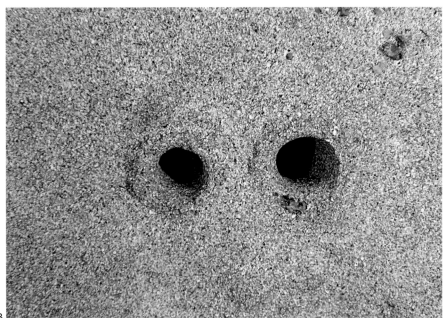

B

including edible species, is much more rewarding, because for the most part these bivalves are not only edible, but also particularly prized. Using shovels, rakes, and other methods refined by experience, fishermen in the area dig up the sea truffle or warty venus *(Venus verrucosa)*, the common cockle *(Cerastoderma edule)*, the European bittersweet *(Glycymeris glycymeris)*, the gray mactra *(Mactra glauca)*, two species of coquina *(Donax vittatus* and *variegatus)*, the variable scallop *(Chlamys varia)*, the saddle oyster *(Anomia ephippium)*, and the yellow razor clam *(Solen vagina)*. These species, or members of the same genera, are also found in the Mediterranean, but usually in the infralittoral band, on seabeds

that are always underwater, below the low tide mark.

If you carefully observe a sandy, shallow seabed through a diving mask, it may often feel like swimming over a desert: a few little fish, an alga, or a small hermit crab carrying a shell its builder left empty are often the only signs of life. But appearances are deceiving. Hidden and protected by the sand is a whole universe of prey and predators from different phyla in the animal world. And mollusks with shells are well represented. For mollusks, a mobile substratum has advantages and disadvantages compared to a fixed one. It is easier to find shelter by diving into a hole and hiding there, but that hole does not provide as much protection

from a predator's attack as a narrow crevice in the rock. When the sea is rough and shallow seabeds are swept by waves, a mobile substratum offers no place to anchor, and digging deeper into the sand may not be enough. Thus, periodically the sea wreaks havoc with benthic animals and hurls immense quantities to shore.

Bivalves have chosen different strategies to populate the seabed. To eat, some species are equipped with vertical siphons that inhale water to capture plankton and suspended detritus; these are known as planktophages and suspension feeders. Other species have a siphon that works horizontally, sucking the detritus lying on the seabed, and are known as detritivores. In any case, you may often note their presence by carefully observing the surface of the sand in the infralittoral band; if you see two little holes, there will be two siphons in action. Snails that prey on bivalves leave a long, sinuous little furrow to mark their passage.

Sometimes a sandy or muddy seabed will have a very large number of bivalves, but of just a few species, while the population of predator mollusks is clearly fewer in terms of individuals, but more numerous in species. Many of the more interesting gastropods for shell collectors come from sandy or muddy seabeds or those with very fine detritus. One example is *Architectonica perspectiva* from the Indopacific, whose umbilicus seems designed by a whimsical architect. A large number of conch species,

90

including the elegant *Babylonia formosae formosae* of the West Pacific; the Naticidae family, great predators of bivalves; many large species from the Cassidae family, in particular *Cassis fimbriata* (reaches 4.7 inches [12 cm] in length) from the Australian province and *Cassis madagascariensis* from the Caribbean (although its name seems to indicate otherwise); and two cassids from the Indopacific, *Phalium areola* and *Phalium bandatum*, with checkerboard-design shells, are among the shells most commonly sold in souvenir shops. But the cassid in this area that played a leading role in the history of art is *Cypraeacassis rufa*, a large shell (over 8 inches [20 cm] long) that has been used to make cameos since ancient times (the artist uses the

black spots, but when it creeps along muddy seabeds, it's very difficult to see, because it is covered by a dark periostracum that resembles the surrounding environment. *Conus tulipa*, which lives in the sand along the Great Barrier Reef of Australia, is not as large as the notorious *Conus geographus* (it is no more than 2.7 inches [7 cm] long), but is just as poisonous, and poses a mortal danger to humans as well.

The sand of the tropics is home to some of the most beautiful representatives of the families Harpidae, Mitridae, Costellariidae, Olividae, and Strombidae. Among the latter, the shells of species from the genus *Lambis* are spectacular for the long, arcuate digitations of their shells. They are popularly known as sea scorpions or spider shells, but their names

deep, is one of the largest and most spectacular representatives of the family, the imperial volute (*Cymbiola imperialis*), which reaches 10 inches (25 cm) in length. The bat volute (*Cymbiola vespertilio*) is common from the Philippines to Australia, on seabeds of sand and mud up to 65 feet (20 m) deep; it takes its name from the interesting bat-wing pattern on its shell. On the sandy seabeds of West Africa, from the Strait of Gibraltar to Senegal, fishing boats with trawls often come up with spectacular booty in the form of *Cymbium* (the species *Cymbium cymbium* may exceed 6 inches [15 cm] in length), volutes with an exceptionally wide aperture. Local populations consume the mollusk as food, while shells in good condition are sold to collectors.

difference in color between the ostracum and the hypostracum to bring the profile of the portraits into relief). Many species of beautiful murices live on sand, mud and detritus, like *Chicoreus cervicornis* from southern Australia and *Chicoreus spectrum* from the Caribbean.

Of the families most prized by collectors, the Conidae family is particularly well represented on sandy or muddy seabeds in the infralittoral and circumlittoral bands. In shallow waters of the Indopacific, the multitude of species includes *Conus virgo,* which prefers muddy seabeds, and *Conus zonatus* and *Conus zeylanicus,* from the Gulf of Bengal in western Indonesia, which come very close to shore. In honor of its name, *Conus leopardus* has a beautiful light shell dotted with little

do them an injustice; unlike most snails of mobile substrata, members of the genus *Lambis* are peaceful herbivores.

On the other hand, most of the lovely, highly prized volutes are voracious carnivores. Because they have no poison glands, they are forced to approach their prey and kill it with blows of their radula, and thus have developed a very unusual characteristic among snails— speed. Those from the genus *Amoria* are almost exclusively from Australia, as only one or two species have reached the southernmost islands of Indonesia. This is also explained by the way volutes reproduce; they do not have a period of larval, planktonic existence, but come into the world as little snails already formed. In the Philippines, on sandy seabeds from 6 to 65 feet (2–20 m)

A. A great scallop (Pecten maximus) on a sandy bed off the English coast: it is moving along calmly, expelling water from the valves near the hinge.

B. The two little holes in the sandy seabed signal the presence of a buried mollusk. They are in fact the openings of the inhaling and exhaling siphons.

C. Two examples of pipi (Plebidonax deltoides), a donax that lives in eastern and southern Australia, buried in the beds of coarse coastal sand at a depth of a few yards. We can clearly see the siphons and the foot.

D. The sandy seabeds of the Indopacific hold much interest for enthusiasts. Here, the photographer has surprised a strombus, who has left evident ruts in the sand before burrowing down.

The Coral Theater

Great coral reefs form only in warm seas. And there are more species of coveted mollusks in these seas than anywhere else, because here are the most beautiful and rare shells in the world. Yet a brief vacation in a tourist area near a coral reef will not

A

A, B, D. The reef has different mollusk habitats. A diver swimming above a garden of Acropora like that of the Great Barrier Reef of Australia in the photo (A) may have the impression that the shells are vacant

and their builders are absent. But this is not so: a myriad of mollusk species find their ecological niche among the corals. Only the very sturdy and massive giant clams (B and D) do not mind being exposed to the sunlight.

necessarily provide an opportunity to see and collect a great number of species, as some places, like the lagoons in Polynesian atolls, are home to very few species. This is due to the great glaciations in the Quaternary period that lowered the sea level, transformed the lagoons into closed salt lakes, and then dried them out, causing the extinction of all existing forms of life, including calm-water bivalves. At the end of each glaciation, when the sea level rose and the waters once again invaded the dried-out lagoons, only the few coral reef bivalves exposed to wave motion were able to repopulate them—but it wasn't a hospitable environment.

B

C

C. A reconstruction of a stretch of the Australian Great Barrier Reef. As with the other illustrations, the various elements are not to scale for reasons of graphical clarity.

1. Tridacna
2. Turbo petholatus
3. Conus imperialis
4. Charonia tritonis *devouring an* Acanthaster planci *starfish*
5. *pearl oyster* Pinctada margaritifera
6. Cypraea vitellus
7. Tridacna squamosa
8. Coralliophila costulans
9. Haliotis ovina
10. Limaria fragilis
11. Acanthopleura gemmata
12. Pteria saltata
13. Gloripallium pallium
14. Calpurnus verrucosus
15. Drupella cornus

D

So sea currents had to carry a sufficient number of larvae from distant coasts for the lagoons of the atolls to once again become home to new populations of rather diversified bivalves.

Despite these periodic catastrophic events, mollusks, along with fish and corals, play an important role on the great stage of marine life that is the reef, in all its forms. And the star is certainly the tridacna. Indeed, while other bivalves tend to hide themselves, the tridacna likes to stand out. From its open valves, we can see its brilliantly colored mantle, running from blue to green to orange to purple, often in contrast with brown or black striped or spotted patterns. The Tridacnidae family lives only in the Indopacific province, with ten species, eight in the genus *Tridacna* and two in the genus *Hippopus*. The tridacna we all know best is the giant clam *(Tridacna gigas)*, which came to Europe in the Middle Ages, when it was placed in churches as a font for holy water. Its shell may exceed 50 inches (130 cm) in length and weigh as much as 550 pounds (250 kg). The first marine biologists to study it were faced with a paradox. All bivalves feed by filtering what they find in the water. But how could a gigantic bivalve live in the waters of the coral reef, which are transparent precisely because there is little suspended organic matter? The research generated by this problem led to the discovery of one of the most fascinating cases of symbiosis, involving the mollusk and single-celled zooxanthellae algae. The mollusk cultivates the algae

A

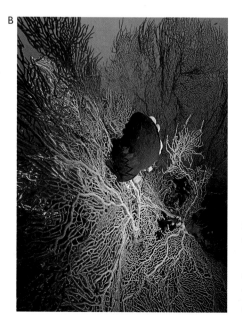

B

A, B. An enthusiast finds the best opportunities to observe shells on the infralittoral level of the coral reef, which is not difficult to visit when the sea is very calm. Nevertheless, you need to be very careful not to break branches of living coral. In A, well camouflaged formations of bivalves, anchored to a large formation of dead coral. In B, a Lopha on a branch of gorgonia.

within the tissues of its mantle, which is exposed to sunlight to permit the algae's chlorophyll-producing system to operate. The clam certainly receives oxygen and organic material from the algae, but how the exchanges between the two symbionts actually occur is still not clear. Certainly, the mollusk avoids drawing on its capital of zooxanthellae, just like a good gardener who lets enough lettuce plants go to seed so he'll have enough for the next harvest. In exchange, the algae receives the giant clam's catabolites—garden compost, so to speak—plus perfect lighting in a well-protected environment. The symbiosis is perfectly analogous to what occurs between zooxanthellae and colonies of coral polyps. Among other things, by absorbing carbon dioxide, as all plants do, the algae reduce the acidity of the water, encouraging the growth of corals as well as mollusks with shells.

This type of feeding has played a role in the evolution of the tridacna, causing a 180-degree rotation of its vertical axis. Thus, unlike the clam, which stands up buried in the sand with the hinge up and the flaps of the mantle down, the tridacna lies buried stomach up among the corals, with the hinge down and the flaps of its mantle clearly visible. And what gives the tridacna's mantle its brilliant colors? It has tiny lenses of organic material known as iridocytes that it uses to maintain the right quantity of light for its algae, just as a gardener

does when he covers or lights a greenhouse. In the past, the tridacna was collected for food: to remove it from the coral branches in which it lived buried, a large section of the coral reef had to be destroyed. Now this precious environment is treated with more respect, and tridacnas are regularly raised for their meat and shells, and as living specimens for aquarium owners.

D

E

C

Thus, you can collect them without feeling guilty, provided you have room for them in your home or aquarium.

In tropical regions, there is a clear distinction within mollusk families between species that prefer waters strongly affected by the proximity of continental masses, and strictly oceanic species. The mollusks that populate coral formations are for the most part members of the latter group, although corals can develop in the immediate vicinity of the coast through so-called barrier reefs, or else grow in the open sea along the edge of the continental shelf (like the Great Barrier Reef in eastern Australia). In both cases, the barriers are formed where the flow of continental waters and thus sediments is nonexistent or extremely reduced (such

C. A large cone photographed in Bali, Conus marmoreus. It is found in the coral reefs of the Indopacific, especially below pieces of dead coral or at the base of colonies of cnidarians. Although it feeds on mollusks and thus does not need a potent poison like that used by others of its genus who prey on fish, there have been cases of poisoning.

D, E. Two bivalves have settled among the corals on the reef.

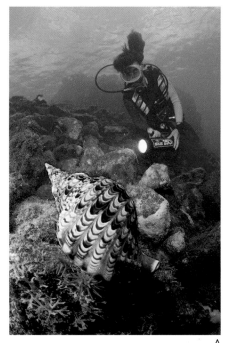

A

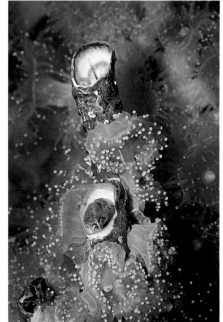

B

of the reef, creating microenvironments enlivened by the flow of the tide; and finally, on the slope facing the open sea, the barrier reef, which is the zone of coral expansion, the area where life is richer and more abundant. In this area as well, as we have noted for rocky coasts, there are differences between the fauna of the midlittoral band, which is periodically left dry by the tide, and the infralittoral band, which is almost underwater. Mobile species, however, move from one level to another, and the tidal pools of the coral reef have a wealth of beautiful shells.

On the coral reefs of the Indopacific, the large *Trochus niloticus* and the pearl oyster, *Pinctada margaritifera*, live on the outer slope. Due to their great

as the Red Sea) and water conditions (variations in salinity and quantity of suspended materials) are not much different from those of coral formations in the open sea, like the ring-shaped ones that form atolls.

The complex coral seascape includes a wide range of substrata and exposure to light, factors that play a major role in mollusk populations. Some of the most important environments include coral sand lagoons, sometimes scattered with dead corals or dotted with isolated formations of live corals, often with a wealth of algae and phanerogamic plants; channels that connect lagoons with the open sea and are dense with coralline, encrusting algae; the maze of passages and tunnels that open within the ridge

D

C

A. The image shows the thrilling encounter of a diver with a great triton (Charonia tritonis).

B. A vermetid, Serpulorbis squamiger *from California. This vermiform shell is cemented to the reef and completely hidden by sponges and algae.*

C. A tiny ovulid crawls along a branch of coral. Mollusks in this family are for the most part associated with gorgonians and soft corals.

D. Well-camouflaged gastropods cling to the coral reef.

E. Tiny parasitic gastropods at work among the spines of a large sea urchin: they feed by sucking liquids from its tissue.

economic importance in the production of pearls and mother-of-pearl, their populations were decimated by uncontrolled harvesting. Now the two species are successfully cultivated, and the natural populations are slowly recovering. The cone family is represented by beautiful species that live primarily at the foot of or in pockets of sand within coral formations. Often they are invisible due to a "camouflage suit" of encrusting coral algae or a periostracum wrapped in green algae. Others, like *Conus nusatella* of the Indopacific, become almost impossible to reach, as they slip under various layers of dead coral. *Conus marmoreus, Conus generalis, Conus litoglyphus,* and *Conus geographus* live in infralittoral

E

coral sands in the Indopacific. The latter species, which hunts fish, is armed with a poison dart that may be lethal even to humans. *Conus jaspideus* and *Conus daucus* live in a similar environment within coral formations in the Caribbean. The Great Barrier Reef of Australia is home to an extraordinary number of cones: *Conus lividus, flavidus,* and *miles* prefer the midlittoral band, while *Conus mustellinus* is found in intertidal areas, including coral rock exposed to light.

Of all shells, the most prized are cowries. Most of the approximately two hundred species of these beautiful shells prefer a coral environment. It is very difficult to spot them during the day, but it is not uncommon to see them at night as they graze on algae around coral formations. On the outer slope of the reef in the southwest Pacific, lives the legendary golden cowrie *(Cypraea aurantium),* a royal emblem in ancient Polynesia, and even now rare and highly prized. There are beautiful variations of color in the tiger cowrie *(Cypraea tigris),* common in much of the Indopacific. There are even completely black specimens, which prefer to live under blocks of dead coral. Widespread in the same area, but less common, is another reef inhabitant, the eyed cowrie *(Cypraea argus),* with its surface scattered with circular patterns that look like the hundred eyes of the mythological Greek monster Argus. The midlittoral band of the reef, down to two meters deep, is

home to the money cowrie *(Cypraea moneta),* quite common along with the gold-auger cowrie *(Cypraea annulus),* which is also found in rocky, non-coralline environments. As we will see, these two Indopacific species, used as money, were of great importance in the international trade of premodern peoples. On the reefs of the Caribbean, there are only about a half dozen species of cowrie. *Cypraea zebra* (which does not have a striped shell as its name might imply, but has round spots, and is in fact known as the measled cowrie), has a special system for caring for its eggs.

The female spreads its mantle over them as if brooding, and periodically removes detritus from them with its proboscis. The ovulid *Volva volva* lives in the coral environment, feeding primarily on gorgonians; it has an extremely elongated form that may be as much as 4 inches (10 cm) in length.

One of the stars in coral habitats is the trumpet shell *(Charonia tritonis),* which may be as long as 18 inches (45 cm). Widespread in other environments as well, and in warm or temperate seas around the world, it was universally used by humans as a musical instrument. But several years ago newspapers also proclaimed it the defender of the reef, as it preys on the crown-of-thorns *Acanthaster planci,* which devours coral. The uncontrolled multiplication of the crown-of-thorns was attributed to overharvesting of tritons. Now the trumpet shell is a protected species.

A. This strange formation of Posidonia oceanica meadow in the Mediterranean Sea is due to the rhizomes, which grow upward to prevent the plant from being suffocated by the accumulation of detritus carried in by the currents. In this manner, tables form, among which channels and wide areas are created, moving the seabed and encouraging the great amount and variety of marine life around it.

B. A beautiful meadow of Posidonia australis, off the coast of western Australia. This environment offers protection to many small living species, in particular the tiny snails that hide beneath the thick leaves, within the maze of rhizomes, or below layers of rotting leaves, the so-called thanato-posidonia habitat.

A

B

Hidden in Underwater Meadows

When you swim over an underwater meadow, either scuba diving or snorkeling, you will see few or no shells. But if you rummage through the sand on the bank of a sheltered basin with a bed rich in vegetation, you will find an often astonishing quantity of empty shells. They are small or even tiny, most of them only a fractions of an inch long, almost all eroded by the surf and made chalk by the sun. But there will be a few fresh ones just washed up among all these, and you'll find it worthwhile to take out a lens and observe them at your leisure, as their sculptures and colors are of a rare elegance.

These are the little inhabitants of algae and marine phanerogams, which offer perfect hiding places, making it very difficult to observe them in nature. To collect them live, the traditional technique is to pull off a tuft of vegetation from the floor and immerse it in a bucket of fresh water. The mollusks will drop to the bottom and it will be easy to collect them, put them in a aquarium, and observe them at your leisure, or return them to their environment after examining and identifying them. But this procedure is not recommended for those areas where sea meadows are at risk.

C. The drawing shows an example of population of the underwater Posidonia oceanica *pasture in the Mediterranean (for illustrative purposes, the animals are not to scale).*
1. Salpa
2. Pinna nobilis
3. Chlamys hyalina
4. Stella chaetaster
5. Natica stercusmuscarum

D

6. Typhinellus sowerby
7. Rissoa
8. angler fish
9. sea horse
10. Haminoea navicula
11. Tricolia tenuis
12. Tricolia pullus
13. Bittium
14. Lima hians
15. Nassarius reticulatus
16. Venerupis senegalensis
17. Solemya togata

D. The triton Charonia lampas, *a large predator common in many seas, devours a bivalve on a seagrass meadow of the Red Sea. This triton did not come to be here due to its movements as an adult (it lives its entire life in a limited area of the seabed), but rather to its life in the planktonic larval state, when it can be carried great distances by the marine current.*

C

A. The shell of this Australian trochid, Cantharidus lehmani, *can be distinguished by its tall shell and beautiful axial coloration. Here it is crawling in a leaf of a marine phanerogam.*

B. A small, graceful trochid from European seas, Calliostoma zizyphinum *customarily grazes on seabed meadows. It is most frequently seen at about 30 feet (10 m) deep.*

A

The most surprising inhabitant of these environments is *Berthellina engeli*, from the Juliidae family, which lives in the Galapagos Islands and along the Pacific coast of Central America (the Panamic malacological province). Its small, greenish, fragile, thin shell is formed of two valves, just like a clam. But what's incredible is that *Berthellina* is a true snail, a gastropod. The apex of one valve has only a hint of the spiral shape that characterizes this class of mollusks, but its body leaves no doubt of its nomenclature: it has a foot used for crawling, a head with two pairs of tentacles, and a mouth with a radula—

C

D

E

essentially, the anatomy of a true snail. But this one can fully retract its body into its shell, closing the valves hermetically like a clam.

In areas of the sea that are relatively sheltered from wave motion, on solid substrata at shallow depths, meadows of algae are exposed directly to the sunlight (photophilic algae). Mollusks take refuge from the light, so the little snails that populate the cracks in the rocks and the detritus at the foot of algae come out primarily at night and begin to creep up the thalli. If sea conditions suddenly deteriorate or if some threatening presence disturbs them, they fall onto the sea floor and head back to their shelters. In the Mediterranean, truly graceful little snails graze on the thalli of photophilic algae. For example, there is *Tricolia pullus,* from the Tricoliidae family. No more than .4 inches (10 mm) long, it has an extraordinary variety of patterns on the glossy surface of its shell. If you observe a collection of these little snails with a 10**X** lens, you'll be amazed at the pattern of spiral or radiating bands, either broken or continuous, undulating or uniform, that combine and contrast tones of red, black, white, and beige. Less colorful, but with just as elegant a design, is a much larger member of the Phasianellidae family (which is closely related to Tricoliidae), from southern Australia, *Phasianella australis,* which lives in meadows of *Cymodocea.*

Meadows of algae and marine phanerogams are the preferred habitats of the Rissoidae family, which has about a hundred species in seas all over the world. They are never particularly colorful, but their sculptures are often

truly elegant. Identifying a rissoid— always with the use of a good lens, or better yet, a stereoscopic microscope, is a fascinating task, as it is to make a specialized collection of them (which has the advantage of fitting into just one drawer). A small and very graceful representative of the Neritidae family, *Smaragdia viridis,* with a beautiful bright green color rather rare for marine shells, frequents both algae and phanerogam meadows on all the Atlantic coasts of Europe, America, and Africa. Mollusks also frequent meadows of photophilic algae, remaining at the base of plants without crawling over or eating them, especially during the juvenile phase. Some species that behave in this manner are a graceful murex, *Ocinebrina edwardsi,* and *Gibberula caelata,* a tiny margin shell that inhabits European seas.

Phanerogam meadows are very different from the photophilic algae environment. Phanerogams are true land plants that have conquered the marine environment. Unlike algae, they flower and bear fruit and anchor to the seabed with roots. To avoid being suffocated by the sand, marine phanerogams like *Posidonia oceanica* grow vertically above

C, D. Pinna nobilis, *one of the largest bivalves in existence, in the* Posidonia oceanica *meadow of the Mediterranean. The byssus the mollusk uses to anchor itself to the bottom was once spun and used to make gloves and other accessories that were particularly light and prized.*

E. We usually think of a chiton as a small animal doomed to crawl along the bottom, but this elegant Ischnochiton elongatus crispus *was instead caught by the camera crawling up a leaf of a large marine phanerogam in the waters of Cape Leeuwin, Australia.*

B

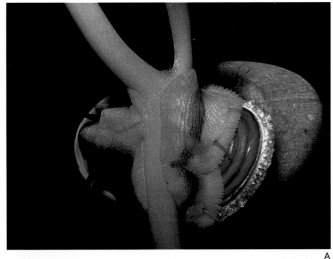

A. This Norrisia
norrisi, *a graceful
trochid from
California, feeds on
sea-tangles and other
algae just below the
lower tidal line. The
brilliant red body of
the animal is quite
characteristic. It is
abundant in its
territory, which
runs from Point
Conception to central
Baja California.*

the sediment that accumulates around
their rhizomes, to form characteristic
table-shaped rises known as mats. This
phenomenon enlivens the seabed,
because channels open up among the
mats where the current carries and
accumulates the hulls of dead shells and
other detritus. Sometimes the mats are
arranged in a circle around a coastal
pool, or follow the slope of the seabed,
forming steps. They thus form micro-
habitats that offer a large variety of
conditions to hundreds of animal and
plant species. Mollusks are abundant
within them.

B. *Two graceful* Alia
carinata *photographed
on the thallus of an
alga. These little
snails from the
Columbellidae family,
less than .4 inches (10
mm) long, live from
southern Alaska to*

*Baja California, on
any type of marine
vegetation, from the
low tide mark to about
16 feet (5 m) deep. In
particular, they can
be found in forests of
great sea-tangles,*
Macrocystis pyrifera.

C. *Trochids from the
genus* Tegula *as they
graze on the sea-
tangle vegetation in
California waters.*

D. *The fantastic
environment of the
underwater forest of*

*sea-tangles. The algae
photographed belong to
the species* Macrocystis
pyrifera, *whose thalli
can rise dozens of
yards from the seabed.
The sea-tangle forest is
home to a thriving
animal life.*

A small, elegant bivalve, *Lissopecten
hyalinus,* attaches to the ribbonlike
leaves of *Posidonia.* It is little more than
.8 inches (2 cm) in diameter, with a
shell color that can vary greatly, but of
such a vitreous consistency that it
sometimes seems transparent. The maze
of *Posidonia* rhizomes is a true underwater forest, shadowy and pulsing with
life. Algae, sea anemones, sponges, and
crustaceans have chosen this habitat. Of
the mollusks, another delicate-appearing
bivalve, *Limaria hians,* about 1 inch
(2.5 cm) high, has long colorful
tentacles that allow it to move through
this labyrinth. *Limaria* also frequents
another *Posidonia* ecological niche
made of masses of dead *Posidonia*
leaves, the so-called thanatoposidonia
habitat. It also lives in the West Indies
and along the Atlantic coasts of Europe
and North Africa.

A rare bivalve, *Solemya togata,* lives
in the muddy sediment of coastal pools
among phanerogam mats. An average
of 2 inches (5 cm) long, it has a glossy
brown periostracum furrowed by dark
green radiating bands. It is not easy to
find, but lives in the Mediterranean, the

Portuguese Atlantic, and as far south as Senegal. The same environment is also home to a gigantic bivalve, *Pinna nobilis,* up to 35 inches (90 cm) high, which lives in the detritus of channels among the mats. In the past it was gathered for its byssus, which was used in the textile industry, and in recent decades it was overharvested for food or rather tasteless souvenirs. Now it is a protected species, and should you ever run across one alive, you should simply photograph it and never tell any casual acquaintances on the beach where you found it. A snail that frequents channels among the mats is *Gyroscala lamellosa,* as elegant as its cousins the wentletraps, also members of the Epitoniidae family. In the same environment, but buried in the sediment, lives a clam, *Venerupis senegalensis,* that looks very similar to the *Lioconcha philippinarum* of eastern Asia, now cultivated in many parts of the world. On the two shores of the Atlantic, in the algae of the infralittoral band, lives the opisthobranch *Bulla striata,* which has an oval-shaped, rather light shell. The last whorl is larger than the preceding ones and completely covers the spire. Along the coast of northern Brazil, algae meadows are home to *Modulus modulus,* an average-sized snail with a rather robust shell and a very distinct head with two long tentacles. Surprisingly, its eyes are about halfway up the tentacles.

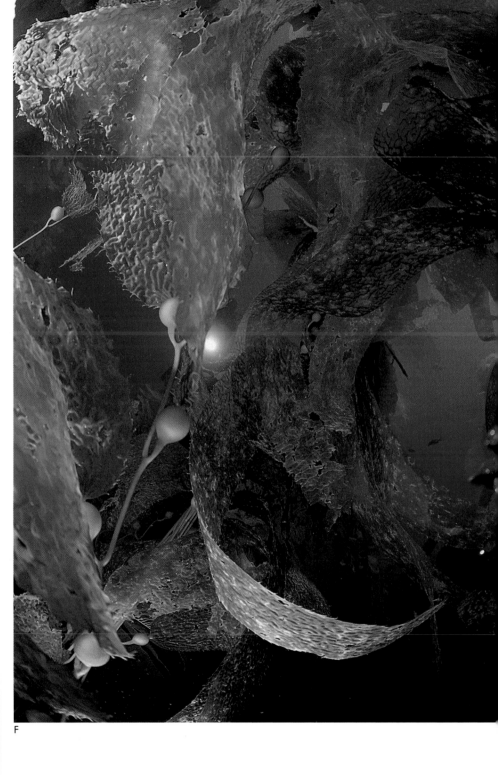

F

E

E, F. The forests of large seaweeds represent a rich pasture for numerous species of gastropods (E) and at the same time offer them excellent places to hide from predators.

The Mangrove Forests

Mangroves mark the border between the marine world and dry land along many tropical coasts less exposed to the surf. Vegetation takes hold along the sandy and muddy beaches of lagoons, at river mouths, in sheltered bays, and on the leeward side of islands. These are extraordinarily productive environments in biological terms: they are home to a myriad of fish, birds, crustaceans and mollusks, who find both food and shelter within them. Mangrove forests are not, however, an ideal coastal environment for mass tourism, which prefers sandy beaches or reefs, coral or otherwise, and always demands clear water. Thus, in coastal areas that have recently been developed and urbanized, mangrove forests are unfortunately destroyed to make room for not only ports and industrial development but swimming beaches and traditional seaside promenades.

In mangrove forests, the trees have adapted to setting their roots in an asphyxiated soil drenched with salty or brackish water. To survive, they have

A

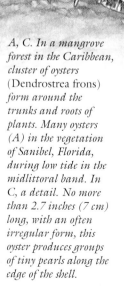

A, C. In a mangrove forest in the Caribbean, cluster of oysters (Dendrostrea frons) form around the trunks and roots of plants. Many oysters (A) in the vegetation of Sanibel, Florida, during low tide in the midlittoral band. In C, a detail. No more than 2.7 inches (7 cm) long, with an often irregular form, this oyster produces groups of tiny pearls along the edge of the shell.

B

B. In this illustration we can see the population of mollusks in a mangrove forest in Florida, in the Caribbean province. For illustrative purposes, the mollusks are not shown in correct proportion to the vegetation or each other.

1. Littorina scabra
2. Neritina virginia
3. Isognomon alatus
4. Cypraea zebra
5. Lucina pectinata
6. Batillaria minima
7. Melongena corona

C

devised ingenious systems—they expel the salt from their tissues using something like pores, which deposit it on the bark, and propagate not by seeds but through little fully developed plants that float on the water until the tide deposits them where they can take root. They breathe oxygen directly from the air, using special aerial branches called pneumotophores, and develop a system for anchoring to unstable ground so they can withstand the flow of the tides.

It is easy to visit only the edge of this extremely interesting natural environment, or degraded areas where the vegetation is sparse. By boat, you can easily traverse the part of the forest facing the sea, but entering it is a very difficult enterprise. The maze of aerial roots and branches is extremely dense, while the sandy or detrital soil, especially where fresh water enters from rivers and streams, quickly develops a layer of black, slimy mud that is absolutely impassable. And collecting shells? In an environment like this, it's better to give

A

B

A. A cluster of oysters of the species Crassotrea virginica *has formed around the aerial root of a* Rhizophora.

B. A population of Terebralia palustris *scattered over a "field" of pneumatophores on the mud of a mangrove formation in Oman.*

C. The mangrove forests of St. George Basin, Kimberley, Australia, feed vast populations of mollusks. The mangrove mollusks from the family of Ellobiidae live on trunks or leaves of mangroves and have adopted aerial respiration.

up the do-it-yourself attitude and let local fishermen give you a hand. Only about a hundred species of mollusk throughout the world have chosen mangrove forests as their habitat. The supralittoral band, which is here represented by mangrove trunks, branches, and leaves, is inhabited by species of pulmonates and prosobranchs that seem to be evolving more toward a terrestrial existence than a marine one. Thus, in Australian mangroves (which line the whole north coast of the continent, from Queensland to northwest Australia), *Littorina filosa*, like various species of the genus from the rocky coasts of temperate zones, spends much of its existence out of the water. The females of this slender snail, about 1 inch (2.5 cm) long with a shell that varies from yellow to red to brown, enter the water only after mating, to lay their eggs. After a brief period in the water, young hatchlings settle on tree branches, from which the males never descend. This choice of aerial life-style has led to a transformation of the mantle cavity into a organ that acts as a lung.

On the other hand, the ellobiids are true pulmonates, and there are various species of them in the mangrove forests of Australia. The most noticeable in form and size is *Ellobium aurismidae*, whose white shell covered with a blackish periostracum can reach a length of nearly 3 inches (7.6 cm). The shell of *Ellobium aurisjudae*, which has a chestnut-colored periostracum, is whitish with a more slender form, and is no more than 2 inches (5 cm) long. The small *Pythia scarabaeus*, no more than 1 inch (2.5 cm) long, is perfectly adapted to dry substrata, and lays its eggs on leaves that are not dampened by the tide, while *Cassidula rugata*, even smaller, frequents the upper band of the midlittoral band, thus living both an aerial and an aquatic life on a daily basis. All ellobiids, who have no operculum, have developed teeth around the aperture of the shell that prevent predators from entering.

While ellobiids are a family of substantially terrestrial mollusks that still long for the marine environment, the potamidids are a clearly marine family, with a shell form and anatomy very similar to the cerithids. They live in estuary environments (hence the name, from the Greek *potamos,* or "river")

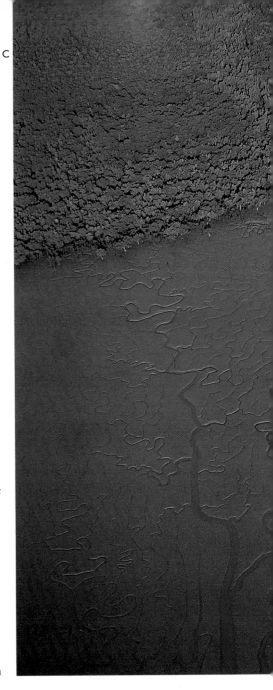

C

and are well represented in mangrove forests. They are all herbivores and feed on tiny algae. In Australia, the large *Pyrazus ebeninus* is quite common and exceeds 4 inches (10 cm) in length. The aborigines used it for food, and the English navigator James Cook, who discovered the continent, found enormous quantities in Botany Bay, where the Gulf of Sydney is today.

Widespread in mangroves throughout much of the Indopacific area, from China to Madagascar, is *Telescopium telescopium*, with its beautiful conical shell, blackish with very thin light stripes, 3.5 inches (9 cm) high. In the same area lives *Cerithidea cingulata*, up to 2 inches (5 cm) high, its elegant shell adorned by a network of axial and spiral stripes, with three little bands of beading in different colors for each whorl. Billions

of shells of this and related species can be found in every square mile in the mangroves of the Philippines.

One potamidid from the West African province, *Tympanotonus fuscatus,* is quite variable in form, with a shell that is sometimes almost smooth and sometimes adorned by a regular band of spines; it lives in the muddy sand of the mangroves, in the midlittoral band, and feeds on the organic surface film.

A nerite from the mangroves of the west central Pacific, *Neritina communis,* is extremely abundant, with shells in elegant designs and colors. About .8 inches (2 cm) in diameter, it is adorned by pink, red, yellow, white, and black bands in primarily zigzag patterns. It's easy to find in souvenir shops. The dark-colored *Nerita lineata,* relatively large for the nerite family, lives in the mid-

littoral band. It is no larger than 1.5 inches (3.8 cm), and many of its shells are inhabited by hermit crabs. *Nassarius olivaceus,* with a brown shell about 1 inch (2.5 cm) long, is a necrophage, and can occasionally be found alive within rotting trunks.

Among the bivalves, an oyster that has colonized the mangroves but has adapted to other situations as well, and is in fact subject to intensive cultivation, is *Saccostrea commercialis,* which, as the scientific name indicates, is quite popular in fish markets. A lucinid, *Anodontia edentula,* lives in the waters at the edge of mangroves in the Indopacific region, deeply embedded in the mud. It is 1.4 inches (3.5 cm) in diameter and has massive, swollen, white, perfectly circular valves. A frequent bivalve in mangroves in the Caribbean, from

Florida to Brazil, is the isognomid *Isognomon alatus:* its valves are not hinged by teeth but by a very long, thick ligament, the resilium, which has parallel segments perpendicular to the edge of the valves, a characteristic common to the entire family.

But the largest bivalve that colonizes the mud of mangrove seabeds is a gigantic teredinid from the genus *Kufus,* which reaches a length of about 35 inches (90 cm) and lives in the south-western Pacific. It digs a tunnel with two small valves and transforms it into a very long calcareous tube. Only the tips of the siphons poke out of the mud, and the creature uses them to circulate the water of the seabed through its organic filters, to remove suspended nourishment and oxygen: local populations gather *Kufus* for food.

A

From the
High Sea

O nce it has decided to leave the
seabed and wander freely
through the immense oceans,
what can a mollusk do with a
shell it inherited from ancestors that
crept lazily over just a few yards?
Wouldn't that shield—made to protect
the exposed side of the body stretched
out on a hard surface—prove perfectly
useless in a three-dimensional space,
where predators can attack in a flash
from any direction? In effect, the

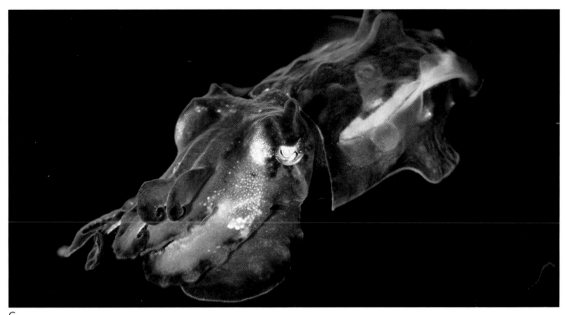

A. More than any other mollusk adapted to a pelagic life, the squid has probably best fulfilled the evolutionary potential of the class of cephalopods. Of the ten arms that crown its siphon, which is a transformation of the ancestral foot, eight of them, which encircle the mouth, are not retractable, while two others, which are much longer, can be retracted completely into two pockets in the mantle. The squid is a very fast swimmer, totally comparable to a fish.

C

solution of getting rid of the shell, which does seem logical according to human experience—swimming with a backpack on your shoulders is possible, but it's easier without it—was the choice of many mollusks that became pelagic, i.e., forsaking the resources of the marine seabed to seek nourishment in the open water. This is what the octopus did. This is what the nudibranchs did, with their beautiful forms and colors that have given them the name of sea butterflies. But there have been many interesting exceptions. In many cases, the question, What do we do with the shell? has led to unpredictable evolutionary responses. There was even a genus of pelagic mollusks that discarded its original shell and then invented a completely new one to protect its young. It is known as the argonaut *(Argonauta)*, a cephalopod that is a distant relative of the octopus. The female, who is a giant compared to the male, builds an ootheca, an egg case, in the form of a little boat, where it lays and keeps its eggs as it swims in the high sea. Sometimes the current pushes it toward the coast and the poor argonaut ends up on the beach.

The purple snail *(Janthina)* is a true snail with a very light, but classically formed shell. It travels under the surface of the sea, attached to a raft it makes by sticking together bubbles of mucus filled with air. To make the bubbles, it stretches out part of its foot from the water. Some species of purple snail (including *Janthina nitens* from European seas) also attach their egg capsules to this raft. They are prolific mothers, and can lay as many as 2 million eggs

each, arranged in about 500 capsules. The purple snail is carnivorous and easily devours colonies of polyps of the Portuguese man-of-war *(Physalia)* and the tissues of jellyfish and other planktonic cnidarians, even though they are protected by stinging cells capable of killing much larger animals. You need to be very lucky to find intact purple snail shells on the beach. On rare occasions, the sea will toss up large quantities, but years may go by before even one arrives along a stretch of coast. About thirty species of purple snail have been described, and they can be found in seas throughout the world, except for polar regions. The snail's mimetic colors run from pale blue to purple. If it feels threatened, it emits a substance that tinges the water violet, thus confusing its predator.

Another planktonic gastropod, Peron's sea butterfly *(Atlanta peroni)*, has an extremely small, fragile, transparent shell. It can swim actively, as it has transformed the front part of its foot,

B. A swimming Argonauta argo. *The ancients imagined that the argonaut used its pseudoshell, which we know is an ootheca, or egg case, to float as if on a true boat. Although the female argonaut is the only one that builds an ootheca, caring for young is a common trait in cephalopods.*

C. This Indopacific cuttlefish, Metasepia pfefferi, *can be distinguished by its bright colors.*

D. This small octopus, Hapalochlaena maculosa, *has a more powerful poison than any related species. It lives in southern Australia.*

B

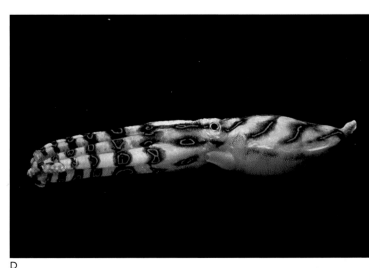

D

A. With its foot transformed into a swimming organ and its sturdy yet extremely light shell, this Haminoea hydatis snail leads an entirely pelagic life.

B. A rare case of a pelagic prosobranch, a Janthina janthina is feeding on the tentacle of a cnidarian, the Portuguese man-of-war, whose scientific name is Physalia utriculus. Small cirripeds have settled on the outside of the shell.

known as the propodium, into a sort of fin. This allows it to venture into deep waters, and it has been found as deep as 9,800 feet (3,000 m) below the surface (on the other hand, if the purple snail loses contact with its raft, it sinks and dies). The central part of the sea butterfly's foot, the mesopodium, instead has a sucker that the animal uses to stick to its prey, which it devours by lacerating its tissues with a radula. *Cavolinia*, an opisthobranch, has pelagic habits and similar swimming abilities, but it uses two lobes of the foot as fins, which have developed outward and laterally. Its small, fragile shell has a globular form quite different from that of snails.

Unlike the argonaut, some cephalopods produce true shells. These include the internal shell produced by the cuttlefish *(Sepia)* and the squid *(Loligo)*, in common parlance known as cuttlebone and pen; the former is calcareous and the latter horny. If all shells were so

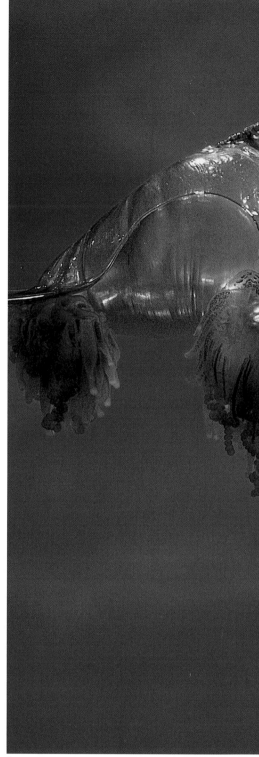

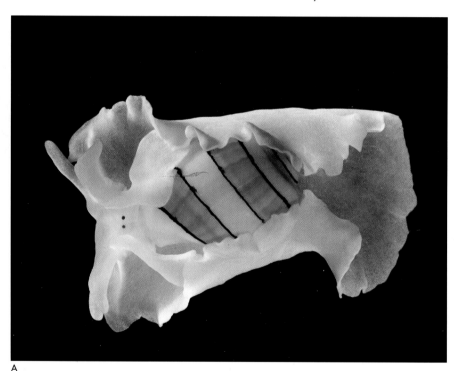

A

B

unattractive, certainly no one would collect them, but they're a necessary part of any naturalist's collection.

A true jewel, and strong point of any collection, is the shell of the nautilus which lives in the Indopacific. The nautilus is a true living fossil that has remained practically unchanged for 500 million years. In this case as well, as in fossil ammonites, the spiral is coiled around a single plane, but the last whorl of the shell coils around the earlier ones and hides them, creating a globular form

of rare elegance. It is no wonder that the shell of the nautilus has always been used by sculptors and goldsmiths. The interior of the shell is made up of little chambers that the animal abandons as it grows, closing them off by a calcareous diaphragm in the center of which it leaves a little hole. A siphon runs through the series of little holes and allows the mollusk to pump gas into the interior of the shell, thus changing its specific gravity and allowing it to move vertically. In other words, it has a mechanism

similar to a fish's air bladder or the immersion chamber of a submarine. For horizontal movement, the nautilus uses the principle of a reaction engine, forcefully expelling water through contractions of its mantle, much as octopuses, cuttlefish, and squid do. But while these distant relatives have a maximum of about ten tentacles, the nautilus has an impressive quantity of from sixty to ninety, but with no suckers. It has four gills, no ink sac, and very primitive eyes. There are three species of nautilus in the warm waters of the southwest Pacific. Fishermen catch it in nets at depths of between 160 and 330 feet (50–100 m), where it wanders in search of its preferred prey, lobsters and shrimp.

The shell of another cephalopod, the spirula has a structure and functions similar to the nautilus, but is much more modest in size and appearance. It is coiled in a flat spiral, but its indentations are disjointed, and most of the spiral is covered by the mollusk's body. The spirula is usually found at between 160 and 1,600 feet (50–500 m) in depth. It is not an impressive addition to a collection, but it is still a naturalistic curiosity.

There are relatively few pelagic species of mollusks, and the overwhelming majority of species in the phylum are part of the benthos and live on seabeds. at least at the adult stage.

During larval existence, most marine mollusks are part of the plankton, and sea currents are used to disperse their multitudinous young.

HOW TO COLLECT SHELLS

Images from the whole chapter: Different criteria can be used to arrange shell collections. According to a tradition that dates back to the "Wunderkammer" of cultured persons of the eighteenth century, the collection is displayed using essentially aesthetic criteria, placing the strangest and most surprising forms in a showcase or in drawers with compartments separated by a sheet of glass. For study purposes, however, after selecting and identifying the materials, it is better to arrange them according to a zoological criterion, i.e., using the classification indicated in manuals, which takes into account the kinship between families of mollusks

based on their descent from common ancestors. Today, as computers become common in private homes, it is certainly appropriate to arrange all significant data on the collection in a good database (thus saving yourself the work of preparing charts, registers, and index cards by hand) and identifying the discovery with just a number. You can thus let the database systematically order the collection, while the shells can be placed in plastic sacks and boxes to protect them from dust and arranged as you like, according to aesthetic criteria or in a way that saves space. Nevertheless, don't forget that shells prefer the dark; exposure to light will fade their colors.

Collecting a shell during a walk along the beach or a dive over a beautiful seabed is an instinctive gesture, as is buying a beautiful one that somehow beckons you from a sales stand in the tropics. For some, the young or the young at heart, the attraction to shells and the worlds they evoke leads them to start a collection. Usually the first shells found, bought, or received as gifts end up in a glass jar or lined up on a shelf as a reminder of a wonderful vacation, an exciting dive, perhaps a happy love affair, but when you make the decision to obtain others, and perhaps also a book to help you identify them and tell you more about them, a collection begins to take shape. At this point, it's best to be sure that your collection will be a success and give you all the satisfaction that a naturalistic collection can provide.

Of course, any plans to make a collection are based on more or less conscious motivations. With shells, one thing should be cleared up immediately: if you want to obtain costly specimens as well, you should know that they are never a good investment of your money. It's true that there are pieces that can cost a very great deal due to their rarity and beauty. But, as experience of the past two centuries has shown, even the rarest and most beautiful shells, whose few known specimens were found only by chance, usually in the stomachs of fish, sooner or later became cheap when fishermen discovered their habitat and sold them in large quantities. A shell collection is very satisfying in terms of beauty and knowledge, calms the soul and takes you to marvelous worlds— but it will never make you rich.

A passion for shells takes a leap in quality when the pleasure of collecting them goes from being aesthetic to naturalistic, and possession of specimens is no longer the only purpose but becomes a tool for learning more about the sea and its creatures, about what

happens in an underwater cave or a forest of oarweed, and how the animal that made those fascinating shells actually functions. The following suggestions are for naturalistic collectors, and are based on the practice of generations of shell enthusiasts.

You should make one decision as soon as you can: what kind of collection do you want? Specialized by family, environment, or geographical area? Needless to say, trying to make a complete or nearly complete collection of all marine shells is an impossible dream; not even the most splendid museums in the world have such a thing. When making this decision, it's a good idea to think about where you live and your life-style. If you have a house near the sea or regularly frequent a stretch of coast or an island, you might aim for a local collection. Done well, it could even become scientifically important, not necessarily due to the discovery of new species, but certainly in deepening knowledge of the environment. Anyone who enjoys spending time at the stereoscopic microscope could aim for a collection of micromollusks: you can obtain bags of detritus collected from seabeds that are true treasure troves of specimens. One advantage of a collection of micromollusks is that the whole collection can fit into a drawer or little more. You can devote your collection to just one family: those with beautiful shells are obviously preferable. The most popular shells for collection in the world are cowries, followed by cones. Only someone who has truly enormous financial resources and the time for international shopping can collect a rare, beautiful, and costly family of shells like the pleurotomarids.

Shells can be contemplated for their many aesthetic values. But to enter the enchanted world of these sea treasures, it's not enough to contemplate them. You need to read them, understand them, recognize them. It's an exercise with various levels of difficulty. It's almost always easy to read adult shells in excellent condition that are at least .4 inches (1 cm) in size, which are usually found in price lists in the collectors' market or in stands at fish markets. But you should practice distinguishing the details of even easy shells, for example, comparing the murices sold in fish markets with those found on the beach. You also need to know how to recognize immature shells and classify them under the right species. Often juvenile forms are very unlike the adult form, and it's easy to classify them as a different species from their parents (an error that even reputable malacologists have committed!). Obtaining examples of intermediate phases by collecting shells of increasing size from detritus and trying to arrange them in order of growth will help you avoid mistakes of this kind. It's also not advisable to practice on washed-up shells that have been bleached by the sun and polished by the beach. When many important details have been eliminated, it's not always easy to identify the shell. Day after day, as you examine large quantities of materials, you'll develop the diagnostic eye you need to write up an index card (or create a computer file) on the shell, with information on where you found it and a naturalistic observation of the seabed visited. For beginner enthusiasts, an important goal is being able to classify the shell by family. From here, consulting malacological atlases by geographical area, or collections of specialized periodicals in the library or local museum, you will be able to identify even less common species (the index published in the final part of this volume is organized so you can identify families, as well as the individual species illustrated).

Is an intact specimen of an adult shell proving hard to identify? That is, is properly reading its characteristics (size, form, ornamentation, color, and glossiness) not enough to classify the species? It could happen. Sometimes even commonplace shells, even the clams sold in fish markets, may have shells with characteristics somewhere between the typical features of two very similar species, and this often generates interesting discussions in meetings of shell enthusiasts. In cases like this, what should you do? If it is only a question of writing up an index card to place the

shell in your collection, don't worry, just note your doubts in anticipation of learning more in the future, knowing that a specimen that may seem doubtful is certainly no less interesting than others. For example, you could note the following for a true clam with a shell that could be either a cultivated Indopacific area species (the Japanese littleneck), always called a true clam in restaurants, or a European clam fished in the open water: *Tapes* cf. *decussatus* (Linneaus 1758), cf. *philippinarum* (Adams & Reeve, 1850) (*cf.* is an abbreviation that means "compare"). Naturally, as connoisseurs know, there are no doubts if you have the whole animal before you instead of a shell: the Indopacific clam has horns (more properly called siphons) that are welded together, while the European clam's siphons are detached.

In truly doubtful cases, an examination of the soft parts is actually the only way to identify a find (i.e., place it under an

already described species) and classify it (i.e., give it a taxonomic position and a name, if it is unknown to science). Today, professional malacologists use sophisticated microscopes to examine the details of the radula or genital apparatus, and also use statistical methods to study diagnostic aspects for entire populations of mollusks. This rigor is gradually giving some order to mollusk nomenclature. In the past, when an examination of only shell characteristics was deemed sufficient to create a new species, many authors published their discoveries as species new to science, when they were in reality only manifestations of normal individual variability or at the most distinctive features of a race or sub-species. This created a great deal of confusion and a mass of synonyms in successive publications.

In any event, until an enthusiast decides to become a researcher he does not need to use a microscope to examine the organs of mollusks to identify his finds. This is in part due to the fortunate fact that there are few cases where shell features cannot be read, and these are micromollusks, especially terrestial and freshwater species and deep marine species, which have small, unattractive shells not desirable in anything but the most specialized collections.

THE INFORMATION
TO KEEP

The first step in starting a good collection is to record all important information about how you found (or acquired) each specimen or lot. Until recently, we would have suggested writing everything on a card in pen, but today it's faster and better to enter every-thing in your home computer database. The box on this page gives you an outline for a typical registration, based on that used for the mollusk census for the coasts of Italy that the Italian Malacological Society performed in collaboration with ENEA (National Agency for Energy and the Environment). It makes no difference if many cards have empty boxes, but it is important for the data to be accurate. In the beginning, it's not even necessary to determine the name of the species. Even in scientific research, this information may be left hanging for years, although a beginner tends to believe it is more important than anything else. If you can't answer the question, What shell is this? write "cf." (compare) followed by the name of a species that seems similar, and go on. It's better to leave an empty space than make an identification you're not sure of. Accurate notes are potentially very useful. Don't forget that many people who began gathering shells for personal pleasure later became full-time scientists, going from shell enthusiasts to malacologists, discovering new species and writing fine pages in the great book of natural science. Even if you have no such ambitions in the beginning, you should start off right. For this reason, when you acquire shells, either as a gift or through exchanges, you should insist on obtaining as much information as possible (including the original files, if they exist), especially information on provenance or locality. This second- or third-hand information should nevertheless be treated with much caution. When in doubt, better to leave a blank space than write something wrong. The safest shells are those you personally collect or receive from experts associated with malacological circles, then come those acquired from specialized merchants who distribute detailed price lists. With rare exceptions, souvenir dealers know little about shells and do not even know what a collector needs.

THE SEARCH FOR SHELLS

An old rule says that shells are where you happen to find them, and in fact luck plays a very important role. But some basic knowledge of marine environments like that presented in this book is always helpful.

It may seem unnecessary, but experience has proved that we need to insist on one thing: be careful as you search, so you don't endanger either yourself or your companions. Exploring an environment requires a great deal of time and should be considered a job rather than a pleasure swim. While you explore environments and gather your finds, the tide rises or falls, and the currents, waves, and wind could change direction or intensity. When you're underwater searching the seabed, the air in your tank always seems to run out faster than you had expected, especially if you are exerting effort, as when turning over rocks and scraping walls, and if you emerge far from the boat or the shore, you may be exhausted. Thus, even in situations that seem easy, work

times and movements should be planned and followed, and you should stay well within the equipment tables and your own energy reserves. In the sea, you should always expect the unexpected.

A NOTE ABOUT CLOTHING AND EQUIPMENT

There are still people who venture onto reefs barefoot and on coral formations wearing only swimming trunks. Don't follow their example when you go looking for shells. An emerged reef should only be explored when the sea is calm, wearing sturdy closed sandals with anti-slip soles, and protecting your head and body from the sun. To keep your hands free, you should tie a plastic bag around your belt for finds that require no special protection, while delicate shells should be carried in a plastic container with a large mouth and screw top. A pair of very thin steel tweezers is indispensable for collecting small specimens in the fissures of rocks.

When you explore a tidal or underwater area, you need to add a mask and mouthpiece, thin gloves that your hands can feel through, and a scuba knife. Water temperature may be dangerous. If you're in temperate waters in summer and early autumn, you'll need an average-thickness wetsuit, about 5 millimeters of neoprene, while in other seasons or when the water is cold, you'll need a thicker, or dry, wetsuit. If you plan to collect micromollusks that may be found on rocks encrusted with calcareous algae, anellids, and bryozoans, you'll need to scrape samples of the surface and collect all the material, which you can examine later at your leisure. You can use a garden trowel with a very short handle, and a steel net with a handle in which you can gather the material removed from the wall.

On tropical coral reefs, you need to wear padded boots as well as a mask, thin gloves, a mouthpiece and flippers, and a very light wetsuit, whatever the temperature of the water is. Clearly, this equipment would be too much for a swimmer, but a shell enthusiast is there to work, and you need to arm yourself against fire coral stings, cuts caused by accidental contact with razor-sharp corals, and the sun, which mercilessly punishes the ignorant and careless.

CLEANING AND CONSERVING THE MATERIAL COLLECTED

The sea is fragrant, but after only a short time everything that comes out of it smells bad. Ideally, all shells collected should be cleaned within 24 hours. If you can't, as is usually the case when you're traveling, the fastest system is to store everything in salt, or even a mixture of 50 percent water and alcohol, in hermetically sealed containers, of course. This method has the drawback of causing the tissues of the mollusks gathered to harden somewhat, which may complicate later cleaning of gastropods with a spiral shell, but it is only a minor problem compared with allowing a bad smell to ruin the pleasure of your trip.

There are differing views on the best method of cleaning your shells. Once it was advised to quickly boil everything collected, but now many believe that boiling can ruin the color and may even crack more fragile shells. If you have a freezer, you can freeze mollusks, and after one or two days bring them back to room temperature and eliminate the soft parts. For bivalves, just cut the adductor muscles from their housing, being careful not to break the hinge. By gently heating the shell, you can close the valves until they meet perfectly and tie the shell in a closed position with sewing thread. After a couple of days or less, you can cut the thread, and the hinge, now dry, will no longer open the valves. If in the future you need to reopen the shell to examine the inside, just briefly heat the hinge, which will become elastic again, and you can repeat the operation when you put the specimen back in the collection. If, despite all precautions, the ligament breaks, or if you want to put back together a shell you have found with its valves separated, just use a bit of flour and water paste on the hinge to put the specimen back together again. It's not a good idea to use a commercial glue; if you need to separate the valves in the future, the flour paste, unlike the glue, can easily be dissolved with a bit of water.

It's a bit more difficult to remove the soft parts from spiral gastropods. You'll need some patience at first, and experience will do the rest. Using a pair

of tweezers, firmly grasp the soft parts and try to remove them from the shell without breaking them. By pulling gently but continuously, without jerking, you'll usually succeed, especially when the animal's tissues are still intact. If despite your efforts fragments of the intestinal tract remain in the bottom of the shell, use a piece of wire to make a spiral that ends in a hook. Working delicately, you'll be able to extract the fragments. It may also help to put the shell under running water. When you're sure that the shell is completely empty inside, it's a good idea to immerse it briefly in a weak bleach solution, which will clean and deodorize it, and then let it dry in the shade on a shelf for several days. Finally, if you note that despite everything, the shell still smells bad, you should drip candle wax inside it and then stop the opening with a cotton ball soaked in perfume. When you prepare a gastropod with an operculum, you should always take this out when you remove the soft parts, allow it to dry along with the shell, and then place it in its natural position before the opening, using a drop of glue to affix it to a cotton ball.

Everything becomes much more simple when you are preparing micromollusks, which are never more than .2 or so inches (5–6 mm) in size. After keeping them in alcohol for a few days, just leave them in the open in the shade to allow the soft parts to dry out without leaving any bad odor. Preparation of chitons requires a bit more care, because these little animals tend to roll up into a ball, making it impossible to distend them without breaking them. Right after you catch them, you need to immobilize them by tying them to a small piece of wood with a bit of thread, before putting them in the freezer. Then you can prepare them or allow them to dry in the open, especially if they are very small, or else remove the soft parts, being careful not to break the girdle or disjoint the eight plates. If you want to highlight the plates to compare and study them, you must very delicately separate them from each other. They should then be glued to a piece of cardboard in the sequence they had on the living animal.

Finally, an expert collector will need to keep the soft parts of a few specimens collected for purposes of anatomical examinations, which are sometimes necessary to determine a species accurately, and are indispensable when you need to classify what you believe to be a species new to science. In this case, you should keep the specimen in a sealed container in a 30 percent ethyl alcohol solution for the first three days, which you can then replace with a 50 percent solution for the next three days, and finally a 70 percent solution for permanent storage.

During cleaning, many collectors are tempted to improve the shell's appearance by removing the periostracum, and trying to eliminate any limestone encrustation with a steel pin, or by running the shell through a diluted acid solution. Souvenir sellers even change the shell's appearance by filing or glazing it. A serious collector would never do this, but even small things like removing the periostracum and encrustations should only be done in moderation. You should keep at least one specimen intact as it was found in nature. And remember that while acid will corrode the encrustation, it will also corrode the shell, which is made of calcium carbonate. If you must use this method to improve a specimen's appearance, the parts you want to preserve, in particular the shell's aperture, should be protected from the acid bath by dripping wax or liquid paraffin over them.

Shells are beautiful to look at, and a collector rightly likes to display at least the most showy or prized pieces. There's one problem. Light and dust deteriorate the surface of the shell, which over time will appear calcined, just like shells that have lain in the sunlight on the beach. If you really want to display some specimens, it's best to do it in a display case with smoked glass, out of direct sunlight.

The best way to conserve shells is to keep them in a chest of low drawers, placing each specimen, along with a label containing its essential data, within a little transparent plastic box. Specialized stores sell all sizes. For micromollusks, the most practical boxes are square, about .75 inch (2 cm) wide and .5 inch (1 cm) high. Very fragile specimens can be held between the box cover and a cotton ball in contrasting color, which will bring out the details of the shell.

In this way, the collection will be easily accessible, but at the same time well protected from accidental blows to the chest and other mishaps. The order in which you arrange the boxes is a personal choice. If you have enough room, it's better to follow systematic order, as museum collections do. In any event, it's practical to keep very large specimens in a special chest with large drawers.

Finally, you need to consider your study equipment. A pair of good magnifying lenses is indispensable, a 5X for your first examination of the shell's details, and a 10X (counting glass) lens to examine the smaller parts. If you want to collect micromollusks, you'll need at least a 20X stereoscopic microscope. You'll want steel tweezers to handle very small specimens, a little paintbrush that you can moisten to handle very delicate parts, a gauge to take precise measurements, boxes, test tubes, little plastic bags, and adhesive labels to keep your material in order. That's more or less all you'll need, plus a good register to note down

EXAMPLE OF RECORD
TO ENTER IN DATABASE
(the "fields" in bold type, the information to be added as a record in regular type):

SERIAL NUMBER: Given to each individual specimen or lot of specimens of the same species and origin as they enter the collection.

DATE OF RECORDING: The date the specimen entered the collection; should be typed in to permit numerical operations.

FAMILY: The scientific name, if necessary indicating any common synonym between parentheses.

SPECIES: Genus, species, author, date of publication, entered according to the conventions of naturalistic literature.

PLACEMENT: The section of the collection in which it is kept; if the collection is strictly systematic, this can be omitted.

SPECIMENS: If it is a lot with more than one item.

IDENTIFIED BY: The name of the person or institution that made the identification.

PURCHASED: Where, when, from whom, price.

GIVEN: By whom, when.

FOUND BY: Name of the collector.

LOCATION: As precise as possible an indication of the place found (may include global positioning coordinates).

DATE: The date found.

TIDE: High, medium, low.

COLLECTION METHOD: By hand from the shore, by hand while diving, with nets or dredges if caught by fishing boats.

DISTANCE FROM THE SHORE: In meters.

AT DEPTH OR ALTITUDE: In meters.

TYPE OF SEABED: Rocky, shingly-pebbly, sandy, muddy, coarse detritus without mud, deep detritus with very fine sand and mud, coral.

ENVIRONMENT: Supralittoral, midlittoral, infralittoral, circumlittoral, lagoon, on algae, on terrestrial or aquatic plants, on *Posidonia*.

ALIVE: Yes, no.

NOTES: Other useful information regarding ecology, behavior, relative abundance or scarcity in the area, etc.

BIBLIOGRAPHICAL REFERENCES: Publications used to identify the species or useful for other information about it.

information, or better yet, a personal computer with a good database.

WRITING SHELL NAMES

According to the conventions of natural science books, genus names are indicated in italics, with the first letter capitalized (for example, *Cypraea*), and the name of the species and any sub-species are indicated in italics with a small first letter (for example, *tigris*). The scientific names of the families are anglicized, with the first letter capitalized (for example, Cypreidae), while common names always appear with a small first letter (cowries). Species with a universally known name are indicated in English (mussel for *Mytilus galloprovincialis*), or by the anglicized scientific name (tiger cowrie for *Cypraea tigris*), when this is commonly known among shell enthusiasts, following the usage of popular publications in the major European languages. The scientific name in Latin is always indicated when the text requires it to be intelligible.

THE SHELLS OF THE SEA

The following list of shells follows the taxonomic order established in K.C. Vaught's *A Classification of the Living Mollusca*. Melbourne, FL: American Malacologosts, Inc., 1989.

Stenoplax conspicua
Conspicuous chiton

ISCHNOCHITONIDAE ▶

Lives in America along the Pacific coast, from Santa Barbara to the Gulf of California, under rocks in the intertidal area. From 2 to 5 inches (5–12 cm) in size. Has a distinctive elongated form and numerous small spines on the girdle.

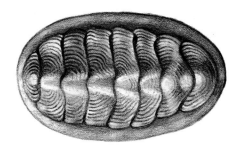

Tonicia elegans
Elegant chiton

CHITONIDAE

This graceful polyplacophore from the South American Pacific coast feeds on the pellicle of algae that forms on rocks. Less than ◀ 2 inches (5 cm) in length. The first chitons appeared on the earth about 570 million years ago.

Chiton olivaceus

CHITONIDAE ▶

The greenish color and fanlike ornamentation on the sides of the plates make it easy to identify this polyplacophore that lives on Mediterranean reefs. It feeds on algae and reaches 1.5 inches (4 cm) in length.

Cryptoplax larvaeformis

ACANTHOCHITONIDAE

Unlike other chitons, *Cryptoplax* has only five imbricate valves, ◀ while the other three are separate. Average in size, it lives in the Indopacific region in the infralittoral band.

Cryptochiton stelleri
Giant Pacific chiton

ACANTHOCHITONIDAE ▶

This is the largest chiton in the world, reaching to over a foot (33 cm) in length. It lives up to 60 feet (18 m) deep, from Alaska to California. To prevent other animals from settling on its plates, it secretes a mucus that expands upon contact with water.

Pleurotomaria hirasei
Hirase's slit shell

PLEUROTOMARIIDAE

This is the most well-known and common of this family of shells, highly prized by collectors. It is 2.7 to 5 inches (7–12 cm) in diameter and lives at depths of about 300 feet (90 m) in the sea ◀ off the island of Honshu, Japan.

Pleurotomaria africana
African slit shell

PLEUROTOMARIIDAE ▶

This large, rare shell is found only along the South African coast, where it lives on the soft floors of the deep sea. The gradual closing of the slit on the last whorl leaves a band that traverses all whorls. Up to 5 inches (12 cm).

Entemnotrochus adamsonianus
Adamson's slit shell
PLEUROTOMARIIDAE

Quite rare, it lives in the Caribbean along steep underwater slopes from 200 to 1,500 feet (60–450 m) deep. The characteristic slit crosses about half of the shell's last whorl, which has a diameter of 6 inches (15 cm). Sometimes it is caught in fish traps.

Haliotis tuberculata lamellosa
Lamellose ormer
HALIOTIDAE

This is the Mediterranean subspecies of the Atlantic *Haliotis tuberculata* that lives from Portugal to the Canary Islands. It is distinguished by its smaller average size 2 inches (5 cm) and more evident lamellae. It lives on reefs in the midlittoral and infralittoral bands.

Haliotis rufescens
Red abalone
HALIOTIDAE

The largest of the abalones, it reaches 12 inches (30 cm) in length. The shell is bulky, reddish on the outside, with a pearly interior with green to pink glints. It lives from Oregon to Baja California. Its flesh is quite tasty.

Diodora graeca
Greek keyhole limpet
FISSURELLIDAE

Can be distinguished from others in its genus because it has few radial ribs. About 1 inch (2.5 cm) in length, it lives from the upper midlittoral to the infralittoral band, on rocky substrata, from the Mediterranean to the coast of England. Rather common.

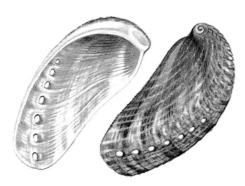

Haliotis asinina
Donkey's ear abalone
HALIOTIDAE

This abalone, common in the Indian Ocean and Pacific, owes its name to the unusually elongated form of the shell, which is robust but light, measuring up to 4 inches (10 cm) in length.

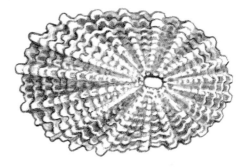

Lottia gigantea
Giant owl limpet
LOTTIIDAE

Lives on the rocky coasts of the Pacific, including above the high tide level, from the Canadian border to Baja California. The interior of the shell is blue-white with a brown spot. It reaches 4.3 inches (11 cm) in diameter.

Patelloida saccharina
Pacific sugar limpet
ACMAEIDAE

Has a depressed profile and more or less stellate margin. Up to 2 inches (4 cm) in diameter. It is quite common along the rocky coasts of the Indian Ocean and the western Pacific, to western Australia.

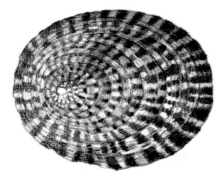

Patella caerulea
Rayed Mediterranean limpet
PATELLIDAE

Mediterranean and Portuguese species, often quite abundant in the midlittoral band of reefs. Its form and color vary widely. It is 1.5 to 2.7 inches (4–7 cm) in length. The interior is shiny gray with bluish glints.

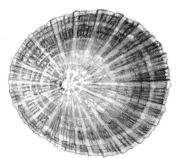

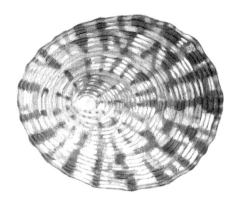

Patella longicosta
Long-ribbed limpet
PATELLIDAE

Has a characteristic stellate form and may be up to 2.3 inches (6 cm) in diameter. Lives along the rocky coast of South Africa, where it is quite common. Calcareous encrustations often hide the dorsal sculpture, giving it a grayish appearance.

Patella ferruginea
Ribbed Mediterranean limpet
PATELLIDAE

The solid, rust-colored ribs make it unmistakable. Lives in western North Africa to the Tyrrhenian coasts, where it has become quite rare due to overharvesting. Reaches 3 inches (8 cm) in diameter.

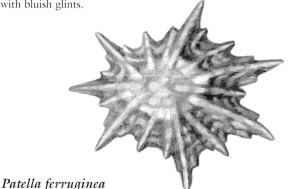

Cellana radians
Common New Zealand limpet
PATELLIDAE

Lives in New Zealand and is the most common of the twenty limpet species in the archipelago. It is 2 inches (5 cm) in diameter, with an extremely fine concentric sculpture and beautiful color, pink outside with glints of mother-of-pearl within.

Cellana exarata
Hawaiian limpet
PATELLIDAE

Lives in Hawaii and can be distinguished by its elegant ray-shaped design formed by black ribs spotted with gray alternating with whitish furrows. It can reach 1.2 inches (3 cm) in height and a maximum of 3 inches (8 cm) in length.

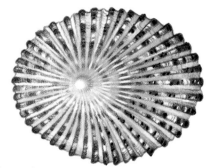

Umbonium giganteum
Giant buttontop
TROCHIDAE

This trochid with a lenticular, biconvex, button-shaped shell, characteristic of the genus, prefers muddy floors of sheltered inlets. Reaches 1.8 inches (4.5 cm) in diameter. Lives in Japan.

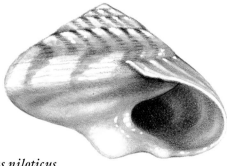

Trochus niloticus
Commercial trochus
TROCHIDAE

This massive trochid from the Indopacific (it can reach 4.7 inches [12 cm] in height in six years) has for many years been raised for its mother-of-pearl. Its natural environment is the surf area of coral reefs.

Tegula regina
Queen tegula
TROCHIDAE

Beautifully ornamented; radial, grayish purple ribs with a golden yellow umbilical region. It lives in California from 16 to 80 feet (5–25 m) in depth. Not common. An average of 1.5 inches (4 cm) in height.

Monodonta turbinatus
Turbinate monodont
TROCHIDAE

Has a solid, globular shell, as wide as it is tall, on average about 1 inch (2.5 cm). Lives in the Mediterranean and on the Atlantic coasts of Portugal and North Africa. A gregarious mollusk, it forms enormous populations on rocks in the midlittoral band.

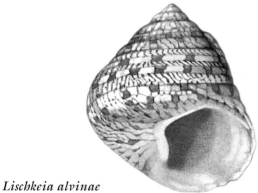

Lischkeia alvinae
TROCHIDAE

The pointed tubercles that traverse the middle band of each whorl give this trochid a particularly elegant appearance. It lives on the coasts of Japan and Taiwan. It is from 1.5 to 2 inches (4–5 cm) wide and is a uniform cream color.

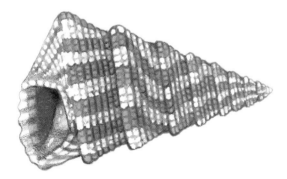

Gibbula magnus
Great topshell
TROCHIDAE

The largest in the *Gibbula* genus, it reaches 1.4 inches (3.5 cm) in diameter. Lives in the Atlantic from Great Britain to Senegal and the Mediterranean, on detrital, sandy and muddy substrata in the infralittoral and circumlittoral bands. Whitish with red spots.

Tectus pyramis
Pyramid top
TROCHIDAE

Robust and greenish-yellow in color, this trochid from the Indopacific is pagoda-shaped when young, quite different from the slender conical form it assumes as an adult. About 3 inches (7 cm) high, it lives in shallow waters on rocks near the reef.

Monodonta articulata
Tessellate trumpet
TROCHIDAE

Abundant on rocks sheltered from waves, in the midlittoral band along the Mediterranean coasts. It reaches 1.4 inches (3.5 cm) in height and may vary in form and color; typically it has white spiral bands with reddish spots on a gray background.

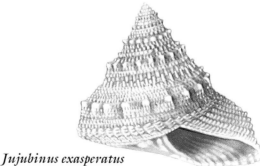

Jujubinus exasperatus
Rough topshell
TROCHIDAE

A small solid shell with an elegant form and quite variable ornamentation. It lives from Great Britain to Morocco to the Mediterranean from phanerogam meadows to coral environments. Fairly common, it reaches .4 inches (1.5 cm) in height.

Gibbula divaricata
Divaricate gibbula
TROCHIDAE

Extremely common throughout the Mediterranean, especially where the rocks of the midlittoral band are protected from waves. Rarely exceeds .8 inches (2 cm) in height. It has a distinctive deep suture that makes the last whorl look detached.

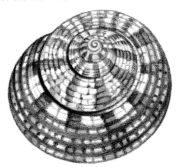

Clanculus pharaonius
Mantle clanculus
TROCHIDAE

This is one of the most common and graceful shells that can be collected in the sand among rocky formations in the Indian Ocean. Reaches 1 inch (2.5 cm) in width. It has distinctive small beading in alternating colors.

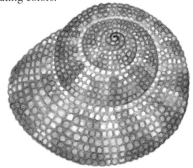

Cittarium pica
West Indian topshell
TROCHIDAE

This solid trochid is common in the tidal areas of the Caribbean islands and is prized by local populations as a food source. Its height and width vary from 2 to 5 inches (5–12 cm). The shell is yellowish white with blackish purple spots. Edible species.

Calliostoma zizyphinum
European painted topshell
TROCHIDAE

Lives in the Mediterranean and off the Atlantic coasts of Europe, as well as in the Azores, from the infralittoral band to the sandy and muddy floors of the circumlittoral band. Not common. Has a conical profile and shell that is rough at the apex and smooth at the base. An average of 1.4 inches (3.5 cm) in height.

Gibbula ardens
Flaming top
TROCHIDAE

Common in the Mediterranean, it lives in meadows of dwarf *Zostera* seagrasses and algae in shallow water. Reaches .8 inches (1.7 cm) in diameter. Apex is pointed, often rose-colored. Ornamentation consists of small spiral cords, from four to seven on the last whorl, often duplicated by an edging.

Clanculus corallinus
Coral topshell
TROCHIDAE

Graceful Mediterranean shell, bright red sometimes tending to brown. About .4 inches (1 cm) in length. Lives in rocky infralittoral and circumlittoral areas. More frequent in warm waters, but never very common.

Phasianotrochus eximius
TROCHIDAE

Lives in the tidal area up to about 130 feet (40 m) deep in the Australian province, where it is rather common. Up to 1.5 inches (4 cm) high. It is red-brown in color with four greenish bands for each whorl.

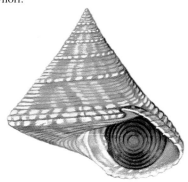

Maurea selecta
Select maurea

TROCHIDAE

Around ten beautiful topshells can be found in New Zealand, including this one, which can be distinguished by the size (3 inches [7cm]) of the light shell, decorated by a series of narrow, dotted spiral bands. It can be found among rocks in shallow water.

Turbo marmoratus
Great green turban

TURBINIDAE

Large, massive shell from the Indopacific, where it lives from 13 to 60 feet (4–20 m) deep. Reaches 7 inches (17.5 cm) in height. The bright green surface and iridescence of the aperture give it a lacquered appearance. Quite popular as a souvenir.

Bankivia fasciata
Banded bankivia

TROCHIDAE

Lives along the southeastern to western coasts of Australia and is distinguished by its slender form and the variability of the elegant ornamentation with colored bands. Specimens, up to .75 inch (2 cm) in size, live along sandy, wave-swept coasts.

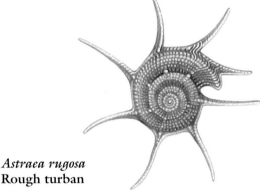

Astraea rugosa
Rough turban

TURBINIDAE

Lives in the circumlittoral band of the Mediterranean and Atlantic southern Europe. When young, it has showy spines that disappear in adult shells. Reaches 2 inches (5 cm) in diameter. The calcareous operculum is considered a symbol of good luck.

Guildfordia yoka
Yoka star turban

TURBINIDAE

Has a depressed structure and reaches 4 inches (10 cm) in diameter. It is spiral-shaped, hexagonal near the apex, and octagonal at the base, where angulations carry appendages as long as the diameter of the shell. Lives in Japan, where it is frequently found at depth.

Angaria delphinus
Common delphinula

TURBINIDAE

This Indopacific and Australian species lives in the circumlittoral band in coral habitats, and assumes different forms depending on the depth and currents in the area. Its spines may vary in length and shape. Up to 2.3 inches (6 cm) in diameter.

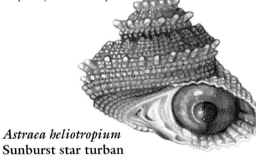

Astraea heliotropium
Sunburst star turban

TURBINIDAE

Seen from above, this large turban from New Zealand looks like a ten-pointed star, giving it its common name of star shell. It reaches 3 inches (8 cm) in diameter and lives in rather deep waters. It is somewhat uncommon.

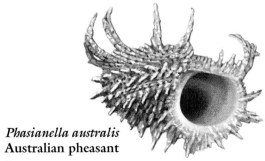

Phasianella australis
Australian pheasant

PHASIANELLIDAE

With its 2.3 inch (6 cm) height, it is the giant of the family that takes its name from the Latin for pheasant, due to its colors being similar to this bird. It lives in southern Australia and Tasmania, where it is common in shallow waters, among algae, on rocks in the infralittoral band.

Tricolia pullus
Pheasant shell
TRICOLIIDAE

Graceful and tiny (it rarely reaches .4 inches [1 cm] in length), it is frequent in the Mediterranean province at shallow depths among algae, on sandy floors. Its color ranges from pink to brown, with slightly undulating oblique flames.

Smaragdia viridis
Emerald nerite
NERITIDAE

This tiny (maximum of .3 inches [8 mm]) shell is distinguished by the bright green color of its surface, adorned with white or purple markings. It is common from the Caribbean to the Mediterranean province. Frequent on algae at shallow depths.

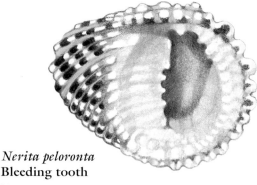

Nerita peloronta
Bleeding tooth
NERITIDAE

This is a very common species on reefs near the low tide mark, from Florida to Brazil. The inner lip of the aperture has white teeth surrounded by an orange or bright red spot. Reaches a maximum of 1.5 inches (4 cm).

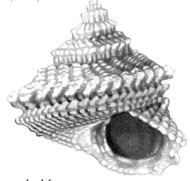

Littorina neritoides
Reef snail
LITTORINIDAE

Forms large colonies in fissures in the rock, up to 6 feet (2 m) above the high tide level. Up to .4 inches (9 mm) high, it is dark, black, or brown with a narrow light band that is sometimes absent. Common in the Mediterranean and Atlantic Europe.

Neritina communis
Zigzag nerite
NERITIDAE

The most colorful inhabitant of the mangroves, common throughout the Southwest Pacific. Its colors usually include yellow, white, black, and all shades of pink, to brick red. The design is extremely varied. The apex is acute, and it is about .8 inches (2 cm) long. It is gathered in great quantities in the Philippines, and can often be found in souvenir shops.

Nerita textilis
Textile nerite
NERITIDAE

Robust, globular shell, adorned by solid spiral ribbing with alternating white and black spots. Found in the Indopacific province, where it is common on rocks in tidal areas. From 1.4 to 2 inches (3.5–5 cm) in length.

Echininus cumingii
LITTORINIDAE

Common in the western Pacific, from Japan to New Caledonia. From .5 to 1 inch (1.2–2.7 cm) high, it has an especially graceful form due to the two robust spiral carinae on the last whorl. It is pink at the apex and creamy white on the rest.

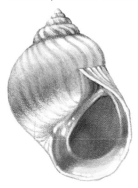

Littorina littorea
Common periwinkle
LITTORINIDAE

Lives in Atlantic Europe and northeast North America. Gray-black with black spiral bands, it reaches 1.2 inches (3 cm) in length. Quite common among the rocks of the lower midlittoral band, it is prized for its meat in France and England.

▶

Rissoa variabilis
RISSOIDAE

This elegant tapered shell is from .27 to .31 inches (7–8 mm) long, and is quite common on meadowy seabeds in European seas and neighboring Atlantic. It can be distinguished by its violet peristome and dotted brown spiral lines, sometimes alternating with solid lines. It has about ten ribs.

Rissoa auriscalpium
RISSOIDAE

Has 7 to 8 flat axial ribs and a varicose lip. Whitish and semi-transparent, it can reach .3 inches (8 mm) in height. It lives in western European seas and can be quite abundant in *Posidonia* meadows in the infralittoral band.

Cerithium vulgatum
European cerith
CERITHIDAE

Robust shell with two spiral series of more or less raised tubercles on each whorl. Variable color, tending to brown. Up to 3 inches (7 cm) high. Quite common in rocky habitats in shallow waters in the Mediterranean and Atlantic, as well as West Africa.

◀ ### *Rissoina spirata*
Spiral risso
RISSOIDAE

An Indopacific species, it entered the Mediterranean from the Red Sea after the Suez Canal was opened. Reported on the coasts of Israel and the Tuscan archipelago. Lives in underwater meadows. Up to .6 inches (1.5 cm) high, it has a turriculate sculpture and is whitish in color.

▶

Rissoa violacea
◀ RISSOIADE

This species is abundant in *Posidonia* meadows throughout the Mediterranean, and north to the Arctic, and its average length is a little under .23 inches (6 mm). The upper whorls are smooth, while the last two have about ten wide ribs. Its color may vary, with spiral bands that may be flesh-colored, violet, or purple. The inner lip has tones of violet.

▶

◀ ### *Manzonia crassa* (formerly *Folinia costata*)
RISSOIDAE

Tiny shell that rarely reaches .1 inches (3 mm) in height. Bluish white, with 12 to 15 thin, oblique ribs that give it an elegant appearance. Lives in the Mediterranean in shallow waters, to about 160 feet (50 m) in depth.

▶

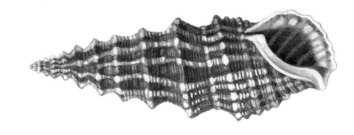

Cerithium nodulosum
Giant knobbed cerith
CERITHIDAE

Solid, with a very marked spiral shape and chalky color. Three black spotted lines run across the tubercles. From 3.5 to 5 inches (9–13 cm) high, it is the giant of the family. Common in the Indopacific on reefs.

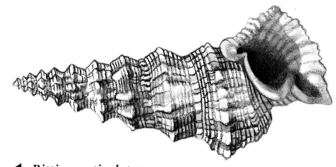

Bittium reticulatum
CERITHIDAE

Ubiquitous species found in the seas of Europe, from a few yards to over 3,000 feet (1,000 m) in depth, in quite varied habitats. Abundant among vegetation. Has whorls traversed by three or four spiral circles and reaches a height of 5 inches (13 mm).

Turritella duplicata
Duplicate turritella
TURRITELLIDAE

Slender shell with a spire of up to fifteen whorls, 6 inches (15 cm) in length. The whorls may be more or less convex and are traversed by two spiral carinae. Lives on sandy and muddy floors of the Indian Ocean and Southeast Asia and feeds on detritus.

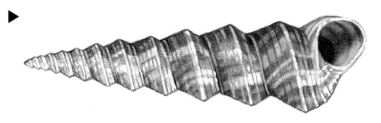

Turritella communis
Common European turritella
TURRITELLIDAE

Lives on sandy and slimy floors of the infralittoral band in sand at a density of 70 individuals per square yard, along the European coasts of the North Sea to the Mediterranean. From 1.5 to 2 inches (4–6 cm) high. Convex whorls traversed by little spiral, yellowish ribs.

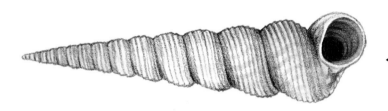

Mesalia opalina
Opal turritella
TURRITELLIDAE

Species from the Atlantic coasts of northwest Africa, recently introduced into the Mediterranean. Lives from 65 to 160 feet (20–50 m) deep. White with red-brown axial flames. From 2 to 3 inches (6–8 cm) high.

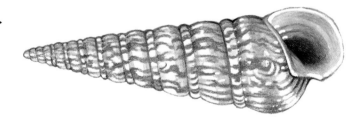

Vermicularia spirata
West Indian wormshell
TURRITELLIDAE

Lives among sponges and other colonial animals in shallow waters of the Caribbean and Florida. The first whorls curl regularly, but after a couple of centimeters elongate in irregular fashion. Common. Up to 5 inches (13 cm) high.

Tenagodus obtusus
SILIQUARIIDAE

Similar to vermetids, but lives freely at shallow depths, with its first whorls in spiral form. A longitudinal furrow crosses the entire shell. Up to 4 inches (10 cm) high, diameter up to 4.3 inches (11 mm). Mediterranean to West Africa.

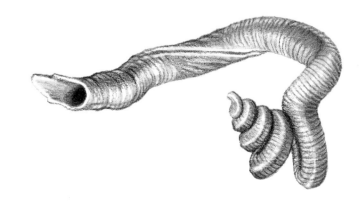

Vermetus triqueter

VERMETIDAE

Lives attached to reefs in the midlittoral band and in trottoir formations. The unattached portion has a single, smooth crest. Diameter up to .2 inches (6 mm). Quite common in the Mediterranean.

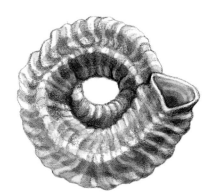

Aporrhais pespelecani
Pelican's foot shell

APORRHAIDAE

Normally has three robust digitations (which appear only in adults), plus that of the siphonal canal. Up to 2 inches (5 cm) in height, it lives in the Mediterranean, Celtic, and Boreal provinces on muddy seabeds. Quite common, it is sold in fish markets.

Aporrhais occidentalis
American pelican's foot

APORRHAIDAE

Lives from Labrador to North Carolina, at gradually greater depths as it moves south, under sand and mud, and feeds on detritus that it sucks up with its proboscis. It is from 1.5 to 2 inches (4–6 cm) high. Has a flared lip, but usually no digitation.

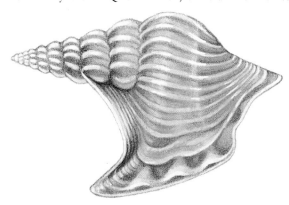

Aporrhais pesgallinae
African pelican's foot

APORRHAIDAE

Lives on sandy and muddy floors in the circumlittoral band along the coasts of West Africa, where it is occasionally caught in fishermen's trawls. Prized for its particularly thin digitations. Around 2 inches (5 cm) high.

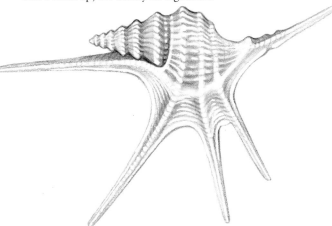

Varicospira cancellata
Cancellate beak-shell

STROMBIDAE

The dense axial ribbing traversing dense spiral striae gives this conch its characteristic reticular design. It is quite small for the family, from 1 to 1.4 inches (2.5–3.5 cm). Frequent in the Philippines.

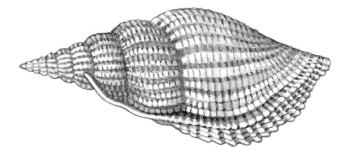

Tibia insulaechorab
Arabian tibia

STROMBIDAE

Lives in the Red Sea and north of the Indian Ocean, in the sand in tidal areas. Six inches (15 cm) long, it has a very slender conical spire with a glossy, yellow-brown surface. From 4 to 5 short digitations on the outer lip.

Tibia fusus
Shin-bone tibia

STROMBIDAE

The extremely large siphonal canal allows this conch to protect the very long siphon it uses to obtain food and oxygen while immersed in sand on the sea floor. Lives in the Philippines. Length 10 inches (25 cm).

Terebellum terebellum
Terebellum conch
STROMBIDAE

Unmistakable due to its projectile form, it is widespread in the Indopacific and quite common. The last whorl is very elongated and has a narrow aperture that widens near the siphon area. It is from 1.5 to 2 inches (4–5 cm) high.

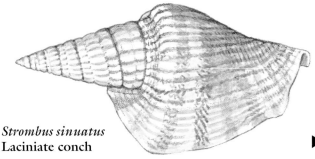

Strombus vittatus
Vittate conch
STROMBIDAE

Lives in the western Pacific near the coasts of Australia on sandy seabeds, up to about 130 feet (40 m) in depth. Average in size (reaches 3.5 inches [9 cm]), with a very slender form, variable outside coloring with a white aperture.

Strombus sinuatus
Laciniate conch
STROMBIDAE

Characteristic of this large species (height from 3.5 to 5 inches [9–12 cm]) is the sort of crest formed by four or five rounded lobes on the back side of the lip. It is white with red-brown decoration. Lives in the Indopacific in coral sand.

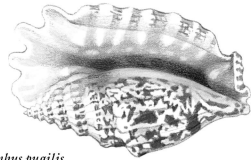

Strombus pugilis
West Indian fighting conch
STROMBIDAE

Lives in shallow waters in the West Indies and southeast Florida, where it is common. Color varies from creamy orange to salmon pink. Has robust spines on the margin of the whorls, with the longest usually located on the second row from the top. About 3 inches (7.5 cm) in height.

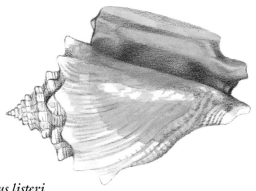

Strombus listeri
Lister's conch
STROMBIDAE

Very elegant, once considered quite rare, but now somewhat frequent in the Indian Ocean. The very elongated spire occupies two-fifths of the total length of 4 to 5 inches (10–13 cm). The lip has a falcate flare.

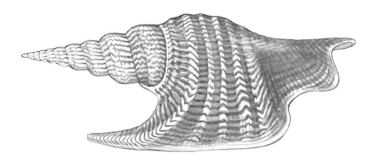

Strombus goliath
Goliath conch
STROMBIDAE

This is the giant of the family: with the spectacular winglike flare of the outer lip of the aperture, it reaches 15 inches (38 cm) in length. It is light brown. Lives in Brazil and is quite rare.

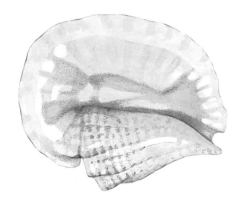

Strombus gigas
Queen conch
STROMBIDAE

Common in the Caribbean from Florida to Venezuela, and known for its delicate meat and the ornamental use of the shell. Lives from 5 to 15 feet (1.5–4.5 m) deep on sand and detritus among the algae on which it feeds. Exceeds 12 inches (30 cm). Common.

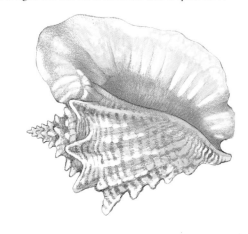

Strombus gallus
Roostertail conch
STROMBIDAE

The posterior elongation of the lip gives this shell from Brazil and the Caribbean an elegant appearance. Color ranges from white to yellow, with red-brown spiral striae. Lives on sandy seabeds among algae. Not common. Five inches (13 cm) in length.

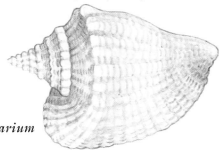

Strombus canarium
Dog conch
STROMBIDAE

Quite variable in size and appearance, with color ranging from whitish to yellow-brown. Pointed spire, outside lip with thickened, smooth aperture. About 2 inches (5 cm) in length. Widespread in the Indopacific. Very common.

Lambis scorpio
Scorpio conch
STROMBIDAE

Lives on coarse sand and detritus in the infralittoral band throughout the Indopacific province. Not common. Length from 4 to 6.6 inches (10–17 cm). The straight outer lip of the aperture is characteristic. Seven digitations.

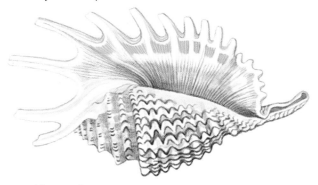

Lambis lambis
Common spider conch
STROMBIDAE

The most abundant of the genus, it lives in the Indopacific from the lower midlittoral band to 33 feet (10 m) in depth. Feeds on algae growing on dead coral or rocks. Reaches 9 inches (23 cm) in length. Females are larger than males.

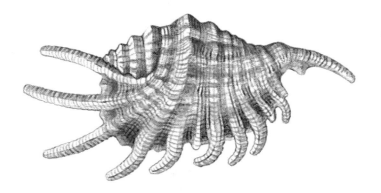

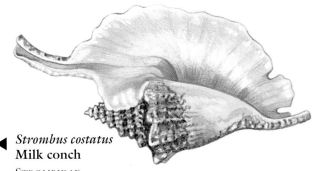

Strombus costatus
Milk conch
STROMBIDAE

This large shell (reaches 7 inches [18 cm] high) lives in shallow waters, on sand and beds of algae, in bays and sheltered lagoons. Common from southern Florida to the West Indies to Mexico and Brazil. Generally white-alabaster in color.

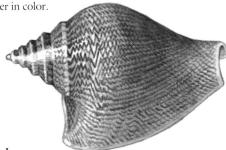

Lambis violacea
Violet spider conch
STROMBIDAE

The rarest and most graceful of the *Lambis* genus. It can be found on the island of Mauritius and other smaller islands off Madagascar. Interior of the aperture is purple, with a dozen digitations on the outside lip. Six inches (15 cm) long.

Lambis millipeda
Millipede spider conch
STROMBIDAE

Lives in the Southwest Pacific, from the Philippines to Java to New Guinea, in shallow waters in coral habitats. It is about 5 inches (12 cm) long, with a dozen principal digitations and a slight difference in form between males and females. Common.

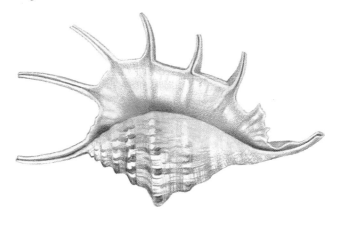

Lambis chiragra
Chiragra spider conch ▶

STROMBIDAE

Reaches 6 inches (15 cm) in length. The apex is pointed. The last whorl is deeply cut by spiral furrows that separate four large ribs. Six principal digitations. Lives in the Indopacific in the sediment around coral reefs.

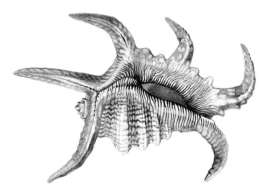

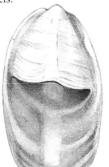

Crepidula fornicata
Common Atlantic slipper ▶

CALUPTRAEIDAE

Lives attached to rocks, other shells, and the carapace of crustaceans. Ranges from .8 to 2.5 inches (2–6.5 cm) in length and has a form that varies depending on substratum. Originally from the American Atlantic, it has spread to European coasts and penetrated the Mediterranean.

◀ ### Crepidula unguiformis
Fingernail slipper

CALUPTRAEIDAE

Tiny, delicate, flattened but variable depending on substratum, it lives in shallow waters, where it adheres to the surface of other shells. Is whitish in color and has a smooth, glossy lower face. From .8 to 1 inch (20–25 mm) long. Mediterranean.

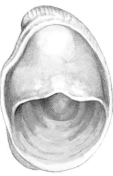

Capulus hungaricus
Fool's cap ▶

CAPULIDAE

Has a curved apex from which extend radial ribs that cut across the growth lines. Lives attached to hard substrata, often on the valves of mussels. Reaches a diameter of 2 inches (5 cm). Common in Europe from the North Sea to the Mediterranean.

◀ ### Calyptraea chinensis
Chinese cup-and-saucer

CALUPTRAEIDAE

Very flat with a pointed apex. The diameter ranges from .4 to .8 inches (10–20 mm). Lives in the infralittoral band, where it adheres to submerged objects, rocks, and other shells. Native to the two shores of the North Atlantic and the Mediterranean.

◀ ### Xenophora crispa
Mediterranean carrier shell

XENOPHORIDAE

Has a flat cone form with a spire covered with various objects that the animal affixes to the sutures among the whorls, such as small shells, organic fragments, and various minerals. Diameter between 1.2 and 1.5 inches (3–4 cm). Lives in the west central Mediterranean. Rare.

Stellaria solaris
Sunburst carrier shell ▶

XENOPHORIDAE

Characterized by 14 long spines. Rarely affixes other objects to the shell, except in the initial whorls. Reaches 3.5 inches (9 cm) in diameter. Lives in the circumlittoral and infralittoral bands of the Indian Ocean and the West Pacific.

Cypraea pyrum
Pear cowrie
CYPRAEIDAE

Widespread in the Mediterranean and on the west coast of Africa. Has a beautiful, varied color that runs from chestnut red to cream to violet, with banded or spotted markings. Lives in shallow waters. Rather common. From 1 to 2 inches (2.5–5 cm) in size.

Cypraea caurica
Caurica cowrie
CYPRAEIDAE

Indopacific species recently introduced to the eastern Mediterranean. Elongated, with color distinguished by three more or less light brown-olive bands with very dark spots. Common. From 1 to 2 inches (2.5–5 cm) in size.

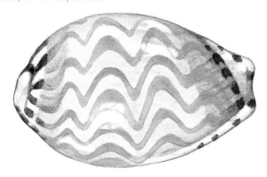

Cypraea friendiithersites
CYPRAEIDAE

Swollen, almost globular form with white base and S-shaped aperture. The back is brown with black spots. Totally black specimens are frequent. Lives along the southern coasts of Australia, where it is not common. From 2.3 to 3.5 inches (6–9 cm) long.

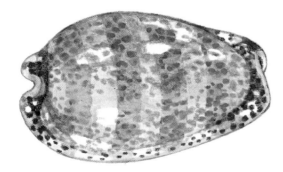

Cypraea mus
Mouse cowrie
CYPRAEIDAE

Found along the Atlantic coasts of Venezuela and Colombia, where it is rather rare. Has a distinctive coloring around the dorsal band, with dark spots that create an irregular pattern on a sand-colored background. From 1.2 to 2.3 inches (3–6 cm) in size.

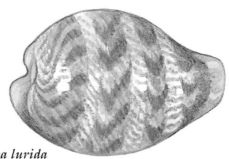

Cypraea lurida
Lurid cowrie
CYPRAEIDAE

Common in the Mediterranean province and West Africa, where it lives from 6.5 to 23 feet (2–7 m) in depth. Nut colored with lighter bands on the back and two black spots on each of the two ends. The base is cream. Rather frequent. From 1.2 to 1.5 inches (3–5 cm) in length.

Cypraea ziczac
Zigzag cowrie
CYPRAEIDAE

Common and abundant throughout the Indopacific, where it lives in shallow waters in the infralittoral band. The back is cream-colored with white bands that create very characteristic V-shaped patterns. Small dark spots on the ends. From .5 to .9 inches (1.2–2.3 cm) in length. Indopacific.

Cypraea nigropunctata
Black-spotted cowrie
CYPRAEIDAE

Has an elongated, subcylindrical form and is small in size (from .9 to 1.4 inches [2.3–3.6 cm]). The back is yellowish, covered with variable, nut-colored spots. There are two blackish spots on the two ends. Lives along the coasts of Peru, Ecuador, and the Galapagos Islands.

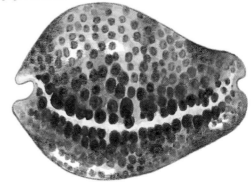

Cypraea moneta
Money cowrie
CYPRAEIDAE

Since the dawn of civilization, this shell has been the one most commonly used for money and ornamental purposes. Has a rather irregular form, with color that runs from white to yellow to green, with a red line. Indopacific and Panamic. About 1 inch (2.5 cm) long.

▶

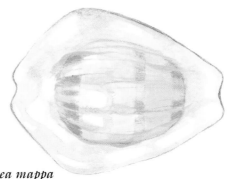

Cypraea mappa
Map cowrie
CYPRAEIDAE

◀

Has a swollen, somewhat pear-shaped form. The pattern on its back is beautiful and varies from individual to individual, with a white stripe that branches out in various directions, resembling a map. Widespread and common in the Indopacific in coral reefs. From 2 to 3.9 inches (5–9 cm) long.

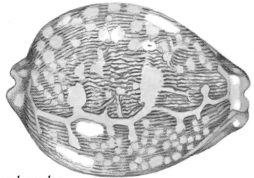

Cypraea leucodon
White-toothed cowrie
CYPRAEIDAE

▶

The white teeth on the cream-colored background of the aperture give this extremely rare cowry its name. Its habitat is unknown. It has been found in the Indian and Pacific Oceans in the intestines of the fish that feed on it. From 2.7 to 3.3 (7–8.5 cm) in length.

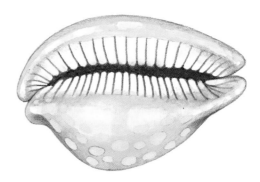

Cypraea hesitata hesitata
Undecided cowrie
CYPRAEIDAE

◀

Lives in deep waters in southeast Australia and Tasmania and is fairly common. Has a white, sinuous aperture that widens in front, while the cream-colored back has irregular brown spots. Four inches (10 cm) long.

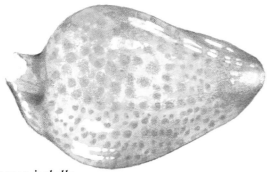

Cypraea isabella
Isabelle cowrie
CYPRAEIDAE

▶

Lives in shallow waters throughout the Indopacific, and is very common. It is little more than 2 inches (5 cm) in length. It has two brownish red spots on the ends: the beige or light gray shell is traversed by dark dotted or segmented lines.

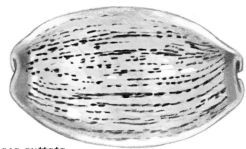

Cypraea guttata
Great spotted cowrie
CYPRAEIDAE

◀

Lives in the Indopacific, where it is very rare, in reef habitats. Has beautiful red stripes around the aperture and edges, and large, infrequent spots on the cream-colored back, sometimes traversed by a lighter stripe. It is about 2 inches (5 cm) long.

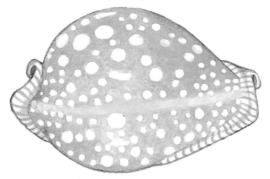

Cypraea granulata
Granulated cowrie
CYPRAEIDAE

▶

Has unusual ornamentation for a cowrie, with beading that runs from the back to the side margin. Its color varies, with little spots that range from brown to orange to lilac. Varies in length from .8 to 1.5 inches (2–4 cm). Lives in Hawaii and Midway.

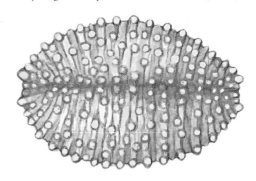

Cypraea fultoni
Fulton's cowrie
CYPRAEIDAE

This cowrie was considered extremely rare until the late 1980s, when its habitat off Mozambique was discovered. It is 3 inches (8 cm) long, with brown spots on the light background of the base, while the back has a beautiful print pattern.

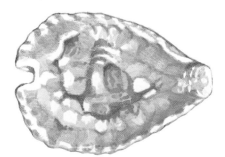

Cypraea depressa
Depressed cowrie
CYPRAEIDAE

Oval-shaped and average in size (from 1 to 2.1 inches [2.5–5.5 cm]), with a beautiful spotted pattern on the back, with zigzag lines running into brown areas. The base is white with brown spots. Lives in the Indopacific in rough waters and reefs.

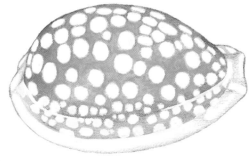

Cypraea cervus
Atlantic deer cowrie
CYPRAEIDAE

The back of this large shell (3.5 to 6 inches [9–15 cm] in size) is a beautiful dappled tawny color, sometimes traversed by a light stripe. The aperture is wider at the front. Lives in the infralittoral band from North Carolina to Mexico and Cuba. Rather common.

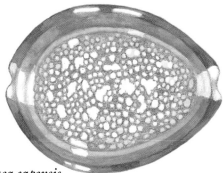

Cypraea capensis
Cape cowrie
CYPRAEIDAE

Oval-shaped and 1 inch (2.5 cm) long, it lives near South Africa. Ornamentation consists of a series of thin, attractive transverse wrinkles on a pink to brown background. Nut-colored central spots. Rather frequent.

Cypraea diluculum diluculum
Dawn cowrie
CYPRAEIDAE

Small (from .5 to 1.2 inches [1.3–3.2 cm] long), and quite lovely, it lives along the entire eastern coast of Africa and islands in the Indian Ocean. Fairly common, it takes refuge under rocks and dead corals on rocky seabeds in shallow water. Its design is quite characteristic, consisting of longitudinal zigzag bands.

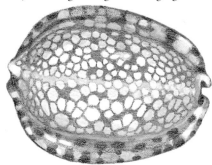

Cypraea cribraria
Sieve cowrie
CYPRAEIDAE

Elongated, with its back speckled with white circles that stand out against the light nut-colored background. The base and margin of the lips are white. Lives in the Indopacific and is relatively common. Length: 1 inch (2.5 cm).

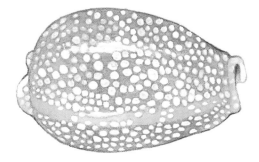

Cypraea caputserpentis
Serpent's head cowrie
CYPRAEIDAE

One of the most common shells in the Indopacific. Found from Japan to Hawaii, Tahiti, and Africa. White spots stand out on a brown network, while two white spots at the ends interrupt the dark band along the margins. One inch (3 cm) long.

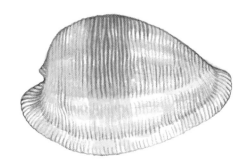

Cypraea aurantium
Golden cowrie
CYPRAEIDAE

▶

Once the insignia of the kings of the Fiji Islands, it is even now one of the most coveted of shells. From 2.3 to 4 inches (6–10 cm) long. Its color is unmistakable: the back is golden orange, with a white base. Lives in caves of coral formations in the Pacific. Extremely rare.

Cypraea argus
Eyed cowrie
CYPRAEIDAE

▶

Cylindrical in form, it is spattered with eyes like the mythological monster that gives it its name. Three transverse bands and two spots on each lip complete the ornamentation. It is 3 inches (8 cm) long. Lives in the Indopacific, where it is rather rare.

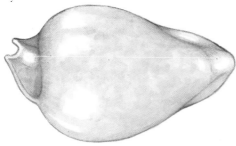

Cypraea annulus
Gold auger cowrie
CYPRAEIDAE

▶

Along with *Cypraea moneta,* it was for centuries used as currency in vast areas of Asia and Africa. Blue-gray inside the gold ring, and cream-colored on the rest of the shell. About .8 inch (2 cm) in length. Indopacific. Common in coral reefs, shallow water.

Ovula ovum
Common egg cowrie
OVULIDAE

▶

Very shiny shell, milk white on the outside, while the interior visible through the aperture is deep red. Lives in the Indopacific in the upper infralittoral band, among the sponges and black corals on which it feeds. An average of 3 inches (7.5 cm) in length.

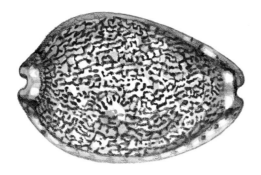

Cypraea armeniaca
Armenian cowrie
CYPRAEIDAE

◀

Has an oval form, with the golden yellow surface scattered with little dark spots and lines. Reaches a maximum of 3 inches (8 cm) in length and is endemic to the waters of Australia. Extremely rare.

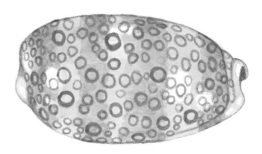

Cypraea arabica
Arabian cowrie
CYPRAEIDAE

◀

The back of this Indopacific shell is traversed by light lines on a brown background variously intersected by transverse lines, resembling Arabic script. It lives in shallow waters under dead corals and rocks. Common. From 1.2 to 3 inches (3–8 cm) in size.

Volva volva
Shuttlecock volva
OVULIDAE

◀

Elongated with a light but robust structure, with no denticles. Lives in the Indopacific, usually associated with soft corals on seabeds off the reef. Color ranges from pink to beige. Quite common, it is about 4.8 inches (12 cm) in length.

Trivia monacha
TRIVIIDAE

Species common from the North Sea to the Mediterranean. Lives on hard substrata at modest depths, and feeds primarily on sea squirts. Up to .5 inches (12 mm) high. Its glossy, corrugated back has from 3 to 4 nut-colored spots on a cream-colored background.

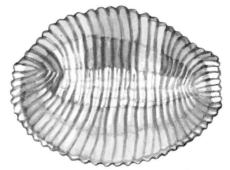

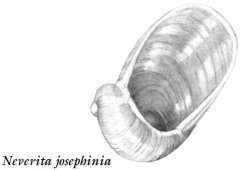

Neverita josephinia
Josephine's moon
NATICIDAE

Flattened, porcelain-like shell with a columellar callus that nearly closes off the umbilicus. White-yellow in color, with a gray-blue spiral band. Mediterranean and western European species common in sands in the infralittoral band. From 1.2 to 1.5 inches (3–4 cm) in diameter.

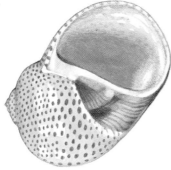

Natica canrena
Colorful Atlantic moon
NATICIDAE

This beautiful naticid, with its shell adorned by four intersecting, cream-colored bands with axial flames, lives in the sand at shallow depths, from North Carolina to the West Indies. From 1 to 2.5 inches (2.5–6.4 cm) in height.

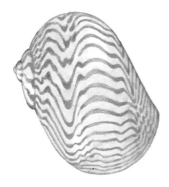

Lunatia
European necklace shell
NATICIDAE

A uniform light nut color, with little spots that form a chain pattern in the suture. The columellar callus is white. Lives on sandy seabeds in the infralittoral band, in the Mediterranean and the Atlantic. Reaches 2 inches (5 cm) in height.

Lamellaria perspicua
Transparent lamellaria
LAMELLARIIDAE

This little mollusk, which has a whitish, transparent, ear-shaped shell with a large aperture, lives in association with colonies of sea squirts, among whom it lays its eggs. The diameter ranges from .5 to .6 inches (12–16 mm). Mediterranean and Atlantic.

Natica stercusmuscarum (formerly Naticarius millepunctatus)
Fly-specked moon
NATICIDAE

Mediterranean species. Characteristically, it has many small chestnut-colored spots that stand out against a very light background. There are, however, albino specimens and those with uniform or banded colors. From 1.2 to 2 inches (3–5 cm) in diameter. Rather common.

Natica lineata
Lined moon
NATICIDAE

Lives on the sandy and muddy seabeds of the coastal Indian Ocean and West Pacific, from Taiwan to the northern Philippines. Small in size (from .8 to 1.2 inches [2–3 cm]), it has a cupola-shaped spire that is quite distinct from the last whorl. Its design includes more or less zigzag axial bands that range from orange to brown in color, on a whitish background.

Tonna tessellata
TONNIDAE

Very common species in the West Pacific and Australia. Has a flattened spire from which the slightly pointed apex emerges. The very deep spiral striae are characteristic. Cream-colored with chestnut-colored spots. From 2.3 to 4 inches (6–10 cm) high.

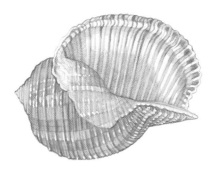

Ficus ventricosus
Swollen fig shell
FICIDAE

Lives in the Panamic province and reaches medium to large size. The pear-shaped appearance is typical of the family, but its form is rendered interesting by a regular succession of spiral ribs in three different heights. The color is light nut brown. Up to 3.5 inches (9 cm).

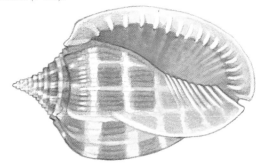

Cypraeacassis testiculus
Reticulate cowrie helmet
CASSIDAE

Lives along the eastern coasts of the Americas and Africa (where, however, it is rare). Has a particular mosaic sculpture created by axial stripes intersecting with spiral stripes. The dorsal color ranges from nut brown to violet. Height runs from 1.2 to 3.5 inches (3–9 cm).

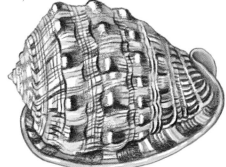

Galeodea echinophora
Spiny bonnet
CASSIDAE

Up to 4 inches (10 cm) in height, it is extremely common in the Mediterranean province, and is even sold in fish markets. It is nut brown on the outside, and white in the aperture. Large spiral ridges with nodules traverse the entire shell.

Tonna galea
Giant tun
TONNIDAE

Cosmopolitan species not found in cold seas. It lives on sandy or detrital floors of the infralittoral and circumlittoral bands. The shell is large, light, and fragile, with colors that vary from yellow to cream to brown. From 4 to 6 inches (10–15 cm) in height.

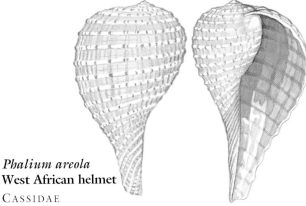

Phalium areola
West African helmet
CASSIDAE

Has a rather slender structure and a thin network on the spire and first part of the last whorl. Color ranges from pink to light nut brown, with four series of chestnut-colored spots. From 2 to 4 inches (5–10 cm) high. Common from eastern Africa to Melanesia and Samoa.

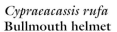

Cypraeacassis rufa
Bullmouth helmet
CASSIDAE

Since ancient times, this shell was most commonly used to make cameos, using the contrast between the red-orange and the cream of the shell's different layers. Common in the Indopacific. Height ranges from 4 to 6 inches (10–15 cm).

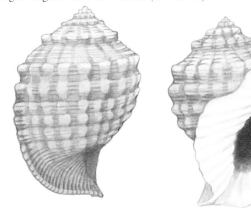

Distorsio anus
Common distorsio
RANELLIDAE

The shell has a truly singular form, with asymmetrical, eccentrically developed whorls on the spire. The edges of the aperture are quite irregular. It lives in the coral reefs of the Indopacific. From 1.5 to 3 inches (4–8 cm) in height.

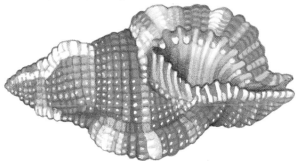

Cymatium corrugatum
Corrugated triton
RANELLIDAE

When the periostracum that forms a velvety brown covering is removed, the shell is white with nut-colored, deeply indented spiral furrows. Its height ranges from 2.3 to 3.5 inches (6–9 cm), unusually to 4.7 inches (12 cm). Lives on sandy beds of the Mediterranean. Not present in the Adriatic.

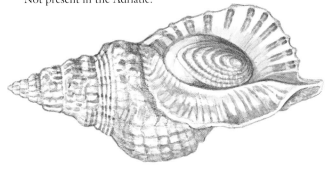

Ranella olearia (formerly *Argobuccinum giganteum*)
Wandering triton
RANELLIDAE

A large (from 6 to 8.5 inches [15–21 cm]), robust, and light shell with a vast distribution, from the eastern Atlantic to the Mediterranean, South Africa, and Australia, on seabeds in the circumlittoral band. Has two series of axial varices in the form of ridges.

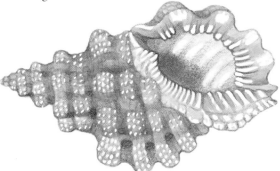

Bursa crumena
Frilled frogshell
BURSIDAE

This elegant representative of an almost exclusively tropical member of the gastropod family lives in the Indopacific. It is pink with violet tones. Sculpture is rather variable. From 2 to 3.5 inches (5–9 cm) high.

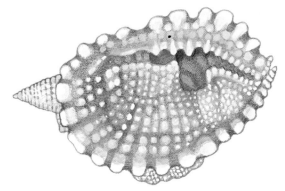

Cymatium rubeculum
Robin redbreast triton
RANELLIDAE

One of the smallest and most graceful of the Ranellidae: its height ranges from 1.4 to 2 inches (3.5–5 cm). The surface, in various shades of red, is covered with beading and traversed by varices. Lives in the Indopacific and Australia near coral reefs.

Charonia lampas (formerly *Charonia nodifera*)
Knobbed triton
RANELLIDAE

A giant among gastropods (reaches a height of more than a foot [40 cm]), used to make horns in ancient times. Is widely distributed in warm seas, not including the Americas. It is found in the western part of the Mediterranean up to a depth of 660 feet (200 m).

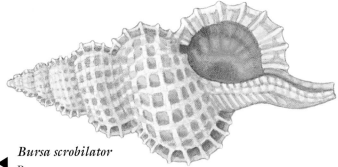

Bursa scrobilator
BURSIDAE

Has a very distinctive aperture, with toothed and furrowed inner edges. Tawny color with darker spots. The varices are often knobby, but may be absent. From 2.7 to 3.5 inches (7–9 cm) in height. Lives in the Mediterranean province and northwest Africa.

Monophorus perversus (formerly Triphora perversa)
TRIPHORIDAE

Has a sinistral shell like all triphorids, and is common from Norway to the Mediterranean. Lives under rocks in the tidal area up to 260 feet (80 m) in depth. Has 16 to 18 spires adorned with three rows of beading. From .8 to 1 inches (2–2.5 cm) high.

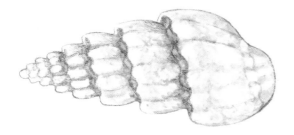

Opalia funiculata (formerly Opalia crenimarginata)
EPITONIIDAE

Lives at the lower edge of the tidal area, at the base of sea anemones from the genus Anthopleura, from southern California to Panama. It is from .4 to .7 inches (10–19 mm) high and is opaque white in color. The ribbing is prominent in the first whorls, and then diminishes.

Opalia crenata
Coarse wentletrap
EPITONIIDAE

Has a thick, white shell and lives in the Mediterranean province and Atlantic coast of North America, where it is extremely rare. About .8 inches (2 cm) high. It has often been found in association with the sea anemone Anemonia sulcata in shallow waters on coarse, wave-swept sand.

Epitonium scalare
Precious wentletrap
EPITONIIDAE

This is one of the legendary rarities in shell collecting. Today, it is fished in the Philippines and Japan from deep seabeds, using trawls, but as fragile as it is, it is difficult to bring it up intact. The whorls just barely adhere to each other. It is from 2 to 2.7 inches (5–7 cm) high.

Epitonium clathrus
EPITONIIDAE

Lives on sandy seabeds in the Mediterranean and the Atlantic in western Europe, feeding on cnidarians, especially sea anemones. An average of 1.5 inches (4 cm) high, the shell has 10 to 12 spires, with nine axial lamellae. Cream colored with brown bands.

Janthina janthina
Common janthina
JANTHINIDAE

Pelagic, cosmopolitan species (except for polar seas). It floats with the currents, using a raft of tiny bubbles of mucus. It feeds on pelagic cnidarians like the by-the-wind-sailor (Vellella). One and a half inches (4 cm) high, the shell is violet with tones of white.

Nucella cingulata
Corded rock shell
MURICIDAE

A South African species of modest dimensions (1 to 1.5 inches [2.5–4 cm]), it is nevertheless unmistakable due to its truly unique sculpture. Each whorl has two distinctly raised whitish cords, except for the last one, which has three. In the spaces between the cords, there are slightly upraised spiral striae. It is pink in color.

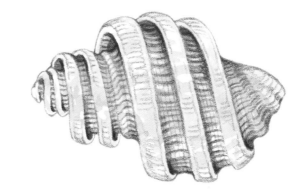

Thais lacera (formerly *Thais haemastoma*)
Red-mouth purpura
MURICIDAE

Lives in the Mediterranean and Atlantic (from Africa to the Bay of Biscay in Africa) in algae-rich reefs, where it preys on bivalves. The more or less knobby shell is often covered with encrustations. The aperture is orange. Up to 4 inches (10 cm) high.

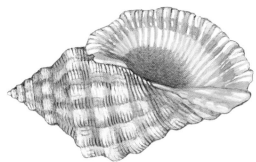

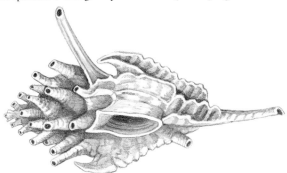

Rapana venosa
Thomas's rapa whelk
MURICIDAE

This Japan, China, and Black Sea murex, which preys on bivalves, as do most members of its family, made news in the early 1960s when it began to invade the Mediterranean. Reaches 4.7 inches (12 cm) in height. The aperture is orange.

Typhinellus sowerby
Frilly typhis
MURICIDAE

Found, but not frequent, on coral seabeds in the Mediterranean and West Africa. Slender and small (no more than .9 inches [2.2 cm]), this shell is noteworthy for the significant wing-shaped flare of the lip of the aperture.

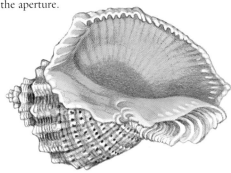

Hexaplex brassica (formerly *Phyllonotus brassica*)
MURICIDAE

Large murex from the Panamic province: may exceed 6 inches (15 cm) in height, and larger specimens with more interesting ornamentation are dredged from deep seabeds. White with three brown spiral bands. The aperture is pink.

Pteropurpura plorator
Weeping murex
MURICIDAE

Comes from the southeast coasts of Japan and is prized for its ornamentation. Three prominent varices traverse the shell axially, creating falcate lobes. The lip of the aperture is flared. It is about 1.4 to 2 inches (3.5–5 cm) high.

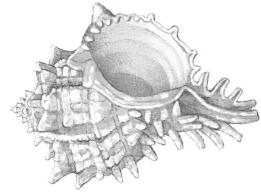

Nucella lapillus
Atlantic dogwinkle
MURICIDAE

Active predator of mussels, and common in the tidal area along the coasts of Europe and North America, from Labrador to New York. Varies in size (from .8 to 2 inches [2 to 5 cm]), color (from whitish to dark brown), and sculpture, which may be more or less prominent.

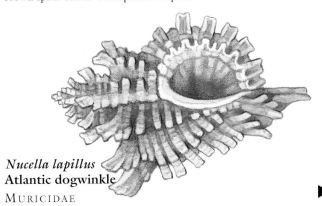

Ocenebra erinaceus
Sting winkle
MURICIDAE

Lives on rocks and port structures, from the tidal zone to shallow depths, and is common on European coasts from the North Sea to the Mediterranean. Feeds on bivalves. Up to 2.3 inches (6 cm) high, with a thick lip adorned by wide crests. Males and females dimorphic.

Hexaplex radix
Radish murex
MURICIDAE ►

Lives along the Pacific coasts from Panama to Ecuador. The surface is white, but the numerous black spines that run from the axial ribs, closely pressed together, give it a blackish appearance. Up to 6 inches (15 cm) in height.

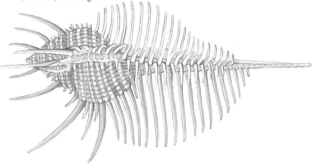

Pterynotus elongatus
Club murex
MURICIDAE ►

The broad, wing-shaped flares and height of the spire give this murex from Japan and the Indopacific a surprising appearance. It is white in color. Lives on detrital and coral seabeds in the open sea. Reaches 3 inches (8 cm) in length.

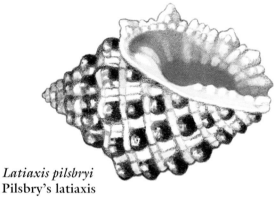

Latiaxis pilsbryi
Pilsbry's latiaxis
MURICIDAE ►

The most prized of the *Latiaxis* of Japan, which are the most beautiful of the genus. It is dredged from deep waters, has a diameter of 1.5 inches (4 cm) and is rare. The tabular spire with flattened spines is characteristic. It is pure white.

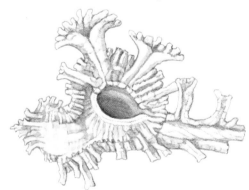

Hexaplex trunculus (formerly *Truncalariopsis trunculus*)
Trunculus murex
MURICIDAE ►

Frequent from the midlittoral band to a depth of 26 feet (8 m), on various types of seabed, in the Mediterranean and Atlantic in the Mediterranean province. The Phoenicians caught it for its purple dye, but today it is used for food. Reaches a length of 3 inches (8 cm).

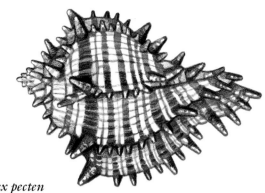

◄ ### Murex pecten
Venus comb murex
MURICIDAE

This is one of the wonders of the realm of mollusks, due to the elegance of its very delicate spines. It is common in the Indopacific on relatively deep seabeds, and is dredged by fishing boats. Up to 6 inches (15 cm) long.

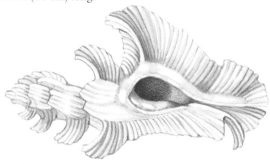

◄ ### Morula uva
Grape drupe
MURICIDAE

A gregarious species: can be found on midlittoral or infralittoral rocks in the Indopacific, usually in groups, or at least in pairs. Up to 1 inch (2.5 cm) high. The last whorl has six rows of black tubercles, while the aperture is violet.

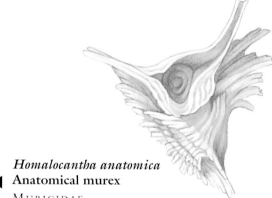

◄ ### Homalocantha anatomica
Anatomical murex
MURICIDAE

This murex, once rare but now regularly collected by fishermen in the open sea off the Philippines, looks like an abstract sculpture made of a little pile of bones. The varices are arranged on three axial rows. About 1.5 to 2 inches (4–5 cm) high.

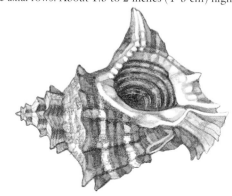

Haustellum haustellum
Spinesbill murex

MURICIDAE

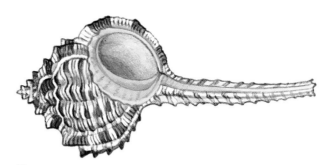

The extremely long siphonal canal, extended for over half the shell's total length (from 2.3 to 6 inches [6–15 cm]) characterizes this Indopacific murex, which seems to prefer sandy or muddy beds at the mouths of rivers.

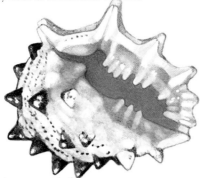

Concholepas concholepas
Barnacle rock shell

MURICIDAE

Lives along the coasts of Peru and Chile. Looks like a capulid and adheres to the rocks of the midlittoral and infralittoral band like a limpet. Harvested in great numbers for food purposes, it is now a protected species. Reaches 3.5 inches (9 cm) in diameter.

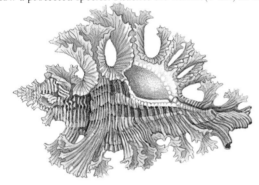

Bolinus brandaris (formerly *Murex brandaris*)
Purple dye murex

MURICIDAE

Lives from 16 to 260 feet (5–80 m) in depth and is common from the Mediterranean to West Africa. The Phoenicians obtained their famous purple dye from it. Today it is collected for food. Reaches a length of 3.5 inches (9 cm) and has widely varying ornamentation.

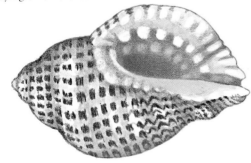

Coralliophila meyendorffi
Lamellose coral snail

CORALLIOPHILIDAE

Is part of a family (Coralliophilidae) of gastropods with no radula, as they feed by sucking the tissues of cnidarians. It is common in the Mediterranean and the Atlantic at shallow depths. It is 1.4 inches (3.5 cm) high and has a rose-colored aperture.

Drupa morum
Purple Pacific drupe

MURICIDAE

This drupe is 1 inch (2.5 cm) high and globular in appearance. There are three or four rows of blackish spines on the last whorl. The sinuous aperture is purple, with white denticles. Common on Indopacific littoral reefs exposed to waves.

Chicoreus palmarosae
Rose-branch murex

MURICIDAE

Rare and elegant, it is found in the Indopacific and Sri Lanka. Its ornate ramifications are arranged in three axial rows that also run along the siphonal canal. The apex and the upper part of the ramifications are pink. It is 2.7 to 4.7 inches (7–12 cm) high.

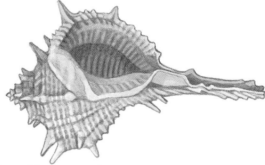

Acanthina punctulata
Spotted unicorn

MURICIDAE

This little murex frequents reefs in the upper midlittoral band in California and western Mexico. From .9 to 1.5 inches (2.2–3.8 cm) high, it has an ornate surface with spiral carinae that intersect with small axial ridges to form a brown checkerboard pattern.

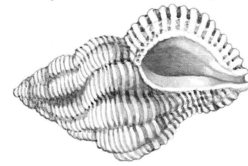

Pollia dorbigny (formerly *Cantharus d'orbignyi*)
Cantharus
BUCCINIDAE

Distinguished by very accentuated spiral stripes and convex whorls. Lives in the Mediterranean on seabeds rich with marine vegetation. The spire is brown with a white area. The aperture is white with violet spots. It is .6 to .7 inches (15–18 mm) in height.

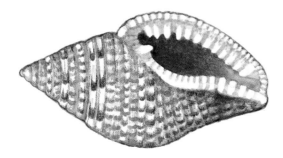

Pisania striata (formerly *Pisania maculosa*)
Tinted cantharus or striate pisania
BUCCINIDAE

Very common in the Mediterranean and Portugal, at shallow depths, especially in areas rich with marine vegetation. About 1.2 inches (3 cm) long, its color varies from white to nut brown to olive green, with a light central band.

Penion dilatatus
Flaming penion
BUCCINIDAE

Members of the *Penion* genus are carnivorous coldwater whelks that live in southern Australia and New Zealand and are caught in fishing trawls. Up to 7 inches (18 cm) long, this whelk has a knobby carina in the middle of its whorls.

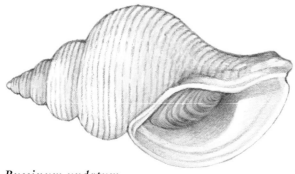

Neptunea contraria
Left-handed neptune
BUCCINIDAE

A sinistral shell species, common in the seas of northern Europe. It is gray, with a surface traversed by dense spiral striae, and from 2.7 to 4.3 inches (7–11 cm) high. Is sometimes caught in fishing boat trawls.

Buccinum undatum
Waved whelk
BUCCINIDAE

In the Mediterranean, relict families live on at great depths, feeding on dead or dying animals. Also common in the shallow waters along both coasts of the North Atlantic. Color runs from white to brown, height to 4.3 inches (11 cm).

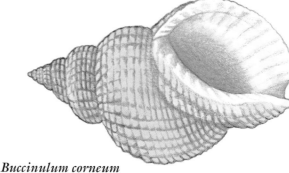

Buccinulum corneum
Spindle euthria
BUCCINIDAE

Lives in the Mediterranean on sandy or muddy seabeds from 16 to 200 feet (5–60 m) deep, feeding on carrion but also other mollusks, worms, and small living crustaceans. Its shell is beige with chestnut flames. About 2 inches (5 cm) in height.

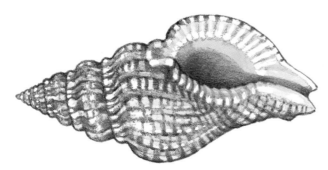

Babylonia canaliculata
MURICIDAE

The spire, with its almost vertical whorls and deeply incised suture, resembles the mythical Tower of Babel that gave its name to the genus. Lives on sandy infralittoral seabeds in the Indian Ocean and is fairly common. From 1.5 to 2.5 inches (4–6.5 cm) high.

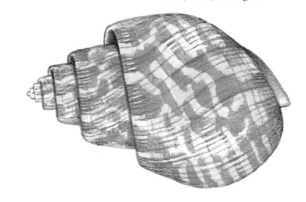

Mitrella scripta
Music dove shell

COLUMBELLIDAE

A Mediterranean species found in rocky habitats among photophilic algae and on sponges. The shell, about .8 inches (2 cm) in length, is brilliant white with reddish speckles. The columella and interior of the lip are orange.

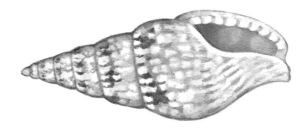

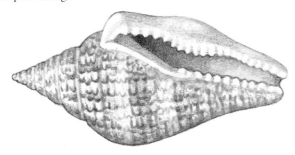

Nassarius mutabilis (formerly *Sphaeronassa mutabilis*)
Mutable nassa

NASSARIIDAE

Species common throughout the Mediterranean province, sometimes abundant. In the Adriatic, it is sold in fish markets. Lives on sandy and oozy seabeds and feeds on carrion, as do the others of its genus. From 1 to 1.5 inches (2.5–4 cm) high. Cream-colored with reddish flames.

Columbella rusticoides
Rusty dovesnail

COLUMBELLIDAE

Lives from southern Florida to northwest Cuba. It is common on vegetation-rich reefs, where it feeds on algae and detritus. Its color varies, but the thick, toothed lip makes it unmistakable. It is .8 inches (2 cm) high.

Nassarius albus
White nassa

NASSARIIDAE

Tiny shell, from .2 to .5 inches (6–13 mm) long, white with a chestnut band under the suture. Prominent axial ribbing and faint spiral ridges. Lives in the sand up to a depth of 100 feet (30 m), from North Carolina to the West Indies.

Nassarius reticulatus (formerly *Hinia reticulata*)
Netted nassa

NASSARIIDAE

Lives on shallow sandy seabeds where it feeds on dead animals, which it can smell from a distance of 100 feet (30 m). Widespread in the Atlantic, from Norway to Morocco, and in the Mediterranean to the Black Sea. An average of 1.2 inches (3 cm) high, with cancellate ornamentation.

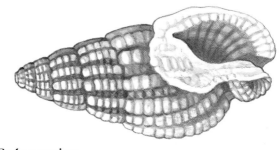

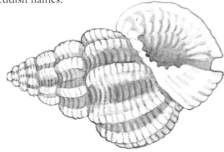

Cyclope neritea
Neritelike dogwhelk

MURICIDAE

Has a flat form, with the lower portion completely covered by a white callus. The upper part is brown, with a variety of flames. It is common in the Mediterranean, Morocco, and Portugal on sandy, shallow seabeds, including littoral ponds. It is .4 to .6 inches (10–15 mm) in diameter.

Dorsanum maniliferum
One-ridge bullia

NASSARIIDAE

This representative of the family Nassariidae is frequent on sandy seabeds along the coasts of South America, from Brazil to Argentina. Distinguished by the beautiful crown of tubercles running along the spire, it is 1.4 to 2 inches (3.5–5 cm) high.

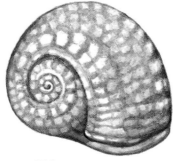

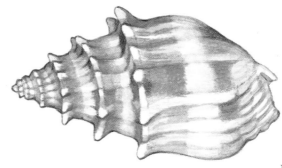

Bullia vittata
Ribbon bullia
NASSARIIDAE

This small necrophage from the sandy and muddy coasts of the Indian Ocean, is from 1.3 to 1.8 inches (3.4–4.5 cm) in size, and has a very elegant, slender form. The beginning of each whorl has a double row of beading, followed by a series of faint spiral striae. Its color ranges from cream to pink.

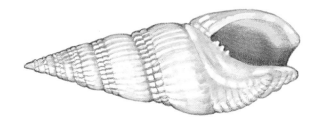

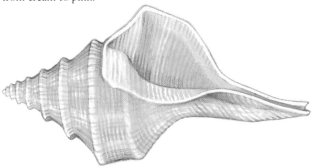

Syrinx aruanus
Australian trumpet
MELONGENIDAE

This is a giant among gastropods, reaching 27 inches (70 cm) in length. Lives in Australia, on shallow muddy seabeds, but can be found at up to 200 feet (60 m) in depth. It is an extremely active predator, especially of other mollusks. Its flesh is edible.

Melongena corona
Crown conch
MELONGENIDAE

Lives in the mud or muddy sand of the midlittoral band, in lagoons and often in mangrove forests, feeding on carrion or preying on bivalves. Quite variable (length from 1 to 8 inches [2.5–20 cm]), including in ornamentation. Common in the Caribbean.

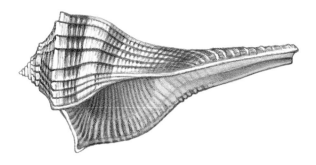

Busycon sinistrum
Lightning whelk
MELONGENIDAE

Sinistral, fusiform shell, with low spire and final whorl that ends in a slightly bent siphonal canal. Dimension varies greatly, from 2.5 to 16 inches (6.5–40 cm). Lives in the sand to a depth of 10 feet (3 m), from North Carolina to Texas.

Pleuroploca gigantea
Horse conch
FASCIOLARIIDAE

This is one of the largest gastropods, reaching 20 inches (.5 m) in height. Preys on other gastropods (by blocking the operculum before it closes) and bivalves. Lives in the Caribbean and southeastern United States on sand and mud in the infralittoral band to a depth of 20 feet (6 m).

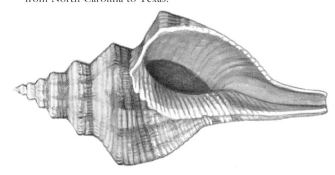

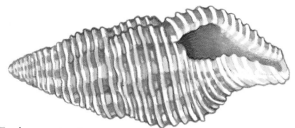

Latirus craticulatus
FASCIOLARIIDAE

Common in the Indopacific. The shell differs from those characteristic of the genus *Latirus* and approaches those of the whelks, with a long spire and short siphonal canal. It is from 1.5 to 2 inches (4–5 cm) long and has white and reddish lines.

Fusinus rostratus
Spindle shell
FASCIOLARIIDAE

Lives in the circumlittoral band and on the continental slope, on seabeds abundant in organic detritus. It is common in the Mediterranean and neighboring Atlantic region. The shell rarely reaches 3 inches (8 cm) in size and is distinguished by a siphonal canal longer than the aperture and prominent axial ribs.

Fasciolaria lignaria
Wooden fasciolaria, knotty tulip

FASCIOLARIIDAE

This predator lives in the Mediterranean, particularly the Canary Islands, from shallow waters to significant depths, preferably on sand and mud, but also on reefs. The shell is about 2 inches (5 cm) long and can easily be distinguished by its large white nodules.

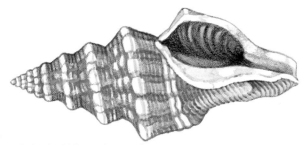

Voluta musica
Common music volute

VOLUTIDAE

This lovely volute, from 1.4 to 3.5 inches (3–9 cm) high, has a beautiful pattern of lines and spots that resembles a musical staff. It lives on coral sand in the Caribbean from 1 to 20 feet (30 cm to 6 m) in depth.

Fasciolaria lilium hunteria
Banded tulip

FASCIOLARIIDAE

Found at depths of from 3 to 30 feet (1–12 m) on seabeds of muddy sand or beds of algae, where it preys on other mollusks. It is common from North Carolina to Texas. Its color varies from blue-green to light mauve, with a dark band. From 2.7 to 3 inches (7–8 cm) high.

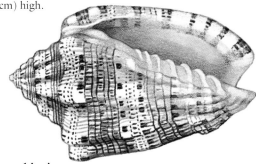

Lyria cumingii
Cuming's lyria

VOLUTIDAE

Small volute (maximum 1.2 inches [3 cm] in size) that lives near Panama and from western Mexico to Peru. Can be found in sub-littoral habitats to 65 feet (20 m) in depth, on soft seabeds. A series of small tubercles increasing in size accompanies the whorls.

Melo aethiopicus
Crowned baler

VOLUTIDAE

Large oval shell, beige-pink in color, with a spire visible only from above because it is embedded in the crownlike ornamentation of the last whorl. From 5.5 to 10 inches (14–25 cm) high, it lives in the Indopacific from the Philippines to northeastern Australia.

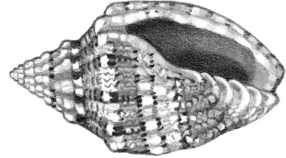

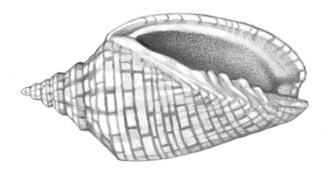

Ampulla priamus
Spotted flask

VOLUTIDAE

A thin, light, very elegant shell with a glossy, light nut-colored surface with darker bands and a series of little square spots. Lives 130 feet (40 m) deep and beyond, in the Atlantic from Vigo, Spain, to Mauritania. From 2 to 2.9 inches (5–7.5 cm) high.

Harpulina arausiaca
Vexillate volute

VOLUTIDAE

A rare volute that lives along the northern coast of Ceylon and the coast of southern India, on seabeds about 65 feet (20 m) deep. From 2.3 to 3.5 inches (6–9 cm) in size, it has a pattern of orange rectangles on cream white that resembles a wall of bricks.

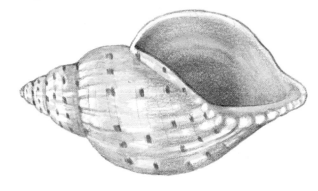

Ericusa sowerby
Sowerby's volute

VOLUTIDAE

Collected by trawls in southeastern Australia and Tasmania on soft seabeds from 65 to 525 feet (20–160 m) deep, this volute is fairly common. Has a very slender structure and can reach 8 inches (25 cm) high. Its pattern varies greatly, with more or less densely arranged lines.

Cymbium cymbium

VOLUTIDAE

Large members of the *Cymbium* genus are regularly fished for food along the coast of Africa from Morocco to Senegal. This species has an almost cylindrical shell with a prominent carina behind the last whorl. It is from 4 to 8 inches (10–15 cm) high.

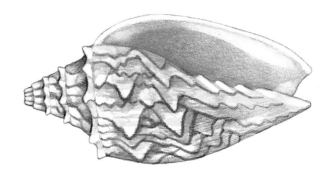

Cymbiola imperialis
Imperial volute

VOLUTIDAE

Always prized for its extraordinary crownlike ornamentation, formed of spines in increasing height located in the middle of the whorls. Lives in the Philippines on sandy seabeds, from 6 to 60 feet (2–20 m) deep. It is from 3 to 8 inches (8–20 cm) high.

Alcithoe swainsoni
Swainson's volute

VOLUTIDAE

Lives in New Zealand on seabeds of sand or mud, from 6 to 300 feet (2–90 m) deep. This family has the habit of remaining buried in the substratum by day and coming out at night in search of prey. It is from 3.5 to 9 inches (9–22 cm) long, with variable colors.

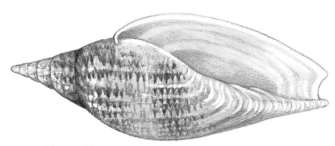

Cymbium olla
Olla volute

VOLUTIDAE

Lives between 150 and 300 feet (45 and 90 m) in depth, from the coast of Spain to Senegal. Its surface is opaque, and the aperture is quite wide and flared. Its color varies from creamy pink to nut brown. Its height ranges from 3.5 to 4.3 inches (9–11 cm).

Cymbiola vespertilio
Bat volute

VOLUTIDAE

This Philippines to northern Australia volute is the most common but also one of the most beautiful of the family, due to the variety of colors and the bat-wing pattern that gives it its name. Lives on sand up to 65 feet (20 m) in depth. From 2 to 4.3 inches (5–11 cm) high.

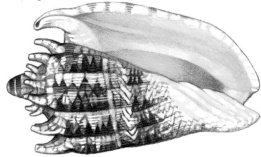

Amoria undulata
Wavy volute

VOLUTIDAE

The genus *Amoria* lives only in Australian waters (and in the far south of Indonesia), on sandy seabeds of the infralittoral and circumlittoral bands. The glossiness and wavy pattern of these shells make them quite beautiful. They range from 2.7 to 4 inches (7–10 cm) long.

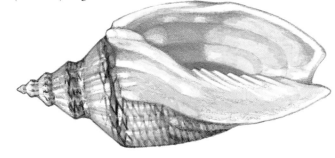

Harpa harpa
True harp

HARPIDAE

▶

Can be distinguished by other members of the genus by the very marked contrast in the spectacular tapestry pattern that adorns the shell of these predators that live on sandy seabeds. There are three spots on the columella. The shell is from 2 to 2.7 inches (5–7 cm) high. Southwest Pacific.

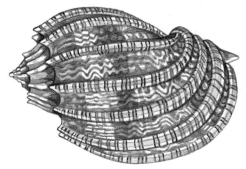

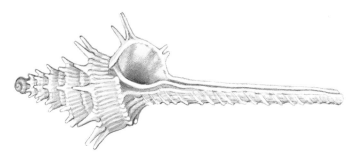

Vasum muricatum
Caribbean vase

TURBINELLIDAE

▶

Has a massive biconical shell and lives in the Caribbean, in shallow waters up to 30 feet (10 m) deep, where it preys on worms and other mollusks. The columella has four or five prominent folds. The shell is about 3 inches (8 cm) high.

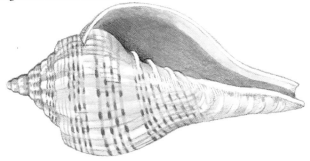

Oliva splendidula
Splendid olive

OLIVIDAE

▶

Lives in the Panamic province, is from 1.5 to 2 inches (4–5 cm) high and is rather rare. The spire is distinct, the suture evident. The color is quite interesting: two triangle-shaped chestnut bands and little spots with a tail run across the cream-colored background.

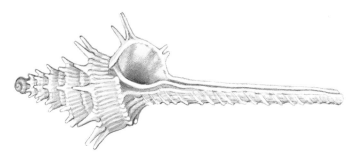

Oliva lignaria
Ornate olive

OLIVIDAE

▶

Species common in the Indian Ocean and West Pacific, including northwestern Australia. An average of 2.3 inches (6 cm) high, it has a subcylindrical form. Its color is highly variable, as is its pattern, which may be indistinct or very marked.

◀ *Turbinella pyrum* (formerly *Xancus pyrum*)
Indian chank

TURBINELLIDAE

This is the sacred shell of the Hindus, who use it in temple ceremonies as a symbol of Krishna. Sinistral specimens are highly prized. Has a pear-shaped structure, is from 2 to 6 inches (5–15 cm) high, and is frequently fished from the seabeds of the Gulf of Bengal.

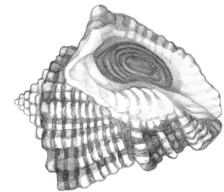

◀ *Columbarium pagoda*
First pagoda shell

VASIDAE

This shell has a very slender structure with a long siphonal canal, and is common along the coasts of Japan. Its height varies from 2 to 3 inches (5–8 cm). A crown of spines appears along the carina of the indentations. There is a second carina near the aperture.

◀ *Oliva peruviana*
Peruvian olive

OLIVIDAE

Has an oval shape, a distinct spire, and a hump near the last whorl. It may be uniformly chestnut in color, but more beautiful specimens are cream-colored with zigzag axial chestnut-colored stripes. Lives in Peru and Chile. From 1.5 to 2 inches (4–5 cm) high.

Baryspira urasima
Urasima ancilla
OLIVIDAE ▶

Lives along the coasts of Japan and remains buried in the sand, with only the siphon emerging to detect the presence of the carrion on which it feeds. Is beautifully colored, with a nut-colored band on cream background. Up to 1.5 inches (4 cm).

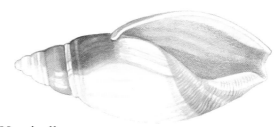

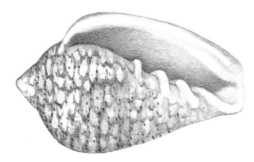

Cryptospira elegans (also called *Marginella elegans*)
Elegant marginella
MARGINELLIDAE ▶

Small (1 to 1.4 inches [2.5–3.5 cm]) and oval, this margin shell from the Bay of Bengal is a true jewel in the elegance of its pattern. The light gray final whorl is traversed by dark gray spiral bands interrupted by axial bands. The aperture is chestnut-colored.

Glabella adansoni
Adanson's marginella
MARGINELLIDAE ▶

Lives on the sandy seabeds of West Africa, where this family of gastropods is very well represented. Has a distinct and developed spire. From .8 to 1.4 inches (2–3.5 cm) high, it has a pattern formed by clear axial lines and spiral spots.

Mitra stictica (formerly *Mitra pontificalis*)
Pontifical miter
MITRIDAE ▶

Lives in coral sediment and under blocks of dead coral, and is common throughout the Indopacific. About 2.3 inches (6 cm) high, it has a ladderlike profile, with cylindrical whorls and a suture that forms a little channel. Groups of red spots form irregular spirals.

◀ ### Marginella rosea
Rosy marginella
MARGINELLIDAE

Slender, with a rather wide aperture, from .8 to 1.4 inches (2–3.5 cm) high, and rather common along the coasts of South and East Africa. Its cream-colored surface is adorned with an intricate pattern of little pink spots, lines, and dots.

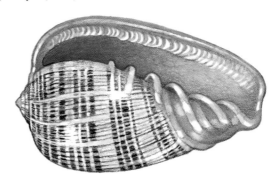

◀ ### Volvarina avena
Orange-band marginella
MARGINELLIDAE

Lives among and under rocks and corals at the edge of the low tide mark to a depth of 300 feet (90 m), and is common from North Carolina to Brazil. From .4 to .6 inches (1–1.6 cm) high, it is pink or yellow in color, with two bands on the last whorl.

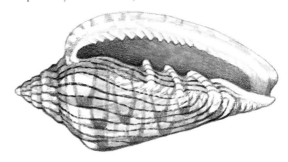

◀ ### Mitra zonata
Zoned miter
MITRIDAE

Found in the Mediterranean province to West Africa, at a minimum of 100 feet (30 m) deep (in the Adriatic) to over 3,300 feet (1,000 m) deep in the Atlantic. Once considered extremely rare, it now seems to be more common. Slender, up to 4 inches (10 cm) long, it has a light nut-colored band on a dark background.

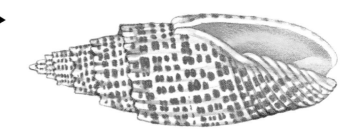

Mitra mitra
Episcopal miter
MITRIDAE

Lives in coral sediment, where it is easy to find by following the furrow it leaves as it moves. It is common throughout the Indopacific and Galapagos, and may reach 7 inches (15 cm) high. Square red markings on a white surface, ivory-colored aperture.

Mitra belcheri
Belcher's miter
MITRIDAE

This is the most beautiful miter in the Panamic province, and is collected on the Pacific coast of Mexico. It is up to 4.7 inches (12 cm) high and rather rare. The slender, dark spire is traversed by a single white spiral furrow, while the aperture is salmon-colored.

Cancilla filaris
File miter
MITRIDAE

This predator (1.2 inches [3 cm] in size) lurks in coral sands and rough detritus at shallow depths. Like all miters, it has a gland that produces a paralyzing poison. It lives in the Indopacific. Its color runs from cream to yellow.

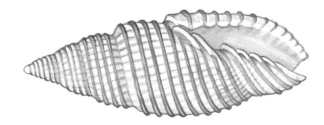

Vexillum subdivisum
Costale miter
COSTELLARIIDAE

Has a slender, spindle-shaped form, with somewhat rounded individual whorls and a rather deep suture. Sinuous axial ribs frame little rectangular markings formed of spiral striae. From 1.4 to 2.3 inches (3.5–5 cm) high, it lives in the Indopacific, where it is not frequent.

Vexillum sanguisugum
Bloodsucker miter
COSTELLARIIDAE

Has a distinctive surface covered with beading formed by the intersection of spiral striae with rounded axial ribs. Standing out on the white background is a little spiral band formed of pairs of red dotted lines on the ribs. It is 1.4 inches (3.5 cm) high and lives in the Indopacific.

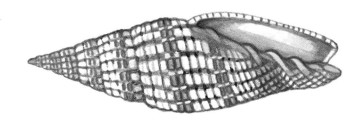

Vexillum ebenus (formerly Mitra ebenus)
Ebony miter
COSTELLARIIDAE

Lives among the vegetation of rocky seabeds or hard substrata in the Mediterranean and western Europe. It is about 1.2 inches (3 cm) high. It is very dark or black, with a pale line running along the whorls. The columella has four little white folds.

Scalptia foveolata
Hollow nutmeg
CANCELLARIIDAE

This small, common South African species, from .8 to 1.2 inches (2–3 cm) high, has a ladder-like profile that is rather unusual for a cancellarid. The spiral sculpture is barely perceptible. Its color may vary, but always includes a darker band.

Cancellaria cancellata
Cancellate nutmeg

CANCELLARIIDAE

Lives in the Senegalese and western Mediterranean province, on detrital or muddy seabeds in the infralittoral and circumlittoral bands. About 1.2 inches (3 cm) high, it has a distinctive cancellate sculpture and a brown band on cream background.

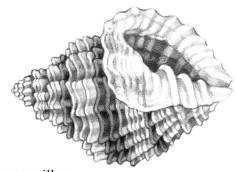

Conus vexillum
Flag cone

CONIDAE

The shell is robust but surprisingly light. Lives hidden among corals under the low tide mark on the side of the reef exposed to the waves, in the Indopacific. Reaches a height of 4.7 inches (12 cm). It is brown with white spots.

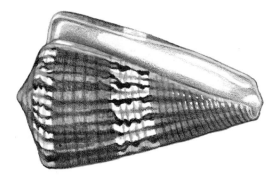

Conus textile
Textile cone

CONIDAE

All members of the *Conus* genus are voracious predators that paralyze their prey by injecting them with poison from a dart on the proboscis. This species, from 1.5 to 5 inches (4–13 cm) high, is even dangerous to humans. Lives in the sand in shallow waters in the Indopacific, where it is common.

Conus regularis
Regular cone

CONIDAE

This species, which is not uncommon along the Pacific coast of Mexico south of Acapulco, has a spire with a distinctive graceful, ladderlike profile, and a slightly concave final whorl. It is from 1.2 to 2.3 inches (3–6 cm) high. It is white with chestnut spots.

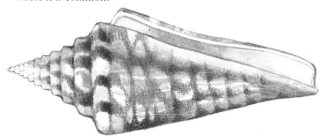

Conus regius
Crown cone

CONIDAE

Common in the Caribbean, as well as Georgia and South Florida, where it lives on rocks and detritus from 1.6 to 15 feet (.5–4.5 m) in depth. It preys on worms, and is from 1.5 to 1.8 inches (4–4.5 cm) high. Its name comes from the crown of tubercles that can be seen behind the last whorl. Color may vary.

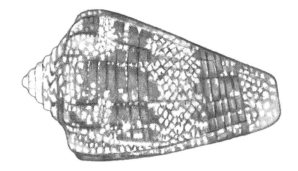

Conus gloriamaris
Glory-of-the-sea

CONIDAE

This was once considered the greatest malacological rarity, but is now found regularly in the Philippines. From 2 to 6 inches (5–15 cm) high, it has an especially graceful straight profile and a dense, fanciful, and particularly elegant pattern.

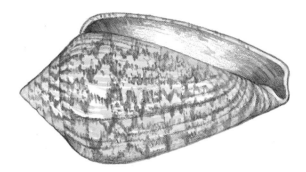

Conus ventricosus (formerly *Conus mediterraneus*)
Mediterranean cone

CONIDAE

Common from the Mediterranean to the Cape Verde Islands in the Atlantic, and quite common in the midlittoral band at shallow depths, especially on rocky seabeds with algae. Its size ranges from .8 inches (2 cm) to, very rarely, 2.7 inches (7 cm). Color is green-chestnut and quite variable.

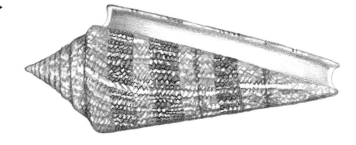

Conus bullatus
Bubble cone
CONIDAE

Lives in the Pacific, from southern Japan to Polynesia, hidden beneath the sand of the infralittoral band. It is from 2 to 2.7 inches (5–7 cm) high, with the last whorl swollen and a flared aperture. Has a reddish pattern on white background. Rare.

Turris babylonia
Babylonia turrid
TURRIDAE

The very slender form and the extremely long siphonal canal of this beautiful turrid, common in the mobile seabeds of the north tropical Pacific, make it similar to a *Fusinus*. Its height varies from 2.3 to 4 inches (6–10 cm). Each whorl has four carinae, with the third more prominent.

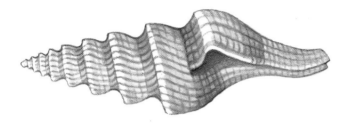

Thatcheria mirabilis
Japanese wonder shell
TURRIDAE

A masterpiece of the architectural ability of mollusks: light, fragile, from 2.3 to 4 inches (6–10 cm) high, it lives from southern Japan to the Philippines at depths of 330 to 660 feet (100–200 m). The acute angle of the shoulder of the whorls gives the shell a pagoda-like appearance.

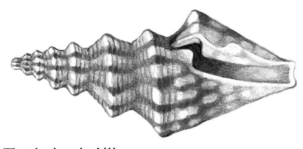

Mangelia vauquelini (formerly *Cythara vauquelini*)
TURRIDAE

Has a glossy, yellow-white surface traversed by about ten axial ribs. A dark band crosses the suture among the whorls, while a reddish spot can be seen on the outer lip. It is from .4 to .5 inches (10–12 mm) high. Mediterranean province.

Fusiturris undatiruga (formerly *Turris undatiruga*)
Wrinkled turrid
TURRIDAE

Beautiful deepwater species that lives in the Mediterranean and along the Atlantic coast of Morocco. From 2 to 2.5 inches (5–6.5 cm) high, it is golden yellow with a chestnut band along the suture. Rather rare. Dense axial ribs obliquely intersect the spiral furrows.

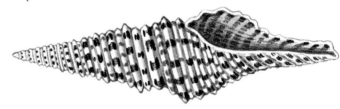

Clavis canicularis
Little dog turrid
TURRIDAE

Like other members of the family, this small turrid (its shell is 1 inch [2.5 cm] high), common in the shallow waters of the Indopacific, preys on small invertebrates by paralyzing them with an injection of poison, but is not dangerous to humans.

Raphitoma purpurea
TURRIDAE

Lives from Norway to the Mediterranean province, in the infralittoral band. It is reddish brown with a white or spotted basal band. An elegant network is formed by the intersection of the axial ribs with the spiral striae. It is from .8 to 1 inch (2–2.5 cm) high.

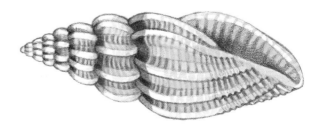

Strioterebrum succincta

TEREBRIDAE

The prominent belt that traverses the whorls of the base distinguishes this small, slender shell (it is from .8 to 1.5 inches [2–4 cm] long). The small axial ribs of each whorl form a transverse network by intersecting the dense spiral striae. Indopacific.

Terebra subulata
Subulate auger

TEREBRIDAE

Widespread species in the Indopacific. Lives in the sand in shallow water, where it uses its poison to prey on small invertebrates. An average of 5 inches (13 cm) long, it is cream-colored with three bands of square chestnut-colored markings.

Terebra dussumieri
Dussumier's auger

TEREBRIDAE

Species is common on the mobile, shallow seabeds of the West Pacific, from Japan to Australia. From 2 to 4 inches (5–10 cm) high; the edge of each whorl is surmounted by a light band. The axial ribs are white, with chestnut intervals.

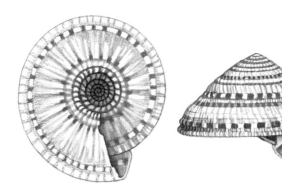

Architectonica perspectiva
Clear sundial

ARCHITECTONICIDAE

Shell with a conical profile and circular base: the very wide umbilicus makes it possible to see the beautiful internal structure. It is rather common in sandy infralittoral and circumlittoral seabeds in the Indopacific. From 1.2 to 1.5 inches (3–4 cm) in diameter.

Turbonilla lactea

PYRAMIDELLIDAE

Like the hundreds of other species in the Pyramidellidae family, this shell from the Mediterranean province has embryonal whorls surrounding an axis different from that of the spire. About .2 to .3 inches (6–8 mm) in height, with straight ribbing, white in color.

Chrisallida doliolum

PYRAMIDELLIDAE

A strong magnifying glass is needed to fully appreciate the sculpture of this little shell, less than a tenth of an inch (2.5 mm) in size. Like all pyramidellids, it is a parasite of other mollusks and invertebrates, and lives in the Mediterranean. Has a swollen profile and prominent ribbing.

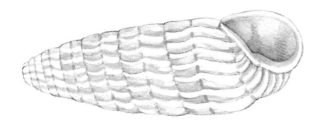

Acteon tornatilis
Lathe acteon

ACTEONIDAE

Species common from the North Sea to the Mediterranean. It lives in shallow waters on sand and mud, as well as on tufts of sea lettuce in harbor areas. The shell is solid, from .6 to 1 inch (1.5–2.5 cm) high, from beige to rose colored, usually with a lighter band.

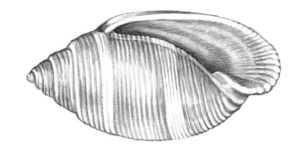

Scaphander lignarius
Woody canoe-bubble

CYLICHNIDAE

As is usually the case for opisthobranchs, this species is not capable of retracting its entire body into the shell. It is a predator and lives in the Mediterranean on slimy seabeds a few dozen yards deep. The shell is from 2.3 to 3 inches (6–8 cm) high.

▶

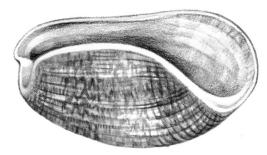

Aplustrum amplustre
Royal paper-bubble

BULLIDAE

This rare shell comes from the sedimentary seabeds of the Indo-pacific. It is light, semitransparent, and has a design of rare elegance. Its bands of color, which vary in width, are orange and black on a cream background. Reaches 1 inch (2.5 cm) in length.

▶

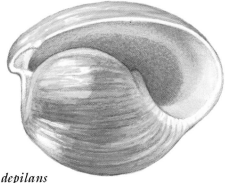

Aplysia depilans
Sea hare

APLYSIIDAE

The mollusk may reach 10 inches (25 cm) in length. Lives in shallow waters, especially where the algae on which it feeds grow most vigorously. The shell, which is completely internal, is reduced to a small translucent plate. It is 2 inches (5 cm) in diameter. Mediterranean.

▶

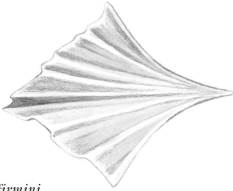

Ovatella firmini

ELLOBIIDAE

The Ellobiidae are lunged gastropods that live in a marine environment, but in the supralittoral band. There are three hundred known species scattered throughout tropical and temperate regions. The one illustrated, .4 inches (11 mm) long, lives in Italy on pebbles in brackish pools.

▶

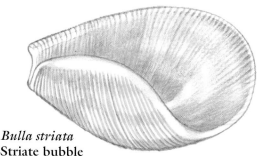

◀ ## Bulla striata
Striate bubble

BULLIDAE

Lives on sandy seabeds, especially *Posidonia* and *Zostera* meadows in the Mediterranean province and western Atlantic. It feeds primarily on algae. The fragile, light shell is chestnut-colored, often with dark marbling. Up to 1 inch (2.5 cm).

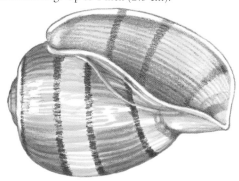

◀ ## Haminoea hydatis

HAMINOEIDAE

The mollusks of this family (which includes about ninety species in tropical and temperate seas) have fragile, translucent shells that at least in part are permanently covered with the lobes of the mantle. Up to .8 inches (2 cm) long. Mediterranean.

◀ ## Clio pyramidata
Pyramid clio

CAVOLINIIDAE

The species of this family of opisthobranchs live in plankton in the open sea. Their shells are completely internal. They can be found on detritus washed up on the beach or collected from the seabed. *Clio pyramidata* is found worldwide. From .4 to .8 inches (1–2 cm) in length.

Siphonaria pectinata (formerly *Siphonaria algesirae*)
Striped false limpet
SIPHONARIIDAE

These mollusks look like limpets, with whom they share habitat and life-style, but the siphonarids, who have both gills and lungs, are very different from the evolutionary perspective. *S. pectinata* is 1.4 inches (3.5 cm) long and lives in the western Mediterranean province as well as Florida, Texas, and the Caribbean.

Spirula spirula
Ram's horn squid
SPIRULIDAE

A pelagic species, it is common in all seas of the world. It has a chambered shell like the nautilus, divided by septa traversed by a siphon, but the shell is almost completely inside the animal. Lives at depths of over 160 feet (50 m). Diameter is from .6 to 1.4 inches (1.5–3.5 cm).

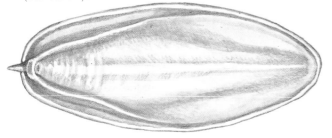

Argonauta argo
Greater argonaut
ARGONAUTIDAE

Pelagic species present in all warm and temperate seas. The shell that the female of this cephalopod builds with a specialized tentacle, is not a true shell, but a parchmentlike structure used to protect its eggs. From 6 to 12 inches (15–30 cm) long.

Nucula nucleus
NUCULIDAE

Common from Norway to Natal and the Mediterranean, where it lives from 16 to 500 feet (5–150 m) in depth, barely covered by silt or muddy or coarse sand. Its foot is better adapted to crawling than burying itself. The shell is .4 to .5 inches (1–1.3 cm) long.

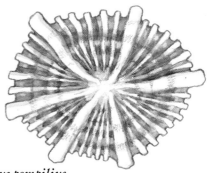

Nautilus pompilius
Chambered nautilus
NAUTILIDAE

Has a chambered shell that is marvelous to look at in cross section due to the perfection of its logarithmic spirals. Lives in the West Pacific at depths of over 160 feet (50 m), where it preys primarily on crustaceans. Its shell is from 4 to 8 inches (10–20 cm) long.

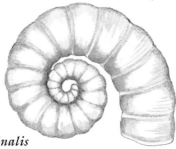

Sepia officinalis
Common cuttlefish
SEPIIDAE

What is commonly known as cuttlebone is the internal shell that testifies to the evolution of cephalopods: the plates in its spongy mass are the equivalent of the septa of *Spirula*. Lives in shallow waters in benthic areas in the Atlantic and Mediterranean. Up to 4.7 inches (12 cm).

Solemya togata
Robe awning clam
SOLEMYIDAE

This is a rather unevolved bivalve that lives in the sand in the infralittoral band, where it feeds on organic detritus. The foot acts as a piston to expel water from the mantle cavity. It lives in the Mediterranean and south to Angola, West Africa. The shell is fragile and rare, 2.3 inches (6 cm) long.

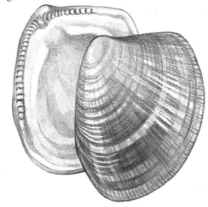

Trisidos tortuosa
Propellor ark
ARCIDAE ▶

This arcid, about 2.3 inches (6 cm) long, that lives from Japan to the East Indies on shallow, muddy seabeds, is distinguished by the fact that the line joining the two valves is not straight but sinuous. Its color ranges from orange to pink.

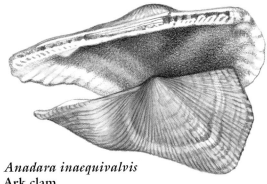

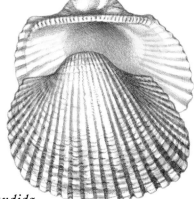

Barbatia candida
White-beard ark
ARCIDAE ▶

Often found in fissures in the rock, where it then assumes the irregular form of the substratum. It is from 1 to 2.5 inches (2.5–6.5 cm) long, with a color that ranges from white to yellowish. The periostracum is brown. It lives in shallow waters from North Carolina to Brazil.

◀ ### *Anadara inaequivalvis*
Ark clam
ARCIDAE

Over recent years, this species, which originated in the Indopacific, has been the villain of a notorious invasion of the Mediterranean. Whitish in color, it is from 2 to 3 inches (5–8 cm) long. Lives buried in sand and mud in shallow waters.

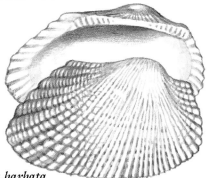

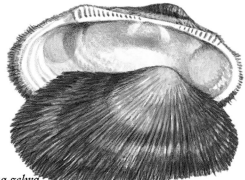

Arca zebra
Turkey wing
ARCIDAE ▶

This is a champion of mimicry: it lives anchored to the rock by its byssus, but allows itself to be covered by encrustations, and the beautiful zebra-striped shell becomes invisible. It is from 1.75 to 3.5 inches (4.4 to 8.9 cm) long and has eyes along the mantle. Lives in the Caribbean, from 3 to 26 feet (1–8 m) in depth.

◀ ### *Barbatia barbata*
European bearded ark
ARCIDAE

Uses its byssus to anchor itself in colonies on reefs, rocks, and sea fans. It is brown, with the periostracum covered by bristles that are more visible at the back end. Lives in the Mediterranean province to northwest Africa, from a few yards to about 1,000 feet (300 m) in depth. It is from 1.5 to 2.3 inches (4–6 cm) long.

Arca noae
Noah's ark
◀ ARCIDAE

Found in the North Sea to the Mediterranean to northwest Africa, and lives attached by its byssus to solid objects, from a few palms to about 330 feet (100 m) in depth. The ventral margin has a byssal gape. From 2.7 to 3.5 inches (7–9 cm) long.

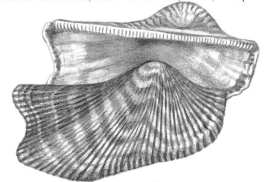

Anadara corbuloides
Basket ark
ARCIDAE ▶

Lives in the Mediterranean province, from Gibraltar to Angola, West Africa, from 100 to 330 feet (30–100 m) deep. The back part of the shell is higher. The radial ribs (an average of thirty-three) appear rough because they are crossed by the transverse sculpture. Length from 2.3 to 2.7 inches (6–7 cm).

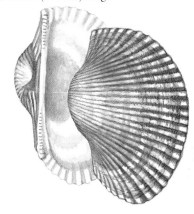

Glycymeris insubrica (formerly *Glycymeris violascens*)
Violet bittersweet ▶
GLYCYMERIDAE

Distinguished from similar species by its lighter, violet gray shell with light radial lines and a form that is generally somewhat square. From 1.7 to 2.3 inches (4.5–6 cm) long, it lives in shallow waters on mobile substrata in the Mediterranean province.

Lithophaga lithophaga
European date mussel ▶
MYTILIDAE

this species uses the acid secretion of its mantle to dig tunnels in calcareous rock. For this reason, unlike other mytilids, it does not need to produce a byssus. The light shell, from 2 to 4 inches (5–10 cm) long, is covered by a brown periostracum. Most of the Mediterranean, Red Sea.

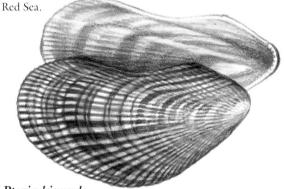

Pteria hirundo
European winged oyster ▶
PTERIIDAE

Has a very distinctive form. Lives from southern England to the Mediterranean to the Azores, from a few yards deep, where it uses its byssus to attach to sea fans, to over 3,280 feet (1,000 m) deep on muddy seabeds. Up to 4 inches (10 cm) long.

Pinctada margaritifera
Pacific pearl oyster ▶
PTERIIDAE

This Indopacific species is now cultivated for its pearls. It lives in the infralittoral band and beyond. Has an almost circular form and lamellae on the rayed sculpture and is greenish gray with yellowish rays. Diameter up to 8 inches (20 cm).

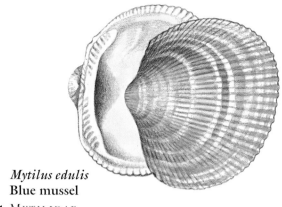

Mytilus edulis
Blue mussel
◀ MYTILIDAE

This is a very widespread species, from Europe to the Americas, Japan, and the Arctic. It is more slender and less dark than the Mediterranean *Mytilus galloprovincialis*, but is highly variable. From 2.3 to 3 inches (6–8 cm) long.

Brachidontes variabilis
◀ MYTILIDAE

As a member of the now numerous group of mollusks that have entered the Mediterranean through the Suez Canal. It is present along all the coasts of Africa. Lives in the midlittoral and infra-littoral bands above the detrital layer. About 1.2 inches (3 cm) long.

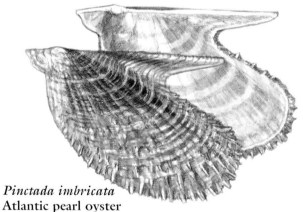

◀ Pinctada imbricata
Atlantic pearl oyster
PTERIIDAE

Lives attached to various supports, using its byssus, from 20 inches (50 cm) to dozens of yards deep, in all warm seas of the world, and entered the Mediterranean through the Suez Canal as early as the nineteenth century. Its diameter ranges from 2.3 to 4 inches (6–10 cm).

Malleus albus
White hammer oyster
MALLEIDAE ▶

Found in shallow waters near coral reefs in the Indopacific. It has no byssus. The hammer-shaped shell (hence the Latin name) is completely white, adorned with lamellae, and rather fragile. Length from 4 to 8 inches (10–20 cm).

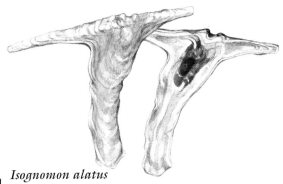

Pinna nobilis
Noble pen shell
PINNIDAE ▶

The largest bivalve in the Mediterranean and one of the largest in the world: the shell can exceed 30 inches (80 cm) in length. Lives anchored and partially buried in *Posidonia* areas, where uncontrolled harvesting has decimated the populations.

Isognomon alatus
Flat tree-oyster
◀ ISOGNOMONIDAE

Uses its byssus to anchor to the roots of mangroves in the Caribbean, including from Florida to Brazil. It is a midlittoral species. The shell is quite flat and round. The ligament forms characteristic comb-like dimples. Diameter ranges from 1 to 4.3 inches (2.5–11 cm).

Ostrea edulis
Edible oyster
OSTREIDAE ▶

A Celtic and Mediterranean province species, it has been cultivated since ancient Rome. It lives on various substrata in the midlittoral and infralittoral bands. The shape of the round shell varies depending on the substratum. Diameter from 2.7 to 4 inches (7–10 cm).

Lima lima
Spiny file shell
◀ LIMIDAE

Lives anchored by its byssus, in fissures in the rocks or among masses in the infralittoral band, in all warm seas in the world, including the Mediterranean. Has a ham form with short spines on eighteen to twenty-two radial ribs. From 1.5 to 2 inches (4–5 cm) long. Many subspecies.

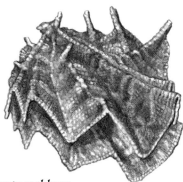

Lopha cristagalli
Cock's-comb oyster
◀ OSTREIDAE

The edges of the valves have four to eight large folds at acute angles that resemble a rooster's crest. Lives attached to rocks and corals, using the aid of special anchoring spines, in the infralittoral band. It is an Indopacific species with a diameter of up to 3.5 inches (9 cm).

Neopycnodonte cochlear
Deepsea oyster
GRYPHAEIDAE ▶

A deep water species (from 100 to over 3,000 feet [30–1,000 m]), it grows by adhering to various solid surfaces, including the thorns of sea urchins, and takes many different forms. In general the top valve (cover) is set into the other one (cup). Occurs throughout eastern Atlantic and Mediterranean. Reaches 3.3 inches (8.5 cm) in size.

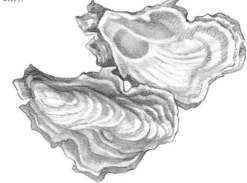

Pecten maximus
Great scallop
PECTINIDAE ▶

Lives in the Atlantic from Norway to the Canaries, on sandy seabeds from shallow waters to 650 feet (200 m) in depth. Prized in fish markets as *coquille de Saint-Jacques*. Has a series of ocelli on the edge of the mantle. About 6 inches (15 cm) in diameter.

Chlamys rubida
Reddish scallop or Hind's scallop
PECTINIDAE ▶

Circular in form, with a diameter that rarely exceeds 2.3 inches (6 cm), it lives on rocky or pebbly seabeds along the western coasts of North America, from Alaska to Monterey, from the low tide mark to about 600 feet (180 m) deep. It is often covered with sponges from the genera *Myxilla* and *Mycale*, which help to camouflage it.

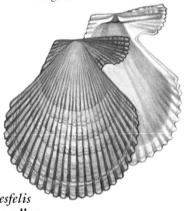

Chlamys pesfelis
Cat's paw scallop
PECTINIDAE ▶

The shell is higher than it is wide, and may be from 2 to 2.7 inches (5–7 cm) in size. The upper valve has eight large radial ribs. The prominent knobs near the edge resemble a cat's paw. Lives in the Atlantic and Mediterranean, from 33 to 750 feet (10–230 m) in depth.

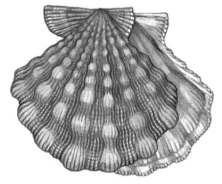

Placopecten magellanicus (formerly *Chlamys magellanicus*)
Sea scallop
PECTINIDAE ▶

It is circular, and the right valve (light) is flatter than the left (reddish). Two to 8 inches (5–20 cm) in diameter, it is sold in fish markets in America. Lives from the Gulf of Saint Lawrence to North Carolina, on sand or shingles, from 60 to 400 feet (18–122 m) deep.

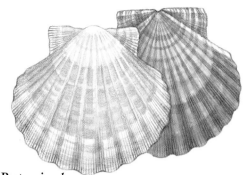

◀ ## Pecten jacobaeus
St. James scallop
PECTINIDAE

Distinguished from *Pecten maximus* by shell edges with angular rather than rounded crests, and by the absence of prominent growth lines. Lives in the Mediterranean on sandy seabeds from 80 to 620 feet (25–190 m) deep. Six inches (15 cm) in diameter.

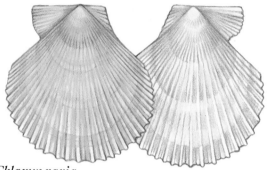

◀ ## Chlamys varia
Variable scallop
PECTINIDAE

Highly variable in color, from white to blackish, including yellow, green, red, marbled, or plain colored. Uses its byssus to anchor to hard substrata from a few yards to over 3,000 feet (1,000 m) deep. Diameter from 1.5 to 2 inches (4–5 cm). Mediterranean, Atlantic, and North Sea.

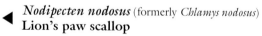

◀ ## Nodipecten nodosus (formerly *Chlamys nodosus*)
Lion's paw scallop
PECTINIDAE

The color varies from orange to red purple, with a diameter from 2.3 to 4.7 inches (6–12 cm). There are 7 or 8 ribs and the large knobs are hollow. It lives on coarse sand or detritus, from 33 to 164 feet (10–50 m) deep, from North Carolina to Brazil.

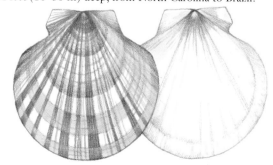

Amusium japonicus
Japanese moon scallop
PECTINIDAE ▶

Orbicular and fragile, it is noteworthy for the color of the upper valve, a mahogany red that contrasts with the straw yellow of the edge of the white lower valve. Lives in Japan, on sand and mud, in the infralittoral band. About 4.3 inches (11 cm) in diameter.

Spondylus gaederopus
European thorny oyster
SPONDYLIDAE ▶

A red sponge, *Crambe crambe,* often hides its upper valve, while the other one adheres to the reef. Spiny appendages are more or less developed. Infralittoral. Diameter from 3 to 5.3 inches (8–13.5 cm). Mediterranean and Senegalese provinces.

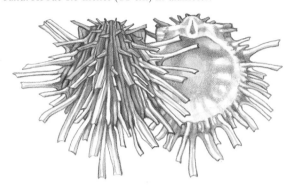

Myrtea spinifera
LUCINIDAE ▶

Widespread species, from Europe to Ceylon and the Azores. Lives on muddy seabeds from the infralittoral band to 3,000 feet (900 m) deep. Dull gray or ivory colored, up to 1 inch (2.5 cm) in diameter. The back dorsal edge has a series of teeth.

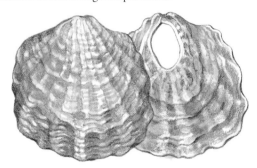

Carditamera floridana
Broad-ribbed cardita
CARDITIDAE ▶

Very robust shell, white or grayish, with prominent radial ribs with beading traversed by chestnut spots, forming concentric bands. Lives on sandy or muddy seabeds from 3 to 25 feet (1–7.5 m) deep, from southern Florida to Mexico. Up to 1.2 inches (3 cm) in length.

◀ Spondylus princeps
Pacific thorny oyster
SPONDYLIDAE

This species adheres to reefs with its right valve, while the free left valve has radial ribs adorned by spectacular paddle-shaped spines up to 1.4 inches (3.5 cm) long. Lives from the Gulf of California to Peru in shallow waters. Up to 5 inches (13 cm) in diameter.

◀ Anomia ephippium
European jingle shell
ANOMIIDAE

Extremely variable; it shapes itself to the substratum to which it adheres. The lower valve has a hole through which the byssus runs. Up to 2.7 inches (7 cm) in diameter. Lives anywhere, down to 500 feet (150 m) deep, from Norway to the Mediterranean to Ghana.

◀ Loripes lacteus
LUCINIDAE

Has a lenticular form; is pure white and from .8 to 1 inch (2–2.4 cm) in diameter. Gathered for food. Lives from England to Senegal and in the Mediterranean, Mauritius, and the Canary Islands. Found on various types of seabeds to 330 feet (100 m) in depth, as well as in brackish lagoons.

Cardita crassicosta
Australian cardita ▶

CARDITIDAE

Has a square shape, with beautiful lamellae with wider tips on the radial ribs. The color is variable: white, yellow, pink, and red. Lives at shallow depths, using its byssus to anchor to the substratum, in the Indopacific and Australia. To 2 inches (5 cm).

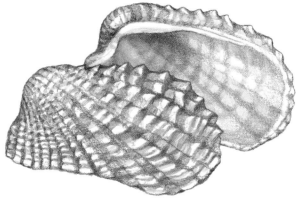

Chama gryphoides ▶

CHAMIDAE

Chamids have one valve, used to adhere to the substratum, which is very concave, and another flat one used as a cover. This species lives in the Atlantic, Mediterranean, and Red Sea, and off Senegal, West Africa, from shallow to very deep waters. Reaches 1.1 inches (2.8 cm) in length.

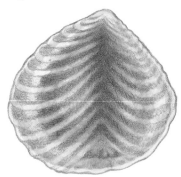

Astarte fusca ▶

ASTARTIDAE

Thick shell with about fifteen concentric furrows, either brown or chestnut. Lives on muddy detrital seabeds in the Mediterranean and Portuguese Atlantic to the Canary Islands, at depths between 100 and 260 feet (30–80 m). Diameter from .8 to 1 inch (2–2.4 cm).

Acanthocardia aculeata
European spiny cockle ▶

CARDIIDAE

The approximately twenty radial ribs that adorn the shell have pointed tubercles, more evident on the back side and along the margins. Lives in the Mediterranean and Celtic provinces off West Africa on sandy or muddy infralittoral seabeds. Diameter from 2.3 to 4 inches (6–10 cm).

◀ Cardita calcyculata

CARDITIDAE

Oblong, distended at the back, white with pink or chestnut spots. The ventral margin is sinuous. It is from .8 to .9 inches (2–2.3 cm) long. Lives in the Portuguese Atlantic and the Mediterranean in the sublittoral band to over 650 feet (200 m) in depth.

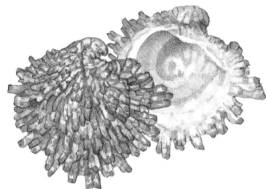

◀ Gonilia calliglypta

ASTARTIDAE

Small, rare, and little known, it has a distinctive frondlike ornamentation on the valves. Lives in the circumlittoral band in the Mediterranean province and neighboring Atlantic, on sandy, slimy and coral seabeds with abundant detritus. Its diameter ranges from .1 to .3 inches (3–5 mm).

Acanthocardia tuberculata
◀ **Tuberculate cockle**

CARDIIDAE

A Mediterranean and Celtic species that lives on fine or coarse sand, including oarweed seabeds, from shallow waters to about 300 feet (100 m) deep. Diameter from 2 to 3 inches (5–8 cm). Has from nineteen to twenty-four rounded ribs, which are knobby toward the front.

Laevicardium crassum
CARDIIDAE ▶

Has a light shell, 1 to 8 inches (2.5–2.8 cm) in size, that is a cream color, often with red spots. Lives in the circumlittoral band on detrital seabeds, but has been found as deep as 6,500 feet (2,000 m). Common in Mediterranean, Senegalese, Celtic, and Boreal provinces.

Cerastoderma edule
Common European cockle
CARDIIDAE ▶

A polymorph species that can adapt to highly diverse salinity conditions, from extremely salty bodies of water to almost fresh water. Lives in shallow waters on sand or mud from the Arctic to Senegal and in the Mediterranean to the Caspian. Reaches 2 inches (5 cm) in length.

◀ ### *Corculum cardissa*
Trueheart cockle
CARDIIDAE

Lives in the midlittoral band on mobile seabeds near coral formations in the Indopacific, and adheres to the substratum with a small byssus. Form is flattened from front to back. Yellow with little red spots. Two inches (5 cm) in diameter.

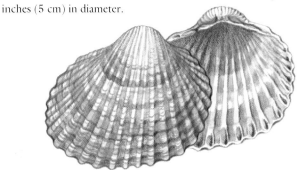

◀ ### *Cardium costatum*
Great ribbed cockle
CARDIIDAE

Large cardiid whose area is limited to the coast of West Africa to southwest Angola. The valves are light, fragile, and white, 4 inches (10 cm) in diameter. Its sculpture consists of about twenty high ribs with a triangular cross section. Lives on mobile circumlittoral seabeds.

Tridacna squamosa
Fluted giant clam
TRIDACNIDAE ▶

Not the largest, but perhaps the most elegant of the small Tridacnidae family. It is adorned with five or six radial ribs with large, paddle-shaped appendages. Reaches 12 inches (30 cm) in length. Lives among corals in the Indopacific.

◀ ### *Hippopus hippopus*
Bear paw clam
TRIDACNIDAE

This tridacnid with a square profile may be up to 16 inches (40 cm) in length. It lives in coral sands near the reef, to a depth of 17 to 20 feet (5 or 6 m), in the Indopacific. It is common where it is not overharvested.

Mactra corallina
Rayed mactra
MACTRIDAE ▶

This mollusk is washed up by rough seas in immense quantities on the sandy coasts of its vast territory, running from Norway to Senegal to the Mediterranean. Its white color is often a background for patterns of dark lines. Its diameter is 1.8 to 2.3 inches (4.5–6 cm).

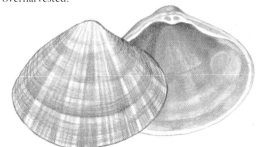

Lutraria lutraria
European otter shell
MACTRIDAE ▶

The two valves are somewhat open at the ends. The shell is whitish in color, with a brownish periostracum and from 4.3 to 4.7 inches (11–12 cm) in size. Lives on mobile seabeds from the sublittoral band to about 160 feet (50 m) in depth, from Norway to Guinea to the Mediterranean.

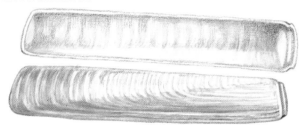

Donacilla cornea
Wedge shell
MESODESMATIDAE ▶

Looks like a donacid, but the inside marginal edge is smooth, not crenulated. Lives in infralittoral sand in the Celtic and Mediterranean provinces. From .7 to 1 inch (1.8–2.4 cm) long and very robust, with a glossy outer surface. Yellow with lighter tones.

Tellina radiata
Sunrise tellin
TELLINIDAE ▶

In America this is known as the sunrise tellin, due to the pink rays on the glossy surface that look like a sunrise. Lives from Florida to the coast of South America, in sand at depths of from 5 to 50 feet (1.5–15 m). From 2 to 4.3 inches (5–11 cm) long.

Tellina pharaonis
TELLINIDAE ▶

Fragile, with a singular appearance, as the cavities of the back margins give it a beaked form. It is a fleshy red color, with concentric white or yellowish bands. Lives in Australia on sandy seabeds at modest depths. Up to 2.3 inches (6 cm).

◀ ### *Solen vagina*
European razor clam
SOLENIDAE

Has almost straight edges and a characteristic single transverse furrow near the front edge, narrowing on the ventral side. An average of 4.9 inches (12.5 cm) long. Sandy infralittoral and circumlittoral seabeds from Norway to Angola to the Mediterranean.

◀ ### *Ensis ensis*
Narrow jacknife clam
PHORIDAE

Has an arcuate, rounded form at the ends. It is yellow-cream in color, with dark streaks. The maximum length is 5 inches (13 cm). Lives from the Arctic to Morocco and the Mediterranean, on fine or slimy sand, up to about 3,000 feet (90 m) deep.

◀ ### *Tellina pulchella*
Red tellin
TELLINIDAE

The back portion is visibly beaked and the ventral margin is a bit sinuous toward the beak. Pink with light radial lines. From .8 to 1.2 inches (2–3.2 cm) long. Lives buried deep in sublittoral sands of the Mediterranean.

Tellina incarnata
Fleshy tellin
TELLINIDAE

▶

Has a compressed form and oval profile in the front portion, while the back is keel-shaped. It is a fleshy orange color, brighter near the umbones. Lives on the mobile seabeds of the Mediterranean and Canary Islands, from the infralittoral band to 200 feet (60 m) deep. From 1.2 to 1.8 inches (3–4.5 cm).

Strigilla carnaria
Large strigilla
TELLINIDAE

▶

The oblique sculpture created by the rough little ribs gives it the Latin name for rasp. It is almost circular in form, and pink in color. It lives in the sand (from 10 to 120 feet [3–37 m] deep) from Florida to Argentina. From .7 to 1.1 inches (1.9–2.8 cm) in size.

Gastrana fragilis
Fragile tellin
TELLINIDAE

The largest specimens reach 1.8 inches (4.5 cm) in length. The shell is dirty white, with dense concentric lines covering the surface. Lives from the Arctic to Morocco and the Mediterranean, on muddy detrital seabeds in the infralittoral and circumlittoral bands.

Solecurtus scupola (formerly Solecurtus strigilatus)
Solecurtus clam
SOLECURTIDAE

▶

Has almost parallel margins and a rectangular appearance. Oblique striae adorn the pink surface, with two lighter radial bands. From 1.5 to 2.7 inches (4–7 cm) in length. Lives in fine sand in the Mediterranean province and off West Africa and the Azores, to depths of 1,500 feet (150 m).

◀

Tellina crassa
Thick tellin
TELLINIDAE

Lives from Sweden to Senegal on coarse or muddy-detrital sand from the infralittoral band to 500 feet (150 m) deep, and also at the western tip of the Mediterranean. Robust shell from 1.5 to 2.7 inches (4–7 cm) long. Light, with little orange spots.

◀

Macoma balthica
Baltic macoma
TELLINIDAE

This little cockle, very common in north temperate to Arctic seas, lives in sand or mud from one inch to 46 feet (14 m) deep. It is from .8 to 1.4 inches (2–3.5 cm) long, and the internal portion is a brighter pink than the outside.

◀

Scrobicularia plana
Flat furrow clam
SCROBICULARIIDAE

This species prefers mud and brackish waters and lives in very sheltered inlets and the mouths of rivers, on shallow seabeds in the Celtic and Mediterranean provinces. The surface is grayish, traversed by growth lines. From 1.5 to 2.1 inches (4–5.5 cm) long.

Pharus legumen
Bean solen
SOLECURTIDAE ▶

Has a fragile shell in the form of a pod, yellowish or flesh-colored. A thin, deciduous epidermis often protrudes at the edges of the valves. From 2 to 2.3 inches (5–6 cm) long, it lives along the coasts of Norway to Senegal and the Mediterranean, from 30 to 3,000 feet (10–100 m) in depth.

Donax trunculus
Truncate donax
DONACIDAE ▶

Lives buried in sandy and muddy seabeds in shallow waters in the Mediterranean and Black Sea, where it is one of the most common species. In some areas it can even be found in fish markets. It is yellowish in color, with lighter rays. Length varies from .8 to 1.5 inches (2–4 cm).

Glossus humanus
Oxhart clam
GLOSSIDAE ▶

The twisted, spiraling umbones are a characteristic of this globular, light shell. Lives in the Mediterranean, Celtic, and Boreal provinces, including North America, from .8 to over 11,500 feet (7–3,500 m) deep, on sand and mud. From 2.7 to 3 inches (7–8 cm) in diameter.

Venerupis philippinarum
Filipino venus
VENERIDAE ▶

This species has spread from East Asia to Europe and western America and has colonized Venice's lagoon. Subject to intensive cultivation. From 1.5 to 2.3 inches (4–6 cm) long, it prefers seabeds of muddy sand in sheltered inlets right below the low tide mark.

◀ ### *Donax variabilis*
Variable coquina
DONACIDAE

Quite abundant in the tidal areas of sandy North American beaches, from New York to northern Mexico. From .5 to 1 inch (1.3–2.5 cm) long, its color varies greatly, with radial and concentric bands that may be pink, violet, yellow, blue, or orange.

◀ ### *Arctica islandica*
Ocean quahog
ARCTICIDAE

This Atlantic species lives along the coasts of western Europe, Iceland, and North America (from Newfoundland to North Carolina), on muddy sand, from 30 to 850 feet (9–260 m) deep. Diameter from 2 to 4.7 inches (5–12 cm). Its color runs from dark olive to black.

◀ ### *Venus verrucosa*
Warty Venus
VENERIDAE

Prized by gourmets, it lives on various seabeds (sand, sandy-rocky) in the western Atlantic and the Mediterranean, from shallow waters to depths of about 300 feet (100 m). Yellowish gray in color, from 1.5 to 2.7 inches (4–7 cm) in diameter.

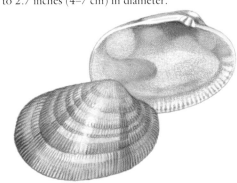

Tapes litteratus
Lettered venus
VENERIDAE ▶

The network of lines that intersect at acute angles on the surface of this venerid resemble an alphabet, giving it its name. From 1.5 to 3.5 inches (4–9 cm) long, it is common on shallow seabeds in the Indopacific, especially in the Philippines.

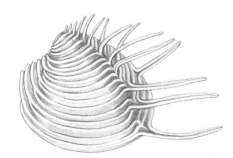

Mercenaria mercenaria
Northern quahog
VENERIDAE ▶

Originally from the Atlantic coast of North America, it was introduced to California for its commercial value. The inside of the valves has a purple spot. About 4 inches (10 cm) long, it lives in sand and mud to a depth of 50 feet (15 m).

◀ ### *Pitar lupanarius*
Prostitute venus
VENERIDAE

Two series of spines rising from the concentric sculpture of the shell distinguish these species. From 2 to 3 inches (5–8 cm) long, it lives in infralittoral sands to 65 feet (20 m) deep in the Pacific, from western Mexico to Peru.

Irus irus
VENERIDAE ▶

The form varies depending on the cavity in the rock in which it lives. From .8 to .9 inches (2–2.3 cm) long, it is adorned with concentric laminae and fine radial striae. Lives on solid infralittoral substrata in Celtic, Mediterranean, and Senegalese provinces, as well as south to South Africa.

◀ ### *Lioconcha castrensis*
Carp pitar venus
VENERIDAE

The shell's tent-shaped decoration, brown or reddish on an ivory surface, suggests a military camp (*castrum* in Latin). It is 1.5 inches (4 cm) long, solid, and common in coral sands near coral reefs in the Indopacific.

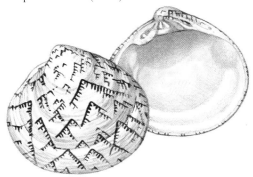

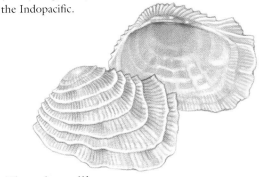

Chamelea gallina
◀ ### Chicken venus
VENERIDAE

Very important for food, this venerid lives on sandy seabeds in the Mediterranean province, at shallow depths. Excessive harvesting has reduced populations in areas where it was extremely abundant. It may reach 1.8 inches (45 mm) in diameter.

Callista chione
Smooth callista
VENERIDAE ▶

Beautiful robust shell, from 2.3 to 4.3 inches (6–11 cm) long, with a very glossy surface, red-brown tending to pink. Harvested for food. Lives on sand to 650 feet (200 m) deep in the Celtic and Mediterranean provinces.

Callanaitis disjecta
Wedding cake venus

VENERIDAE

Characterized by its rich ornamentation of thin, rather fragile laminae. It is rosy white in color. Reaches 1.5 inches (3.5 cm) in length. Lives in the infralittoral band at shallow depths, in muddy sand in southern Australia.

Mya arenaria
Softshell

MYIDAE

Oval form, thin valves open at the two ends, a chalky white color. From 1 to 5.5 inches (2.5–14 cm) long. An important food species, it lives in sand and mud from the tide mark to 230 feet (70 m) deep. North Atlantic and northwest United States.

Petricola lithophaga

PETRICOLIDAE

Lives in cavities that it digs in rocks or other hard substrata, or in fissures it finds in the infralittoral band. A fragile, whitish shell, truncated in front and elongated in back. From .6 to 1 inch (1.5–2.6 cm) long. Mediterranean and Celtic provinces.

Corbula gibba

CORBULIDAE

Globular shell with a smaller right valve that fits into the left valve. From .4 to .6 inches (10–16 mm) long. Lives in sand and mud, from the littoral band to 6,500 feet (2,000 m) deep. Celtic, Mediterranean, Senegalese, and Boreal provinces.

Panopea abrupta (formerly *Panopea generosa*)
Pacific geoduck

HIATELLIDAE

The valves of this large shell (from 3.5 to 9 inches [9–23 cm]) touch only at the umbo and do not enclose the whole mollusk, which may weigh nearly 8 pounds (3.5 kg). Lives buried in the mud in tranquil, shallow inlets from Alaska to Mexico.

Hiatella arctica
Arctic hiatella

HIATELLIDAE

Widespread throughout the northern hemisphere, it lives in holes that it digs in soft rock, or in fissures, from an inch or so to abyssal depths. Small, robust, from .7 to 1 inch (1.7–2.5 cm) long. The left valve is smaller than the right one.

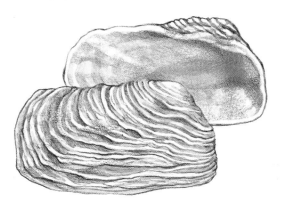

Pholas dactylus
European piddock
PHOLADIDAE

Digs tunnels up to 10 inches (25 cm) long in the rock, but also in other substrata, provided they are hard enough. The shell is white, fragile, open, and from 3 to 4.3 inches (8–11 cm) long. Lives in the infralittoral band from Norway to Cape Verde and in the Mediterranean.

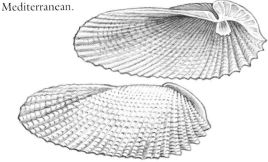

Teredo navalis
Common naval shipworm
TEREDINIDAE

The animal has the form of a worm and lives in tunnels that it digs in wood of any kind, causing damage to boats and structures. The shell is reduced to two anterior plates (about .2 inches [6 mm]) and two blades that protect the siphons. The tube can be longer than 20 inches (50 cm). Cosmopolitan.

Cuspidaria rostrata
Rostrate cuspidaria
CUSPIDARIIDAE

The rostrum that gives this mollusk its name is an open, tubular extension that protects the siphons. The fragile white shell with cream-colored periostracum is .8 to 1.2 inches (2–3 cm) in length. Lives on muddy and clayey seabeds from 100 feet (30 m) in depth and beyond. Atlantic and Mediterranean.

Dentalium dentalis
European tusk
DENTALIIDAE

The shell, fragile-looking and quite varied in color (from white to gray to rose), has ten thin, rounded ribs in the apical portion, while the aperture is circular. Lives in the Mediterranean and Adriatic, from 3 to 650 feet (1–200 m) in depth. One inch (2.5 cm).

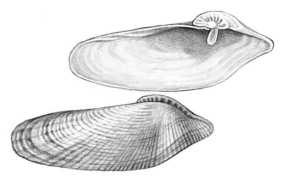

Cyrtopleura costata
Angel wing
PHOLADIDAE

Americans call it the angel wing, due to the lightness and elegance of its pure white shell, from 4 to 8 inches (10–20 cm) long. Lives buried in muddy sand from the tidal line to 60 feet (18 m) deep, from Massachusetts to Brazil.

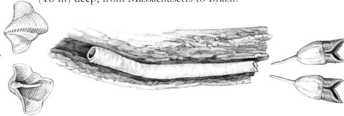

Penicillus australis
CLAVAGELLIDAE

The two valves are reduced to tiny open plates, while the body is protected through the construction of a calcareous shell. Lives buried in sand in shallow water. The tube is about 8 inches (20 cm) long. Indopacific.

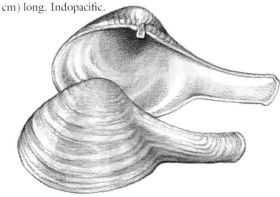

Dentalium elephantinum
Elephant tusk
DENTALIIDAE

This is the most showy shell in the entire class of scaphopods. Bright green ringed with black, with very prominent ribs, it is 8 inches (70 cm) long. Lives in the Indopacific, from the Philippines to Australia, in sandy seabeds about 100 feet (30 m) deep.

Cadulus jeffreysi
GADILIDAE

Tiny, glossy, translucent shell, .12 to .15 inches (3–4 mm) in length. Has a small swelling in the middle-anterior portion and a thickening to the back. Lives in the circumlittoral band, generally on mud, in Mediterranean, Celtic, and Boreal provinces.

This large Hyotissa hyotis *from the Indopacific, which lives in coral formations from the tidal zone to about 65 feet (20 m) deep, is not a true oyster. It reaches 8 inches (20 cm) in diameter. The specimen photographed is camouflaged by a sponge on its shell.*

PHOTOGRAPHIC CREDITS

INDEX

(Page numbers in *italics* refer to illustrations.
Page numbers in **boldface** refer to main descriptions of specific shells.)